Secure Horizons: Ar.
tion to Cybersecurity

Table of Content

Chapter 1: The Digital Battlefield

- Define various cyber threats and their potential impact.
- Explore the motivations behind cyber-attacks.
- Examine common cyber-attack methods (e.g., phishing, malware, DDoS).
- Provide real-world examples to illustrate each type.
- Identify common vulnerabilities in digital infrastructure.
- Discuss the importance of patch management and system updates.
- Introduce popular cybersecurity frameworks (e.g., NIST, ISO/IEC 27001).
- Explain how these frameworks contribute to a secure digital environment.
- Explore the role of human error in cybersecurity incidents.
- Discuss strategies to enhance cybersecurity awareness among users.

Chapter 2: Building the Cyber Defense Framework

- Define the concept of risk in cybersecurity.
- Discuss the importance of risk assessments for effective defense.
- Outline the key components of a comprehensive cybersecurity strategy.
- Address the integration of prevention, detection, and response mechanisms.
- Explore the significance of security policies in a cyber defense framework.
- Discuss compliance requirements and their role in cybersecurity.
- Examine best practices for securing networks.
- Discuss the implementation of firewalls, intrusion detection systems, and other protective measures.
- Detail the importance of having a well-defined incident response plan.
- Provide a step-by-step guide to developing and implementing an effective response strategy.

Chapter 3: Unraveling Encryption: Shielding Your Data

- Explain the basics of encryption and its role in securing data.
- Explore different encryption algorithms and their applications.
- Discuss secure communication protocols (e.g., SSL/TLS) and their importance.
- Explore the use of VPNs for secure data transmission.
- Detail the importance of encrypting data at rest.
- Discuss techniques for securing data stored on various devices and platforms.
- Explore the critical role of key management in maintaining the integrity of encryption.
- Discuss best practices for key generation, storage, and distribution.
- Provide insights into emerging trends in encryption technology.
- Discuss the challenges and opportunities posed by quantum computing on current encryption methods.

Chapter 4: Navigating Threat Landscapes: Cybersecurity Threats and Trends

- Discuss the ever-evolving nature of cybersecurity threats.
- Highlight the challenges posed by emerging technologies.
- Define APTs and their sophisticated strategies.
- Explore notable examples of APTs in recent cybersecurity history.
- Uncover the various forms of social engineering used in cyber-attacks.
- Provide guidance on recognizing and mitigating social engineering threats.
- Investigate the prevalence and impact of ransomware attacks.
- Discuss preventive measures and effective response strategies.
- Explore current trends shaping the cybersecurity landscape.
- Discuss the impact of technological advancements and geopolitical factors.

Chapter 5: Securing the Human Element: Cyber Hygiene and Awareness

- Emphasize the role of individuals in maintaining good cyber hygiene.
- Provide practical tips for securing personal and professional digital environments.
- Discuss the significance of ongoing training programs for individuals and employees.
- Provide guidance on creating effective cybersecurity awareness initiatives.
- Explore the risks associated with social media use in cybersecurity.
- Offer guidelines for secure social media practices to minimize vulnerabilities.
- Discuss the security implications of using personal devices for work.
- Provide recommendations for securing personal devices to enhance overall cybersecurity.
- Highlight the importance of fostering a cybersecurity-conscious culture.
- Discuss organizational strategies for embedding cybersecurity awareness into everyday practices.

Chapter 6: The Role of Artificial Intelligence in Cybersecurity

- Explore how artificial intelligence is revolutionizing threat detection.
- Discuss the use of machine learning algorithms to identify and respond to cyber threats.
- Examine the role of AI in automating incident response processes.
- Discuss the benefits and challenges associated with relying on AI for rapid response.
- Introduce the concept of behavioral analytics in cybersecurity.
- Discuss how AI-driven anomaly detection enhances the identification of unusual patterns and potential threats.
- Explore how artificial intelligence is applied to enhance identity and access management.
- Discuss the role of AI in authentication and authorization processes.
- Address the ethical implications of using AI in cybersecurity.
- Discuss the importance of responsible AI practices and avoiding biases.

Chapter 7: Incident Response: Strategies for a Cyber Crisis

- Discuss the importance of having a dedicated incident response team.
- Outline the key roles and responsibilities within the team.
- Provide guidance on identifying and classifying cybersecurity incidents.
- Discuss the significance of rapid detection for effective response.
- Detail strategies for containing and eradicating cybersecurity threats.
- Discuss the importance of isolating affected systems to prevent further damage.
- Outline effective communication protocols for internal and external stakeholders.
- Discuss transparency and accountability in communicating cybersecurity incidents.
- Discuss the importance of post-incident analysis for continuous improvement.
- Provide a framework for remediating vulnerabilities and strengthening future incident response efforts.

Chapter 8: Emerging Technologies and Future Trends in Cybersecurity

- Explore the potential impact of quantum computing on cybersecurity.
- Discuss strategies for adapting current security measures to quantum-resistant standards.
- Examine the role of blockchain in enhancing decentralized security.
- Discuss its applications in securing transactions and data.
- Investigate the cybersecurity challenges posed by the Internet of Things (IoT).
- Provide solutions and best practices for securing IoT devices and networks.
- Explore emerging innovations in cloud security.
- Discuss the evolving landscape of cloud-based cybersecurity solutions.
- Discuss the evolving role of individuals in shaping the future of cybersecurity.
- Explore the integration of human-centric approaches in technological advancements.

Introduction

In an age marked by the pervasive influence of digital transformation, safeguarding sensitive information stands as an imperative task. The advent of "Secure Horizons: An Introduction to Cybersecurity" signals a crucial gateway into the intricate realm of preserving digital landscapes. In this comprehensive guide, the aim is not merely to scratch the surface but to delve deep into the complexities that shroud the domain of cybersecurity. In a world where the digital realm is both a boon and a potential peril, this guide emerges as a beacon, offering an invaluable understanding of the multifaceted strategies required to navigate and secure our digital future.

As technology seamlessly integrates into every aspect of our lives, the significance of cybersecurity cannot be overstated. "Secure Horizons" embarks on a mission to demystify the intricacies that often render the subject intimidating. This guide does not merely dwell on theoretical principles but takes a practical approach, providing readers with tangible tools and knowledge to fortify their defenses in the dynamic landscape of cyberspace.

The evolution of digital interconnectedness has birthed new challenges and complexities that demand a proactive approach to cybersecurity. Through "Secure Horizons," readers are equipped with insights that empower them to comprehend the motives behind cyber-attacks, the ever-evolving types of threats, and the vulnerabilities inherent in digital systems. By mapping the digital landscape comprehensively, from traditional IT setups to the expansive realm of cloud computing and IoT devices, the guide aims to cultivate a holistic understanding of the diverse terrain where cyber threats proliferate.

Motivated by the belief that knowledge is the most potent defense, "Secure Horizons" unfolds its chapters as a journey through the digital battlefield. The initial chapters explore the various forms of cyber threats, decoding their underlying motivations and shedding light on the vulnerabilities that adversaries exploit. The guide doesn't shy away from examining the historical evolution of cyber warfare, tracing its trajectory from early hacking endeavors to the sophisticated state-sponsored attacks witnessed today.

As the journey progresses, readers are ushered into the construction phase of cybersecurity defenses. The guide intricately details the formulation of a robust cyber defense framework, delving into risk management, strategy design, and the crucial role of security policies. It emphasizes the need for organizations and individuals alike to not only comprehend the threats they face but also to actively engage in risk assessments and develop strategies that encompass prevention, detection, and response mechanisms.

The exploration doesn't stop there. "Secure Horizons" extends its reach into the specialized domains of encryption, addressing the paramount need to shield data. Unraveling the intricacies of encryption, the guide navigates through secure communication protocols, data encryption in storage, and the crucial management of cryptographic keys. It anticipates future trends, considering the impact of quantum computing on encryption methods, ensuring that readers are not only equipped for the present but also prepared for the challenges that lie ahead.

The guide places a significant emphasis on the human element in cybersecurity. It recognizes that even the most sophisticated technological defenses can be compromised if individuals lack awareness and adherence to cyber hygiene practices. Chapters dedicated to securing the human element delve into the importance of cyber hygiene, training programs, and the adoption of secure practices in personal and professional contexts. It advocates for the cultivation of a cybersecurity culture that permeates through every level of an organization.

"Secure Horizons" then turns its gaze to the symbiotic relationship between artificial intelligence (AI) and cybersecurity. In an era where threats evolve at an unprecedented pace, the guide explores how AI powers threat detection, incident response, and behavioral analytics for anomaly detection. It navigates through the ethical considerations inherent in deploying AI for cybersecurity, emphasizing the need for responsible practices.

As the guide advances to address incident response strategies, it acknowledges the inevitability of cyber crises and provides readers with a roadmap for effective response. From establishing incident response teams to implementing communication protocols and conducting post-incident analyses, "Secure Horizons" ensures that individuals and organizations are not only prepared for cyber crises but can emerge stronger from them.

The final chapters peer into the future, where emerging technologies and trends shape the landscape of cybersecurity. From the potential impact of quantum computing to the revolutionary role of blockchain, the guide illuminates the paths that technological innovations may tread. It scrutinizes the security challenges posed by the Internet of Things (IoT) and envisions a future where a human-centric approach remains pivotal in shaping the cybersecurity narrative.

In essence, "Secure Horizons: An Introduction to Cybersecurity" is more than a guide; it is a comprehensive compendium that empowers individuals and organizations to navigate the complexities of the digital era securely. By combining theoretical insights with practical tools, this guide transcends traditional cybersecurity literature, ensuring that readers not only understand the intricacies but are also armed with the knowledge and tools needed to fortify their digital horizons. As we stand at the precipice of a digitally driven future, "Secure Horizons" beckons, inviting all to embark on a journey toward a safer, more secure digital landscape.

Chapter 1: The Digital Battlefield

Define various cyber threats and their potential impact.
Cyber threats encompass a wide range of malicious activities that exploit vulnerabilities in computer systems, networks, and digital infrastructure. One prominent threat is malware, a term encompassing various forms of malicious software such as viruses, worms, and Trojans. These programs can infiltrate systems, compromise data integrity, and disrupt operations. The potential impact of malware is vast, ranging from data theft and financial loss to the impairment of critical infrastructure and the compromise of national security.

Another significant cyber threat is phishing, a deceptive technique where attackers impersonate legitimate entities to trick individuals into divulging sensitive information. Phishing attacks can lead to unauthorized access to personal or corporate accounts, identity theft, and financial fraud. The psychological manipulation employed in phishing campaigns often makes them difficult to detect, amplifying their potential for harm.

Ransomware has emerged as a particularly pernicious cyber threat, involving the encryption of a victim's data with a demand for payment in exchange for its release. The impact of successful ransomware attacks is severe, causing not only financial losses but also operational disruptions, reputational damage, and, in critical sectors like healthcare, endangering lives by compromising access to essential services.

Denial-of-Service (DoS) and Distributed Denial-of-Service (DDoS) attacks pose threats to the availability and functionality of online services. By overwhelming servers or networks with excessive traffic, attackers can render websites and online platforms inaccessible, disrupting business operations, and causing financial losses. The potential consequences extend beyond inconvenience to affecting public services, e-commerce, and even essential infrastructure like power grids.

Advanced Persistent Threats (APTs) are sophisticated and targeted attacks often orchestrated by nation-states or well-funded cybercriminal groups. APTs involve a prolonged and stealthy compromise of a specific target with the intent of espionage, data theft, or sabotage. The potential impact of APTs on national security, intellectual property, and corporate secrets is substantial, with consequences ranging from economic espionage to the compromise of critical infrastructure.

Data breaches, involving unauthorized access to sensitive information, can result from various cyber threats and have profound consequences. Stolen data, including personal details, financial records, or intellectual property, can be exploited for identity theft, financial fraud, or corporate espionage. The reputational damage incurred by organizations in the aftermath of a data breach can be long-lasting, eroding trust among customers, partners, and stakeholders.

Supply chain attacks have become increasingly prevalent, targeting vulnerabilities in the interconnected networks of suppliers and vendors. Attackers exploit weak links in the supply chain to infiltrate larger organizations and compromise their systems. The potential impact is widespread, affecting not only the primary target but also causing cascading disruptions throughout the supply chain, leading to financial losses, operational setbacks, and compromised product integrity.

Zero-day exploits target unknown vulnerabilities in software before developers have had a chance to patch them. Cybercriminals or state-sponsored actors can exploit these vulnerabilities to gain unauthorized access to systems. The potential impact of zero-day exploits is significant, as they allow attackers to bypass existing security measures and compromise systems without detection. This can lead to data breaches, espionage, and the disruption of critical services.

Social engineering attacks leverage human psychology to manipulate individuals into divulging sensitive information or taking specific actions. These attacks can take various forms, including impersonation, pretexting, or baiting. The potential impact of social engineering extends beyond technological vulnerabilities, affecting individuals' behavior and decision-making, making it a challenging threat to mitigate through technical means alone.

Finally, Internet of Things (IoT) vulnerabilities introduce new dimensions to cyber threats. As more devices become interconnected, the potential for exploitation increases. Cybercriminals can compromise IoT devices to launch attacks on larger networks or gain unauthorized access to personal data. The impact can range from privacy breaches and surveillance to the disruption of critical infrastructure reliant on IoT technology.

In conclusion, the diverse landscape of cyber threats poses multifaceted challenges to individuals, businesses, and governments. The potential impact of these threats spans financial losses, operational disruptions, reputational damage, and even threats to national security. A comprehensive and proactive approach to cybersecurity is essential to mitigate these risks and safeguard the increasingly interconnected digital world from the ever-evolving landscape of cyber threats.

Explore the motivations behind cyber-attacks.

The motivations behind cyber-attacks constitute a multifaceted landscape, intricately woven with technological, economic, political, and ideological threads. To understand this complex realm is to embark on a journey through the digital underbelly, where motivations serve as the driving forces behind the myriad cyber threats that permeate our interconnected world. At the forefront of these motivations lies the pursuit of economic gain, an insidious force that propels cybercriminals to exploit vulnerabilities and launch attacks with the primary objective of financial enrichment. Ransomware attacks, a prevalent manifestation of this profit-driven motivation, involve the malicious encryption of data followed by demands for payment, creating a lucrative criminal enterprise. Financial fraud, including the theft of sensitive information for identity theft or credit card fraud, stands as another testament to the allure of monetary gain within the cybercrime ecosystem.

Simultaneously, the geopolitical stage witnesses the choreography of state-sponsored cyber-attacks, where the motivations extend beyond financial incentives to encompass strategic advantages, intelligence gathering, and geopolitical influence. Nations engage in cyber-espionage to bolster their positions, gaining a competitive edge or disrupting the operations of rival states. Cyber-attacks become potent tools of coercion, offering a means to achieve strategic objectives without resorting to traditional military avenues. The Stuxnet worm, a sophisticated cyber weapon believed to be a product of state-sponsored efforts, exemplifies the intersection of cyber and geopolitical motivations, underscoring the gravity of such endeavors on the international stage.

Ideological motivations, often characterized by hacktivism, form another layer of the cyber threat landscape. Individuals or groups driven by specific causes or dissenting views employ cyber-attacks as a means of expression, protest, or advancing particular ideologies. These hacktivist groups target entities they perceive as unethical or oppressive, with motivations ranging from environmental concerns and human rights advocacy to political activism. The actions of hacktivists, typically symbolic and disruptive, seek to raise awareness or voice dissent in the digital realm, adding a dimension of ideological fervor to the motivations behind cyber-attacks.

Within the corporate domain, cyber-attacks fueled by motivations of competitive advantage and corporate espionage introduce a different dynamic. Companies strategically engage in cyber-espionage to gain insights into the intellectual property, strategies, or products of their competitors. The theft of trade secrets, research and development data, or proprietary information becomes a means to secure a significant advantage in the cutthroat global marketplace. These cyber-attacks within the corporate arena reflect economic motivations but with a focus on gaining a competitive edge through covert means.

Beyond individual actors, organized criminal organizations play a significant role in the cyber threat landscape, motivated by a nexus of economic gain, power, and influence. Cyber-attacks become instrumental in facilitating various illicit activities, including drug trafficking, money laundering, and extortion. The digital realm offers these criminal entities an anonymous and global platform to operate, challenging law enforcement agencies worldwide to combat the ever-evolving landscape of cyber-enabled criminal activities.

The surge in hacktivism and cyber-attacks with ideological motivations mirrors the increased interconnectivity of the global community. Activists and dissenters leverage the digital landscape to amplify their voices and influence societal change. However, the lines between hacktivism, cybercrime, and state-sponsored activities blur, complicating the attribution of cyber-attacks and making it challenging to categorize motivations with certainty. This ambiguity adds a layer of complexity to the motivations behind cyber-attacks, where the underlying ideologies may intertwine with other geopolitical or economic interests.

A distinctive layer of motivation emerges when cyber-attacks are orchestrated for strategic disruption. Critical infrastructure, including power grids, transportation systems, or healthcare facilities, becomes the target in these instances, aiming to cause widespread chaos and disruption. Nation-states or non-state actors deploy these attacks to weaken the social fabric, undermine trust in institutions, or create vulnerabilities that can be exploited for geopolitical gain. This strategic disruption goes beyond individual gain, reflecting motivations deeply embedded in political and strategic agendas.

The attractiveness of cybercrime is amplified by the anonymity it affords and the ability to operate across borders with minimal physical risk. The interconnected nature of the internet empowers malicious actors to launch attacks from virtually anywhere, complicating efforts to identify and apprehend them. The borderless nature of cyberspace allows these actors to exploit legal and jurisdictional gaps, posing a significant challenge for international efforts to combat cyber threats.

As the technological landscape continues to evolve, so too do the motivations behind cyber-attacks. Emerging technologies, such as the Internet of Things (IoT) and artificial intelligence, present new avenues for cyber threats. The motivations may shift to exploit vulnerabilities in these technologies, ushering in a potential era of more sophisticated and destructive cyber-attacks. Understanding the evolving landscape of cyber threats and motivations is paramount for developing adaptive and effective cybersecurity measures. In this intricate dance between defenders and adversaries, a comprehensive comprehension of the motivations driving cyber-attacks becomes a cornerstone in fortifying the defenses that safeguard individuals, organizations, and nations in the digital age. The quest for resilience requires a nuanced understanding of these motivations, empowering stakeholders to navigate the ever-shifting terrain of cyber threats with vigilance and strategic acumen.

Examine common cyber-attack methods (e.g., phishing, malware, DDoS).

Cyber-attacks have evolved into a sophisticated array of methods, each tailored to exploit vulnerabilities and compromise the security of digital systems. One prevalent method is phishing, a deceptive technique wherein attackers masquerade as trustworthy entities to trick individuals into revealing sensitive information such as usernames, passwords, or financial details. Phishing often involves emails, messages, or websites that appear legitimate, enticing users to unknowingly divulge confidential data. The success of phishing relies on social engineering tactics that exploit human psychology, making it a persistent and widespread cyber threat.

Malware, a portmanteau of "malicious software," constitutes another pervasive cyber-attack method. It encompasses a diverse range of harmful software designed to infiltrate, damage, or gain unauthorized access to computer systems. Viruses, worms, trojans, ransomware, and spyware are among the various types of malware, each serving distinct purposes. Viruses replicate themselves within host files, worms spread autonomously across networks, trojans disguise themselves as legitimate software, ransomware encrypts files demanding payment for decryption, and spyware clandestinely monitors and collects sensitive information. The versatility and adaptability of malware make it a constant and evolving threat to cybersecurity.

Distributed Denial of Service (DDoS) attacks represent a method aimed at disrupting the regular functioning of a targeted system or network by overwhelming it with a flood of traffic. Attackers orchestrate DDoS attacks by deploying a multitude of compromised devices, forming a botnet that inundates the target with an excessive volume of requests. The sheer scale of this traffic exhausts the system's resources, rendering it incapable of responding to legitimate user requests. DDoS attacks can be financially motivated, ideologically driven, or used as a diversionary tactic while other malicious activities, such as data theft, occur. Mitigating DDoS attacks involves implementing robust security measures and employing traffic filtering technologies to distinguish between legitimate and malicious traffic.

Social engineering represents a category of cyber-attack methods that exploits human psychology and manipulation to deceive individuals into divulging confidential information or performing actions that compromise security. Techniques within social engineering include pretexting, where attackers create fabricated scenarios to extract information, and baiting, which involves offering something enticing to trick individuals into taking malicious actions. Other social engineering tactics include quid pro quo, where attackers offer a service or benefit in exchange for information, and tailgating, which involves unauthorized physical access to secured premises by following authorized individuals. Social engineering attacks underscore the importance of cybersecurity awareness and education to empower individuals to recognize and resist manipulation attempts.

Man-in-the-Middle (MitM) attacks occur when an unauthorized third party intercepts and potentially alters communication between two parties without their knowledge. This form of attack enables the attacker to eavesdrop on sensitive information, including login credentials, financial details, or confidential communications. Common MitM techniques include packet sniffing, where attackers capture and analyze data packets traversing a network, and session hijacking, where attackers seize control of an active session between two parties. Encrypting communications and implementing secure protocols are essential countermeasures to mitigate the risk of Man-in-the-Middle attacks.

Another prevalent cyber-attack method involves exploiting software vulnerabilities through the deployment of exploits. Exploits target weaknesses or bugs in software, leveraging them to gain unauthorized access, execute arbitrary code, or perform other malicious actions. The success of exploits often depends on the timely patching of software vulnerabilities by developers and system administrators. Zero-day exploits, which target vulnerabilities before they are officially discovered and patched, pose a particularly challenging threat. Cybersecurity measures such as regular software updates, vulnerability assessments, and intrusion detection systems are crucial in mitigating the risks associated with exploit-based attacks.

SQL injection attacks represent a method wherein attackers manipulate a web application's database by injecting malicious SQL code into input fields. If the application fails to adequately validate or sanitize user inputs, attackers can exploit this vulnerability to execute arbitrary SQL commands. The consequences of successful SQL injection attacks include unauthorized access to databases, data manipulation, and potentially the compromise of sensitive information. Mitigating SQL injection risks involves employing secure coding practices, input validation, and parameterized queries to prevent the injection of malicious code.

Cross-Site Scripting (XSS) attacks exploit vulnerabilities in web applications by injecting malicious scripts into web pages viewed by other users. These scripts execute within the context of the victim's browser, enabling attackers to steal information, session cookies, or perform actions on behalf of the victim. Reflective XSS involves the immediate execution of the injected script, while stored XSS stores the script on the target server, affecting users who later access the compromised page. Mitigating XSS attacks involves input validation, output encoding, and implementing secure coding practices to prevent the injection of malicious scripts.

Advanced Persistent Threats (APTs) constitute a sophisticated and prolonged form of cyber-attack characterized by a continuous and stealthy intrusion into a targeted network. APTs typically involve highly skilled adversaries who gain unauthorized access to a system, remain undetected for extended periods, and exfiltrate sensitive information gradually. APTs often employ multiple attack vectors, including phishing, malware, and social engineering, to achieve their objectives. Detecting and mitigating APTs require robust cybersecurity measures, including network monitoring, endpoint detection and response (EDR) solutions, and threat intelligence.

Cryptojacking represents a more recent cyber-attack method that involves unauthorized cryptocurrency mining using the computing resources of unsuspecting individuals or organizations. Attackers deploy malware to infect systems, harnessing their processing power to mine cryptocurrencies such as Bitcoin or Monero. The impact of cryptojacking includes increased energy consumption, reduced system performance, and potential hardware damage. Mitigating cryptojacking involves employing robust antivirus solutions, regularly updating software, and implementing network security measures to detect and prevent the unauthorized use of computing resources.

In conclusion, the landscape of cyber-attack methods is diverse and continually evolving, reflecting the relentless ingenuity of malicious actors seeking to exploit vulnerabilities in digital systems. From phishing and malware to DDoS attacks, social engineering, and advanced persistent threats, each method poses unique challenges to cybersecurity. Mitigating these risks requires a holistic and adaptive approach, encompassing technological solutions, regular education and awareness programs, and the implementation of best practices in secure coding and system administration. In the dynamic and interconnected digital era, the battle against cyber threats demands vigilance, innovation, and a collective commitment to fortifying the foundations of a secure and resilient digital ecosystem.

Provide real-world examples to illustrate each type.
Phishing:

A notorious real-world example of phishing is the 2016 attack on the Democratic National Committee (DNC) during the U.S. presidential election. Russian state-sponsored hackers used deceptive emails to trick individuals within the DNC into divulging their login credentials. The phishing emails, appearing to be from legitimate sources, contained malicious links that, when clicked, directed recipients to fake login pages where their usernames and passwords were harvested. This attack had far-reaching consequences, exposing sensitive information and influencing the political landscape.

Malware:

The WannaCry ransomware attack of 2017 serves as a prominent example of malware exploitation. WannaCry exploited a vulnerability in Microsoft Windows systems, spreading rapidly across the globe. Once a system was infected, the malware encrypted files and demanded a ransom in Bitcoin for their release. The attack affected various organizations, including the National Health Service (NHS) in the UK, causing widespread disruption to healthcare services. The incident underscored the destructive potential of malware and the importance of timely software updates to patch vulnerabilities.

DDoS (Distributed Denial of Service):

In 2016, the Internet infrastructure company Dyn fell victim to a massive DDoS attack. The attackers harnessed a botnet of compromised Internet of Things (IoT) devices, overwhelming Dyn's servers with an immense volume of traffic. The attack caused widespread outages, affecting major websites and services, including Twitter, Reddit, and Netflix. This incident highlighted the vulnerability of critical Internet infrastructure to large-scale DDoS attacks and the need for enhanced cybersecurity measures to mitigate such threats.

Social Engineering:

One of the most infamous cases of social engineering is the 2013 Target data breach. In this attack, cybercriminals gained access to

Target's network by compromising a third-party HVAC vendor. Using a phishing email, the attackers tricked an employee of the vendor into clicking a malicious link, providing the initial entry point. The subsequent compromise resulted in the theft of credit card information and personal data of millions of Target customers. This example illustrates how social engineering can exploit human vulnerabilities to infiltrate even well-secured networks.

Man-in-the-Middle (MitM):

A classic example of a Man-in-the-Middle attack occurred in 2013 when security researchers discovered the "DarkHotel" campaign. Operating predominantly in Asia, this campaign involved intercepting hotel Wi-Fi networks to position as a MitM. When unsuspecting guests connected to the compromised Wi-Fi, the attackers intercepted communications, injecting malware into the victims' devices. This sophisticated campaign targeted high-profile individuals, demonstrating the potential for MitM attacks to compromise sensitive information in public spaces.

Exploits:

The Equifax data breach of 2017 is a notable example of a cyberattack leveraging exploits. Attackers exploited a vulnerability in Apache Struts, a web application framework used by Equifax. Failing to patch the vulnerability promptly, Equifax provided an entry point for attackers who gained unauthorized access to sensitive personal information of 147 million people. This incident underscores the critical importance of prompt software updates and patching to mitigate the risk of exploits.

SQL Injection:

The 2014 data breach of the U.S. healthcare provider Community Health Systems is an illustrative case of SQL injection. Attackers exploited a vulnerability in the company's systems, injecting malicious SQL code to exfiltrate sensitive patient data. The compromised data included names, addresses, and Social Security numbers of approximately 4.5 million individuals. This incident highlighted the consequences of inadequate web application security and the potential impact of SQL injection on sensitive healthcare information.

Cross-Site Scripting (XSS):

In 2018, British Airways fell victim to a significant XSS attack that affected its website. Attackers injected malicious scripts into the airline's payment page, compromising sensitive customer information during the booking process. This incident showcased the potential impact of XSS attacks on reputable and heavily trafficked websites, emphasizing the need for robust security measures to protect against such vulnerabilities.

Advanced Persistent Threats (APTs):

One of the most sophisticated APTs in recent history is the 2015 breach of the U.S. Office of Personnel Management (OPM). Believed to be orchestrated by Chinese state-sponsored actors, the attack compromised highly sensitive personnel records of millions of government employees. The APT involved persistent and stealthy infiltration, allowing the attackers to maintain access over an extended period. This case exemplifies the strategic and patient nature of APTs, emphasizing the need for comprehensive defense strategies against such persistent threats.

Cryptojacking:

In 2018, the Coinhive cryptojacking script gained notoriety for being illicitly deployed on numerous websites without users' consent. Websites unknowingly hosted the script, harnessing visitors' computing resources to mine cryptocurrency for the attackers. This covert exploitation of users' computational power led to increased energy consumption, slowed system performance, and sparked debates on the ethical implications of cryptojacking. The incident underscored the need for vigilance in securing websites against unauthorized code injections.

In examining these real-world examples, it becomes evident that cyber threats manifest in various forms, exploiting diverse vulnerabilities across different sectors. The lessons learned from these incidents emphasize the importance of proactive cybersecurity measures, including regular software updates, employee training, and the implementation of robust defense mechanisms, to safeguard against an evolving and sophisticated cyber threat landscape.

Identify common vulnerabilities in digital infrastructure.

Common vulnerabilities in digital infrastructure pose significant challenges to the security and integrity of systems, networks, and data. Understanding these vulnerabilities is crucial for developing effective cybersecurity strategies to mitigate the ever-present threat landscape in the digital realm.

One prevalent vulnerability is related to outdated or unpatched software. Systems running software with known vulnerabilities become easy targets for cyber attackers who exploit these weaknesses to gain unauthorized access, execute malicious code, or conduct other nefarious activities. The Equifax data breach in 2017 serves as a stark example, where attackers exploited a vulnerability in the Apache Struts web application framework due to the company's failure to apply a patch promptly. This incident underscores the critical importance of timely software updates and patch management to address known vulnerabilities and enhance overall system resilience.

Insecure configurations represent another common vulnerability that can be exploited by cyber adversaries. Digital infrastructure often involves complex configurations of hardware, software, and network components. Inadequate or misconfigured settings can create security gaps that attackers can exploit. For instance, default configurations that are not altered may expose unnecessary services or ports, providing potential entry points for attackers. The exposure of critical systems due to misconfigurations was evident in the 2016 Dyn DDoS attack, where insecurely configured Internet of Things

(IoT) devices became part of a botnet that overwhelmed the DNS provider's infrastructure.

Weak authentication mechanisms contribute significantly to vulnerabilities in digital infrastructure. Inadequate password policies, reliance on default credentials, and the absence of multi-factor authentication (MFA) can expose systems to unauthorized access. The compromise of user credentials through techniques like credential stuffing, where attackers use previously leaked passwords, is a persistent threat. The prevalence of weak authentication was evident in the Yahoo data breaches, where attackers exploited weak password security measures, leading to unauthorized access and the compromise of millions of user accounts.

Phishing attacks, leveraging human vulnerabilities, represent a substantial and persistent vulnerability in digital infrastructure. Phishing involves deceptive tactics to trick individuals into divulging sensitive information such as usernames, passwords, or financial details. Despite advancements in cybersecurity awareness, sophisticated phishing campaigns continue to exploit human psychology and trust. The 2016 attack on John Podesta, Hillary Clinton's campaign chairman, is a notable example. Podesta fell victim to a phishing email, resulting in unauthorized access to his email account and the subsequent leak of sensitive campaign information.

Software vulnerabilities, including those within applications and web services, present an ongoing challenge to digital infrastructure security. Flaws in the code can be exploited by attackers to execute arbitrary code, compromise data, or gain unauthorized access. The Heartbleed vulnerability in the OpenSSL cryptographic library in 2014 exposed a significant security flaw, allowing attackers to extract sensitive information from the memory of affected servers. This incident underscored the importance of secure coding practices, regular code audits, and comprehensive vulnerability assessments in safeguarding digital infrastructure.

Insufficient data encryption practices expose digital infrastructure to the risk of unauthorized interception and tampering. Inadequate encryption of sensitive data during transmission or storage can result in data breaches and compromises. The notorious 2013 Target data breach is an illustrative example. Attackers intercepted unencrypted payment card information during transmission, leading to the compromise of millions of customer records. Implementing robust encryption protocols, including Transport Layer Security (TLS) for secure communication, is essential in protecting data from unauthorized access.

Inadequate network security measures, including weak firewalls, unsecured Wi-Fi networks, and insufficient intrusion detection systems, create vulnerabilities in digital infrastructure. The lack of effective network segmentation and monitoring allows attackers to move laterally within a network once initial access is gained. The 2017 NotPetya ransomware attack, which spread rapidly within poorly segmented networks, exemplifies the impact of insufficient network security. Strengthening network security through robust firewalls, secure Wi-Fi configurations, and continuous monitoring is essential for mitigating such vulnerabilities.

The integration of Internet of Things (IoT) devices into digital infrastructure introduces a new set of vulnerabilities. Many IoT devices lack robust security features, making them attractive targets for attackers seeking entry points into larger networks. The 2016 Mirai botnet attack capitalized on insecure IoT devices, compromising them to launch massive distributed denial-of-service (DDoS) attacks. Securing IoT devices involves addressing issues such as weak default credentials, insufficient update mechanisms, and the potential for remote exploitation.

Human factors, including insider threats and social engineering, contribute significantly to vulnerabilities in digital infrastructure. Insiders with malicious intent or unintentional lapses in security practices can pose substantial risks. The 2013 Edward Snowden case highlighted the potential impact of insider threats, where a contractor leaked classified information. Social engineering tactics, such as pretexting or impersonation, exploit human trust to gain unauthorized access. Comprehensive training programs and user awareness campaigns are essential in addressing human-related vulnerabilities.

Supply chain vulnerabilities in digital infrastructure pose a growing threat, as interconnected systems rely on a complex ecosystem of vendors and partners. Malicious actors can target the supply chain to compromise software or hardware before it reaches end-users. The SolarWinds cyberattack in 2020 exemplifies the supply chain vulnerability, where attackers compromised software updates to gain unauthorized access to numerous organizations. Strengthening supply chain security involves rigorous vetting of vendors, secure software development practices, and continuous monitoring of the supply chain ecosystem.

Inadequate incident response and recovery capabilities represent a vulnerability that can exacerbate the impact of cyber incidents. Without a well-defined and tested incident response plan, organizations may struggle to contain and remediate security breaches effectively. The 2017 WannaCry ransomware attack demonstrated the importance of robust incident response, as organizations with efficient recovery processes were able to minimize the impact. Developing and regularly testing incident response plans is essential for reducing the potential fallout from security incidents.

In conclusion, common vulnerabilities in digital infrastructure encompass a broad spectrum of technological, human, and organizational weaknesses. Timely software updates, secure configurations, robust authentication practices, and effective network security measures are crucial in addressing these vulnerabilities. Furthermore, addressing human-related factors through cybersecurity awareness training and implementing comprehensive supply chain security measures are essential components of a holistic cybersecurity strategy. As the digital landscape evolves, organizations must remain vigilant, continually adapting their cybersecurity measures to mitigate emerging threats and vulnerabilities.

Discuss the importance of patch management and system updates.

Patch management and system updates are integral components of robust cybersecurity strategies, playing a crucial role in safeguarding digital systems, networks, and data from evolving threats. These proactive measures are essential for addressing vulnerabilities, enhancing system resilience, and maintaining the overall security posture of organizations in the dynamic and ever-evolving landscape of cyber threats.

Timely and consistent patch management is fundamental to the security of software and applications running on digital systems. Software vulnerabilities, whether discovered by security researchers or malicious actors, represent potential entry points for cyber attackers. Patching involves the release and application of updates, often containing security fixes and improvements, to address these vulnerabilities. The significance of patch management is underscored by numerous high-profile incidents where organizations fell victim to cyber attacks due to the exploitation of known vulnerabilities. For instance, the Equifax data breach in 2017 resulted from the company's failure to apply a patch promptly, allowing attackers to exploit a vulnerability in the Apache Struts web application framework. Effective patch management could have prevented or mitigated the impact of such incidents, emphasizing its critical role in minimizing the attack surface and reducing the risk of exploitation.

System updates extend beyond individual applications, encompassing operating systems and firmware. Operating system updates are central to maintaining the security and stability of the entire computing environment. These updates often address not only security vulnerabilities but also performance enhancements, compatibility improvements, and new features. Neglecting operating system updates can expose systems to a variety of risks, as attackers may exploit unpatched vulnerabilities to compromise the underlying infrastructure. The importance of timely system updates was evident in the WannaCry ransomware attack of 2017, where unpatched Windows systems became targets for exploitation. Organizations that had applied the necessary updates were protected from the ransomware's devastating impact, highlighting the critical role of system-wide updates in preserving the integrity of digital infrastructure.

The rapid evolution of cyber threats necessitates a proactive approach to patch management and system updates. Cybercriminals continuously seek to exploit newly discovered vulnerabilities, making it imperative for organizations to stay ahead of the curve. Security researchers and software vendors regularly release patches and updates to address emerging threats and fortify defenses. The delay in applying these updates can leave organizations susceptible to attacks that leverage the latest techniques and vulnerabilities. Continuous monitoring of security advisories and prompt application of patches are essential for maintaining a resilient security posture and adapting to the dynamic threat landscape effectively.

In addition to addressing known vulnerabilities, patch management and system updates contribute to regulatory compliance and risk mitigation. Many regulatory frameworks, such as the General Data Protection Regulation (GDPR) and the Health Insurance Portability and Accountability Act (HIPAA), require organizations to implement security measures to protect sensitive data. Regularly updating systems and applying patches aligns with these regulatory requirements, demonstrating a commitment to data security and privacy. Furthermore, effective patch management is a key element of risk management strategies, reducing the likelihood of security incidents and the associated financial and reputational consequences. By systematically addressing vulnerabilities through updates, organizations enhance their resilience to cyber threats and establish a foundation for comprehensive risk mitigation.

The importance of patch management extends to the broader ecosystem of third-party software and applications. Many organizations rely on a diverse range of software solutions to meet their operational needs. Each of these applications represents a potential vector for cyber attacks if not properly maintained. Vendors regularly release updates to address security vulnerabilities, improve functionality, and address compatibility issues. A comprehensive patch management strategy involves not only monitoring and applying updates to core systems but also managing the patching process for all software in use. This holistic approach helps create a cohesive security posture that mitigates risks across the entire digital infrastructure.

Effective patch management requires a balance between timeliness and thorough testing. While the urgency of addressing vulnerabilities is paramount, rushing updates without proper testing can introduce unforeseen issues and disrupt critical business operations. The testing phase allows organizations to assess the impact of updates on their specific environments, ensuring compatibility with existing systems and applications. This balance is particularly crucial in environments where system downtime or disruptions can have severe consequences, such as healthcare, finance, or critical infrastructure. By establishing rigorous testing procedures, organizations can confidently deploy patches that enhance security without compromising operational continuity.

Automation plays a pivotal role in streamlining and enhancing the efficiency of patch management processes. Automated patch deployment tools enable organizations to expedite the application of updates across large and diverse IT environments. This not only accelerates the response to emerging threats but also reduces the window of opportunity for attackers to exploit vulnerabilities. Automation also helps ensure consistency in patching practices, minimizing the risk of human error. However, it is essential to combine automation with robust monitoring and testing to maintain a comprehensive and adaptive approach to patch management.

Patch management is not a one-time task but an ongoing, cyclical process. Continuous monitoring of the threat landscape, timely assessment of vulnerabilities, and the application of updates based on risk priorities are essential elements of a proactive and adaptive patch management strategy. Organizations should establish clear policies, procedures, and communication channels to facilitate collaboration between IT teams, security teams, and other stakeholders. Regular training and awareness programs for staff members can enhance their understanding of the importance of prompt updates and their role in maintaining a secure digital environment.

In conclusion, patch management and system updates are cornerstones of effective cybersecurity practices, playing a pivotal role in mitigating vulnerabilities, reducing the attack surface, and enhancing the overall resilience of digital infrastructure. The timely application of patches, spanning from individual applications to operating systems and firmware, is critical in addressing known vulnerabilities and adapting to the dynamic threat landscape. This proactive approach not only safeguards organizations against cyber threats but also contributes to regulatory compliance, risk mitigation, and the establishment of a robust security posture. As organizations navigate the complex cybersecurity landscape, prioritizing and investing in comprehensive patch management practices is essential for safeguarding the integrity, confidentiality, and availability of digital assets in an interconnected and evolving digital era.

Introduce popular cybersecurity frameworks (e.g., NIST, ISO/IEC 27001).

Cybersecurity frameworks serve as essential guidelines and structures for organizations seeking to establish robust cybersecurity practices. Among the most widely adopted frameworks are the National Institute of Standards and Technology (NIST) Cybersecurity Framework and the International Organization for Standardization and the International Electrotechnical Commission (ISO/IEC) 27001. These frameworks provide comprehensive methodologies, best practices, and standards to help organizations assess, implement, and continually improve their cybersecurity posture.

The NIST Cybersecurity Framework, developed by the U.S. National Institute of Standards and Technology, offers a flexible and risk-based approach to cybersecurity. It is organized around five core functions: Identify, Protect, Detect, Respond, and Recover. The "Identify" function involves understanding and managing cybersecurity risks, while the "Protect" function focuses on implementing safeguards to secure critical assets. The "Detect" function emphasizes the timely identification of cybersecurity events, and the "Respond" function guides organizations in effectively mitigating and recovering from incidents. The "Recover" function addresses strategies for restoring services and systems to normal operations. The NIST framework encourages organizations to customize and adapt its principles to their specific needs and risk profiles, fostering a scalable and adaptable cybersecurity strategy.

ISO/IEC 27001, on the other hand, is an international standard that provides a systematic approach to managing information security. It establishes the criteria for an Information Security Management System (ISMS), outlining the requirements for organizations to identify, assess, and manage information security risks effectively. ISO/IEC 27001 is part of the broader ISO/IEC 27000 family of standards, offering a comprehensive set of guidelines for information security management. The standard encompasses areas such as risk management, access control, cryptography, and incident response. ISO/IEC 27001 is widely recognized for its emphasis on continual improvement, requiring organizations to regularly assess and update their security measures. Certification to ISO/IEC 27001 signifies that an organization has implemented an ISMS in line with international best practices.

The Center for Internet Security (CIS) Critical Security Controls, formerly known as the SANS Critical Security Controls, is another prominent framework designed to assist organizations in enhancing their cybersecurity posture. Developed by a global community of security experts, these controls provide a prioritized set of actions that organizations can take to mitigate the most prevalent cyber threats. The controls cover areas such as secure configuration, continuous vulnerability assessment, data protection, and incident response. The CIS Critical Security Controls are recognized for their practical and actionable guidance, enabling organizations to prioritize their efforts based on the most immediate and impactful threats.

The Payment Card Industry Data Security Standard (PCI DSS) is a specific framework tailored for organizations that handle cardholder information. Developed by the Payment Card Industry Security Standards Council (PCI SSC), PCI DSS outlines requirements for securing payment card transactions. The standard covers aspects such as network security, access controls, encryption, and regular security testing. Compliance with PCI DSS is mandatory for entities involved in processing or transmitting payment card data, and noncompliance can result in fines and restrictions on card processing capabilities. PCI DSS serves as a crucial framework for the financial industry, ensuring the security of payment card transactions and protecting cardholder data.

The Federal Risk and Authorization Management Program (FedRAMP) is a U.S. government initiative that standardizes the security assessment, authorization, and continuous monitoring of cloud services. FedRAMP aims to streamline the adoption of cloud services across federal agencies by providing a standardized approach to security assessments and authorizations. Cloud service providers seeking to offer services to the federal government must undergo a rigorous assessment process to achieve FedRAMP authorization. The framework encompasses security controls, risk management, and continuous monitoring, ensuring that cloud services adhere to stringent security standards. FedRAMP plays a pivotal role in promoting the adoption of secure cloud solutions within the federal government.

The Health Insurance Portability and Accountability Act (HIPAA) Security Rule is a framework specifically designed for the healthcare industry in the United States. Part of the broader HIPAA legislation, the Security Rule outlines requirements for protecting electronic protected health information (ePHI). Covered entities, including healthcare providers, health plans, and healthcare clearinghouses, must implement safeguards to secure ePHI and ensure the confidentiality, integrity, and availability of patient information. The Security Rule covers areas such as access controls, audit controls, and encryption. Compliance with the HIPAA Security Rule is essential for organizations handling electronic health records, safeguarding patient data from unauthorized access and breaches.

The European Union's General Data Protection Regulation (GDPR) is a regulatory framework that focuses on the protection of personal data. While not exclusively a cybersecurity framework, GDPR mandates robust data protection measures and has significant implications for cybersecurity practices. GDPR applies to organizations that process the personal data of EU residents, irrespective of the organization's location. The regulation emphasizes principles such as data minimization, purpose limitation, and the right to erasure. Organizations must implement measures to ensure the security and confidentiality of personal data, including the use of encryption, regular risk assessments, and incident response capabilities. GDPR serves as a global benchmark for data protection, influencing cybersecurity practices worldwide.

The Cybersecurity Maturity Model Certification (CMMC) is a framework developed by the U.S. Department of Defense (DoD) to enhance the cybersecurity posture of defense contractors. CMMC introduces a tiered certification model, ranging from Level 1 (Basic Cyber Hygiene) to Level 5 (Advanced/Progressive). The framework incorporates practices from existing standards, including NIST SP 800-171, and introduces additional requirements. CMMC aims to ensure that defense contractors implement adequate cybersecurity measures to protect sensitive defense information and Controlled Unclassified Information (CUI). The certification process involves third-party assessments, providing a more comprehensive evaluation of an organization's cybersecurity maturity.

In conclusion, these cybersecurity frameworks play pivotal roles in guiding organizations toward establishing and maintaining effective cybersecurity practices. Whether focusing on general cybersecurity principles, industry-specific requirements, or regional regulations, these frameworks provide valuable blueprints for risk management, security controls, and continual improvement. Organizations often choose frameworks based on their specific needs, industry affiliations, or regulatory obligations. As the cyber threat landscape evolves, adherence to these frameworks becomes increasingly crucial for mitigating risks, protecting sensitive information, and ensuring the resilience of digital systems in an interconnected and dynamic environment.

Explain how these frameworks contribute to a secure digital environment.

Cybersecurity frameworks play a pivotal role in contributing to a secure digital environment by providing organizations with structured methodologies, best practices, and standards that guide the establishment, implementation, and continual improvement of robust cybersecurity measures. These frameworks serve as comprehensive roadmaps, addressing various aspects of cybersecurity, including risk management, security controls, and regulatory compliance. By aligning with and implementing these frameworks, organizations can fortify their defenses, mitigate vulnerabilities, and foster a resilient security posture in the face of evolving cyber threats.

The National Institute of Standards and Technology (NIST) Cybersecurity Framework, with its five core functions - Identify, Protect, Detect, Respond, and Recover - contributes to a secure digital environment by offering a holistic and adaptive approach to cybersecurity. The "Identify" function assists organizations in understanding and managing their cybersecurity risks, promoting a proactive stance toward potential threats. The "Protect" function guides the implementation of safeguards to secure critical assets, ensuring the confidentiality, integrity, and availability of sensitive information. The "Detect" function emphasizes the timely identification of cybersecurity events, enabling organizations to respond swiftly to potential incidents. The "Respond" function provides guidance on effective incident mitigation, and the "Recover" function focuses on strategies for restoring services and systems to normal operations. NIST's framework fosters a dynamic cybersecurity strategy that adapts to the organization's risk profile and evolving threat landscape.

ISO/IEC 27001, as an international standard for information security management, contributes to a secure digital environment by providing organizations with a systematic and comprehensive approach to managing information security risks. The standard outlines a structured Information Security Management System (ISMS) that includes risk assessment, risk treatment, and continual improvement processes. ISO/IEC 27001 emphasizes a risk-based approach, enabling organizations to identify and prioritize security controls based on their specific risk landscape. By implementing the standard, organizations establish a framework for protecting sensitive information, ensuring the security of data assets, and aligning with international best practices. The certification process for ISO/IEC 27001 provides external validation of an organization's commitment to information security, fostering trust among stakeholders and partners.

The Center for Internet Security (CIS) Critical Security Controls, designed by a global community of security experts, contributes to a secure digital environment by offering a prioritized set of actions that organizations can take to mitigate prevalent cyber threats. These controls cover critical areas such as secure configuration, continuous vulnerability assessment, data protection, and incident response. By focusing on a prioritized list of actionable controls, the CIS Critical Security Controls enable organizations to address immediate and impactful threats efficiently. The framework's practical guidance facilitates the implementation of security measures that have a direct and measurable impact on an organization's cybersecurity posture, contributing to a more resilient and secure digital environment.

The Payment Card Industry Data Security Standard (PCI DSS) is dedicated to securing payment card transactions, making a significant contribution to a secure digital environment, particularly within the financial industry. PCI DSS provides a set of requirements for securing cardholder information, covering aspects such as network security, access controls, encryption, and regular security testing. Compliance with PCI DSS is mandatory for entities handling payment card data, ensuring that organizations implement robust security measures to protect sensitive financial information. By adhering to PCI DSS requirements, organizations contribute to a secure digital environment for financial transactions, instilling confidence among consumers and preserving the integrity of payment card systems.

The Federal Risk and Authorization Management Program (FedRAMP) contributes to a secure digital environment by standardizing the security assessment, authorization, and continuous monitoring of cloud services within the U.S. federal government. FedRAMP

ensures that cloud service providers adhere to rigorous security standards, promoting the adoption of secure cloud solutions across federal agencies. By establishing a standardized approach to security assessments, FedRAMP enhances transparency and trust in cloud services, contributing to a secure digital environment for government
operations. The framework's focus on continuous monitoring aligns
with the dynamic nature of cybersecurity threats, providing ongoing
assurance of the security of cloud services.

The Health Insurance Portability and Accountability Act
(HIPAA) Security Rule is dedicated to securing electronic protected
health information (ePHI) within the healthcare industry. HIPAA
contributes to a secure digital environment by establishing requirements for access controls, audit controls, and encryption to protect
patient data. Compliance with the HIPAA Security Rule is essential
for healthcare organizations handling electronic health records, contributing to a secure and confidential healthcare ecosystem. By implementing measures to safeguard ePHI, organizations adhere to
the principles of privacy and security in healthcare, fostering trust
among patients and ensuring the integrity of health information.

The European Union's General Data Protection Regulation
(GDPR) contributes to a secure digital environment by establishing
principles and requirements for the protection of personal data.
While not exclusively a cybersecurity framework, GDPR mandates
robust data protection measures, including encryption, regular risk
assessments, and incident response capabilities. By adhering to
GDPR, organizations contribute to a secure digital environment for
personal data, respecting individual privacy rights and mitigating the
risk of data breaches. The regulation's emphasis on transparency, accountability, and the right to erasure enhances the overall security
and trustworthiness of digital ecosystems.

The Cybersecurity Maturity Model Certification (CMMC)
contributes to a secure digital environment by enhancing the cyber-

security posture of defense contractors. Developed by the U.S. Department of Defense (DoD), CMMC introduces a tiered certification model, requiring contractors to implement security controls based on the sensitivity of the information they handle. By certifying defense contractors based on their cybersecurity maturity, CMMC ensures that sensitive defense information and Controlled Unclassified Information (CUI) are adequately protected. The framework's focus on maturity levels promotes continual improvement, contributing to a more resilient and secure defense industrial base.

In conclusion, these cybersecurity frameworks collectively contribute to a secure digital environment by offering organizations structured methodologies, best practices, and standards that address diverse aspects of cybersecurity. Whether focused on risk management, regulatory compliance, or industry-specific requirements, these frameworks provide organizations with guidance to fortify their defenses, mitigate vulnerabilities, and establish resilient security postures. By aligning with these frameworks, organizations contribute to the overall trustworthiness and security of digital ecosystems, fostering a safer environment for sensitive information, critical operations, and interactions in an interconnected and dynamic digital landscape.

Explore the role of human error in cybersecurity incidents.

Human error stands as a significant and recurrent factor in cybersecurity incidents, playing a pivotal role in the ever-evolving landscape of digital threats. Despite advancements in technology and the implementation of sophisticated cybersecurity measures, the fallibility of individuals remains a persistent challenge. The multifaceted nature of human error encompasses a range of actions, from inadvertent mistakes to conscious but misguided decisions, and it poses a substantial risk to the security and integrity of digital systems, networks, and data.

One prevalent form of human error in cybersecurity incidents is the lack of awareness and understanding among users regarding potential threats and security best practices. Users who are not adequately informed about the latest phishing techniques, social engineering tactics, or the importance of strong passwords may inadvertently fall victim to cyber attacks. This lack of awareness creates vulnerabilities that attackers exploit, leading to incidents such as unauthorized access, data breaches, and financial losses. Addressing this aspect of human error requires comprehensive cybersecurity education and training programs that empower users with the knowledge and skills needed to recognize and respond to potential threats.

Phishing attacks, which rely on the manipulation of individuals through deceptive emails, websites, or messages, often succeed due to human error. Despite increased awareness of phishing tactics, individuals may still succumb to well-crafted and convincing phishing attempts. Clicking on malicious links, downloading infected attachments, or providing sensitive information in response to phishing emails are common instances of human error that open the door to cyber threats. Organizations need to prioritize user awareness training, simulate phishing scenarios, and implement robust email filtering solutions to mitigate the impact of phishing attacks and reduce the likelihood of human error.

Misconfigured systems and applications, often a result of human oversight, constitute another dimension of human error in cybersecurity incidents. System administrators or developers may unintentionally expose critical assets to the internet, leave default credentials unchanged, or overlook security configurations, creating opportunities for attackers to exploit vulnerabilities. These misconfigurations can lead to unauthorized access, data exposure, and service disruptions. Implementing strict change control procedures, conducting regular security audits, and automating configuration manage-

ment processes are crucial steps in minimizing the impact of misconfigurations caused by human error.

Password-related human errors, such as using weak passwords,
sharing credentials, or failing to update passwords regularly, remain
persistent challenges in cybersecurity. Despite the emphasis on password security, individuals often exhibit lax practices that expose systems to unauthorized access. Weak or easily guessable passwords are
susceptible to brute-force attacks, and the reuse of passwords across
multiple accounts increases the risk of credential compromise. Organizations must enforce strong password policies, implement multi-
factor authentication (MFA), and educate users on the importance
of creating and safeguarding secure passwords to mitigate the impact
of these common human errors.

In the context of insider threats, human error takes on a more intentional but misguided form. Employees or contractors with privileged access may inadvertently or deliberately engage in activities
that compromise the confidentiality, integrity, or availability of sensitive information. Whether through accidental data leaks, improper
handling of confidential data, or intentional sabotage, insider threats
underscore the need for organizations to implement robust access
controls, conduct thorough background checks, and monitor user
activities to detect and respond to potential security incidents.

Social engineering exploits psychological tactics to manipulate
individuals into divulging sensitive information or taking actions
that compromise security. Phishing, pretexting, and baiting are examples of social engineering techniques that leverage human tenden-
cies, such as trust and curiosity, to achieve malicious objectives. Human error in the form of trusting an impostor's identity, clicking on
malicious links, or sharing confidential information during a seemingly legitimate interaction can result in significant security breaches. Organizations must educate users about social engineering tac-

tics, encourage skepticism, and implement technical controls to identify and block social engineering attempts.

The use of removable media, such as USB drives, poses another avenue for human error in cybersecurity incidents. Malicious actors may exploit individuals' curiosity or lack of awareness by distributing infected USB drives or enticing users to plug unknown devices into their systems. This human error can lead to the unintentional introduction of malware, unauthorized access, or the exfiltration of sensitive data. Implementing strict policies on the use of removable media, conducting regular security awareness training, and deploying endpoint protection solutions are crucial measures to mitigate the risks associated with human errors involving removable media.

In the realm of software development, coding errors and insecure coding practices introduce vulnerabilities that can be exploited by attackers. Human error in the form of overlooking input validation, neglecting security best practices, or failing to conduct thorough code reviews can lead to the release of software with exploitable weaknesses. These vulnerabilities may result in unauthorized access, data breaches, or the compromise of critical systems. Organizations must prioritize secure coding practices, conduct regular code reviews, and implement automated security testing tools to identify and remediate coding errors introduced by human oversight.

The complexity of technology and the rapid pace of innovation contribute to human error in the configuration and management of security tools and systems. Security administrators may misconfigure firewalls, intrusion detection systems, or antivirus solutions, creating gaps in the organization's defense mechanisms. Additionally, delays in applying security patches or updates can result from human oversight, leaving systems exposed to known vulnerabilities. Implementing rigorous change management processes, automating routine security tasks, and regularly auditing security configurations are essential strategies to address human errors in the administration of security tools.

In incident response and crisis management, human errors can exacerbate the impact of security incidents. Ineffective communication, delayed response times, or the mishandling of sensitive information during an incident can lead to prolonged downtime, increased financial losses, and reputational damage. Organizations must prioritize incident response planning, conduct regular simulations and drills, and provide training to response teams to minimize human errors during critical phases of incident management.

The role of human error in cybersecurity incidents extends beyond individual actions to encompass organizational culture, leadership, and resource allocation. Organizations that fail to prioritize cybersecurity, allocate insufficient resources, or lack a proactive security culture are more susceptible to human errors that result in security incidents. Leadership commitment, ongoing investment in cybersecurity measures, and the establishment of a cybersecurity-aware culture are critical components in reducing human errors and creating a resilient security posture.

In conclusion, human error represents a complex and multifaceted challenge in the realm of cybersecurity incidents. Whether through lack of awareness, misconfigurations, password-related issues, social engineering manipulation, or intentional insider actions, human errors contribute significantly to the success of cyber attacks. Mitigating the impact of human errors requires a holistic approach that encompasses education and training, technical controls, policy enforcement, and a commitment to creating a security-conscious organizational culture. As organizations continue to navigate the evolving threat landscape, addressing the human element in cybersecurity remains a critical imperative to enhance overall resilience and safeguard against a wide array of potential security incidents.

Discuss strategies to enhance cybersecurity awareness among users.

Enhancing cybersecurity awareness among users is a critical component of a comprehensive cybersecurity strategy, as users play a pivotal role in safeguarding digital assets and systems. Effective awareness initiatives go beyond mere dissemination of information; they aim to instill a culture of security, empower users to recognize and respond to threats, and foster a collective responsibility for cybersecurity. Several strategies can be employed to enhance cybersecurity awareness, ranging from targeted training programs to leveraging advanced technologies and promoting a culture of continuous learning and vigilance.

One foundational strategy is the implementation of robust cybersecurity training programs that cater to users at all levels within an organization. These programs should cover a broad spectrum of topics, including the identification of phishing attempts, password hygiene, safe browsing practices, and the importance of software updates. The training content should be engaging, easily digestible, and tailored to the specific roles and responsibilities of different user groups. Interactive simulations, such as phishing exercises, can provide hands-on experience, helping users recognize and avoid potential threats in a controlled environment. Regular, ongoing training sessions are essential to reinforce key concepts and ensure that users stay informed about evolving cybersecurity risks.

Utilizing a multi-modal approach to training can enhance its effectiveness. In addition to traditional classroom-style training, organizations can leverage e-learning platforms, webinars, and other online resources to provide accessible and flexible learning opportunities. Mobile-friendly training modules enable users to access cybersecurity education on-the-go, accommodating diverse learning preferences and schedules. Gamification, where training incorporates elements of games and competition, can make the learning experience more engaging and enjoyable, motivating users to actively participate and retain key cybersecurity principles.

Fostering a culture of cybersecurity awareness requires active leadership involvement and commitment. Leaders should communicate the importance of cybersecurity regularly and visibly endorse security initiatives. Executives and managers can lead by example, demonstrating secure behaviors and emphasizing the shared responsibility of every employee in maintaining a secure digital environment. An organization's leadership should allocate resources for cybersecurity awareness initiatives, including budget, personnel, and time, signaling a top-down commitment to prioritizing security.

Engaging in open and transparent communication about cybersecurity incidents and threats can contribute to awareness. Regularly sharing information about emerging threats, recent security incidents, and their resolutions helps users stay informed and vigilant. Creating channels for reporting potential security concerns or incidents, and ensuring that users are aware of these reporting mechanisms, encourages a proactive approach to security. Establishing a feedback loop where users receive updates on the outcomes of reported incidents fosters a sense of accountability and reinforces the importance of their contributions to the overall security posture.

Incorporating cybersecurity awareness into the onboarding process for new employees is crucial. Providing comprehensive training from the outset sets expectations for security practices from the beginning of an individual's tenure with the organization. This initial training can cover fundamental security principles, policies, and procedures, laying a strong foundation for ongoing awareness efforts. Additionally, including cybersecurity as a recurring topic in regular staff meetings or team briefings ensures that awareness remains a consistent and integral part of the organizational culture.

Tailoring cybersecurity awareness programs to the specific needs and risks of different departments or job roles enhances their relevance and impact. Not all users face the same cybersecurity challenges, and customization ensures that training addresses the unique threats associated with each role. For example, finance teams may receive specialized training on financial fraud prevention, while IT personnel may focus on system vulnerabilities and secure coding practices. This targeted approach not only makes training more effective but also reinforces the idea that cybersecurity is a shared responsibility across the organization.

Regularly assessing and measuring the effectiveness of cybersecurity awareness initiatives is essential for refining and improving these programs over time. Conducting periodic evaluations, such as phishing simulation assessments, can provide valuable insights into user behavior and identify areas that require additional focus. Surveys and feedback mechanisms can gauge user perceptions of the training content and identify any gaps in understanding. Analyzing trends in incident reports and security-related helpdesk tickets can also provide valuable feedback on the impact of awareness initiatives and areas for improvement.

Leveraging advanced technologies, such as artificial intelligence (AI) and machine learning, can enhance cybersecurity awareness efforts. AI-powered tools can analyze user behavior and identify patterns indicative of potential security risks. These tools can provide real-time feedback to users, alerting them to suspicious activities or potential phishing attempts. Additionally, gamified learning platforms that incorporate AI algorithms can adapt to individual learning styles, providing personalized training experiences that resonate with users. Embracing innovative technologies not only enhances the effectiveness of awareness programs but also underscores the organization's commitment to staying ahead of evolving cybersecurity threats.

Promoting a secure mindset beyond the confines of the workplace is crucial, especially in an era where remote work and personal device usage are prevalent. Extending cybersecurity awareness initiatives to cover home network security, secure remote work practices, and the protection of personal devices reinforces the importance of security in both professional and personal contexts. Providing resources and guidelines for securing home networks, recognizing potential threats in personal email accounts, and securing personal devices against cyber threats contributes to a more holistic approach to cybersecurity awareness.

Collaborating with external partners, industry associations, or government agencies can provide additional resources and perspectives to enhance cybersecurity awareness initiatives. Participating in industry forums, sharing best practices, and staying informed about the latest cybersecurity trends contribute to a broader understanding of the threat landscape. Engaging in collaborative efforts to promote cybersecurity awareness, such as participating in cybersecurity awareness months or initiatives, amplifies the impact and reach of awareness campaigns.

Recognizing and celebrating achievements in cybersecurity awareness can motivate and reinforce positive behaviors. Establishing recognition programs or acknowledging individuals and teams for their contributions to maintaining a secure environment fosters a positive and supportive culture. This positive reinforcement not only encourages individuals to remain vigilant but also establishes a sense of pride and ownership in the collective effort to enhance cybersecurity within the organization.

In conclusion, enhancing cybersecurity awareness among users is a multifaceted endeavor that requires a combination of strategic, cultural, and technological approaches. From targeted training programs to leadership commitment, continuous evaluation, and collaboration with external partners, organizations must adopt a comprehensive and adaptive approach to cybersecurity awareness. By cultivating a culture of security, providing tailored training, leveraging advanced technologies, and promoting a collective responsibility for cybersecurity, organizations can empower users to become vigilant defenders against the ever-evolving landscape of cyber threats.

Chapter 2: Building the Cyber Defense Framework

Define the concept of risk in cybersecurity.

The concept of risk in cybersecurity embodies the dynamic and complex landscape of potential harm or adverse events stemming from vulnerabilities, threats, and the exploitation of weaknesses within an organization's digital ecosystem. In the context of cybersecurity, risk is a multifaceted construct that involves assessing the likelihood and impact of various threats on the confidentiality, integrity, and availability of information and resources. It encompasses the identification, analysis, and mitigation of potential risks that could compromise the security posture of an organization. This comprehensive understanding of risk serves as the foundation for effective cybersecurity management, guiding decision-making processes, resource allocation, and the implementation of protective measures.

At its core, risk in cybersecurity is rooted in the interplay between threats and vulnerabilities. Threats represent potential malicious actions or events that can exploit vulnerabilities and cause harm to an organization's assets or operations. These threats can manifest in various forms, including cyberattacks, data breaches, malware infections, or even natural disasters that may impact digital infrastructure. Vulnerabilities, on the other hand, are weaknesses or gaps in security defenses that could be exploited by threats. These vulnerabilities can exist in software, hardware, network configurations, human behavior, or even in the organizational processes that govern cybersecurity.

Risk assessment, a fundamental component of cybersecurity risk management, involves the systematic evaluation of potential threats and vulnerabilities to determine the level of risk associated with specific assets or processes. This assessment takes into account factors such as the likelihood of a threat exploiting a vulnerability and the potential impact on the organization if such an exploitation occurs. The goal is to quantify and prioritize risks based on their significance, allowing organizations to focus their resources on addressing the most critical and impactful threats.

In the realm of cybersecurity, risks extend beyond the technical domain and encompass a wide range of factors, including human behavior, regulatory compliance, and the broader business context. For instance, the actions of users within an organization can introduce risks through inadvertent mistakes, lack of awareness, or intentional malicious activities. Non-compliance with industry regulations and legal requirements can expose organizations to regulatory penalties and reputational damage, constituting a form of risk. The evolving nature of technology and the business environment introduces uncertainties that further contribute to the complexity of cybersecurity risk.

Risk mitigation strategies in cybersecurity aim to reduce the likelihood and impact of identified risks. These strategies involve a combination of preventive, detective, and corrective measures designed to strengthen security defenses, monitor for potential threats, and respond effectively to security incidents. Common mitigation techniques include implementing robust access controls, conducting regular security awareness training for users, deploying intrusion detection and prevention systems, encrypting sensitive data, and maintaining up-to-date security patches.

The concept of risk in cybersecurity is closely linked to the notion of the risk appetite and risk tolerance of an organization. The risk appetite defines the amount and type of risk that an organization is willing to accept in pursuit of its objectives, considering factors such as business goals, compliance requirements, and industry norms. Risk tolerance, on the other hand, establishes the threshold beyond which risks are deemed unacceptable. Organizations must align their cybersecurity efforts with their risk appetite and tolerance, striking a balance between innovation and security to support business objectives while minimizing potential harm.

Cybersecurity risk is also intertwined with the broader concept of enterprise risk management (ERM), which encompasses the identification, assessment, and prioritization of all risks facing an organization. Cybersecurity risk, while a crucial component of ERM, is just one facet of the overall risk landscape that organizations must navigate. The integration of cybersecurity risk management into the broader ERM framework enables organizations to make informed decisions that consider cybersecurity alongside other strategic, operational, financial, and compliance-related risks.

The concept of risk in cybersecurity is inherently forward-looking and requires organizations to anticipate and adapt to the ever-evolving threat landscape. Threat actors continually evolve their tactics, techniques, and procedures, necessitating a proactive and adaptive approach to risk management. Cybersecurity risk is not a static phenomenon; it is influenced by technological advancements, organizational changes, and the emergence of new threat vectors. As such, organizations must engage in continuous monitoring, threat intelligence gathering, and scenario planning to stay ahead of potential risks and ensure the resilience of their cybersecurity defenses.

Cybersecurity risk also extends to the supply chain, as organizations increasingly rely on third-party vendors and partners for various services and technologies. The interconnected nature of modern business ecosystems means that a security breach in one part of the supply chain can have cascading effects on multiple organizations. Managing cybersecurity risk in the supply chain involves assessing

the security practices of vendors, implementing contractual obligations for security compliance, and establishing contingency plans to
respond to potential disruptions.

In conclusion, the concept of risk in cybersecurity encapsulates
the dynamic interplay between threats, vulnerabilities, and the potential impact on an organization's digital assets and operations. It
involves a comprehensive and forward-looking assessment of potential risks, considering technical, human, regulatory, and business factors. Effective cybersecurity risk management requires organizations
to quantify, prioritize, and mitigate risks in alignment with their risk
appetite and tolerance. The evolving nature of technology and the
threat landscape necessitates a proactive and adaptive approach to
cybersecurity risk, integrating it into the broader framework of enterprise risk management. As organizations navigate the complexities of the digital age, understanding and managing cybersecurity
risk becomes a foundational element for ensuring the security, resilience, and sustainability of their digital ecosystems.

**Discuss the importance of risk assessments for effective de-
fense.**

Risk assessments play a pivotal role in the realm of cybersecurity,
serving as a cornerstone for effective defense strategies in the face
of evolving and sophisticated threats. The importance of risk assessments lies in their ability to systematically identify, evaluate, and prioritize potential risks to an organization's digital assets, allowing for
informed decision-making and targeted mitigation efforts. By comprehensively understanding the landscape of threats and vulnerabilities, organizations can tailor their defensive measures, allocate resources judiciously, and establish a resilient cybersecurity posture
that aligns with business objectives and risk tolerance.

At the core of the importance of risk assessments is the proactive
identification of potential threats and vulnerabilities within an organization's digital ecosystem. Cyber threats are dynamic and continu-

ally evolving, ranging from common malware attacks to sophisticated nation-state-sponsored campaigns. Through a systematic risk assessment process, organizations can stay ahead of emerging threats by anticipating the tactics, techniques, and procedures employed by adversaries. By understanding the specific threat landscape relevant to their industry, geography, and business model, organizations can develop a threat intelligence-informed defense strategy that addresses the most pertinent risks.

Risk assessments provide a structured framework for evaluating the likelihood and potential impact of identified threats. This quantitative and qualitative analysis enables organizations to prioritize risks based on their significance, allowing for a more focused and efficient allocation of resources. Not all risks are equal, and by distinguishing between high-impact, high-likelihood risks and those with lower potential impact, organizations can tailor their defensive measures to address the most critical vulnerabilities and threats. This prioritization is crucial in an environment where resources are finite, and organizations must make strategic decisions to optimize their cybersecurity efforts.

The importance of risk assessments extends beyond technical vulnerabilities to encompass the human element within an organization. Users, whether through inadvertent mistakes or intentional malicious activities, can introduce significant risks. Risk assessments help organizations understand the human factors contributing to cybersecurity risk, such as user awareness, behavior, and potential insider threats. By recognizing these vulnerabilities, organizations can design targeted training programs, implement access controls, and develop a security culture that empowers users to be active participants in the defense against cyber threats.

Organizations operate within a regulatory landscape that imposes various compliance requirements related to cybersecurity. Risk assessments play a crucial role in ensuring regulatory compliance by identifying gaps in security measures and providing a basis for im-plementing controls that align with legal and industry standards. The consequences of non-compliance can include financial penalties, reputational damage, and legal ramifications. Through risk assess-ments, organizations can demonstrate due diligence in addressing cybersecurity risks, thereby satisfying regulatory requirements and building trust among stakeholders.

The dynamic nature of technology and the business environment requires organizations to continually adapt their defense strategies. Risk assessments provide a mechanism for organizations to conduct scenario planning and assess the potential impact of emerging tech-nologies on their cybersecurity posture. Whether adopting cloud computing, Internet of Things (IoT) devices, or artificial intelli-gence, organizations must evaluate the associated risks and imple-ment security measures that align with their risk appetite. Risk as-sessments enable organizations to anticipate and address risks asso-ciated with technological advancements, ensuring that the adoption of new technologies does not compromise overall cybersecurity re-silience.

Risk assessments contribute to the development of incident re-sponse and recovery plans by identifying potential scenarios and their associated risks. Understanding the impact and likelihood of different cybersecurity incidents allows organizations to formulate effective response strategies, ensuring a swift and coordinated reac-tion to security breaches. Incident response plans, informed by risk assessments, enhance an organization's ability to contain, eradicate, and recover from security incidents, minimizing potential damages and downtime.

In addition to understanding external threats, risk assessments shed light on the vulnerabilities inherent in an organization's inter-nal processes and procedures. This includes examining the security controls in place, the effectiveness of security policies, and the robustness of access management. By evaluating internal vulnerabilities, organizations can enhance their overall security posture, identifying and addressing weaknesses that might be exploited by both internal and external actors. This holistic approach ensures that the entire cybersecurity ecosystem is considered in defense strategies.

Risk assessments are instrumental in fostering a culture of continuous improvement within an organization's cybersecurity framework. Through regular assessments, organizations can track changes in the threat landscape, assess the effectiveness of implemented controls, and refine their defense strategies accordingly. This iterative process allows organizations to adapt to emerging threats, learn from past incidents, and stay proactive in the ever-changing field of cybersecurity. The dynamic nature of risk assessments aligns with the evolving cyber threat landscape, emphasizing the importance of continual evaluation and adjustment in the pursuit of robust defense.

The interconnected nature of modern business ecosystems introduces supply chain risks that can have cascading effects across multiple organizations. Risk assessments help organizations evaluate the cybersecurity practices of third-party vendors, partners, and suppliers, recognizing potential vulnerabilities and threats that may affect the integrity of the supply chain. By extending risk assessments to the broader ecosystem, organizations can implement measures to mitigate supply chain risks, ensuring a more comprehensive and collaborative defense against cyber threats.

Another crucial aspect of the importance of risk assessments is their role in supporting strategic decision-making within organizations. Cybersecurity is not solely a technical concern; it is intrinsically linked to broader business objectives and risk management. Risk assessments provide executives and decision-makers with the necessary insights to align cybersecurity strategies with overall business goals. This strategic alignment ensures that cybersecurity is integrated into the organization's broader risk management framework, contributing to the sustainability and success of the business.

In conclusion, the importance of risk assessments for effective defense in cybersecurity cannot be overstated. These assessments provide a systematic and comprehensive approach to identifying, evaluating, and prioritizing potential threats and vulnerabilities. By understanding the dynamic threat landscape, organizations can tailor their defense strategies, allocate resources judiciously, and establish a resilient cybersecurity posture. Risk assessments enable organizations to proactively manage cybersecurity risks, anticipate emerging threats, and foster a culture of continuous improvement. In an era of evolving cyber threats, organizations that prioritize risk assessments are better equipped to navigate the complexities of the digital landscape and safeguard their assets, operations, and reputation.

Outline the key components of a comprehensive cybersecurity strategy.

A comprehensive cybersecurity strategy is essential for organizations to safeguard their digital assets, protect sensitive information, and mitigate the evolving threat landscape. Such a strategy encompasses a holistic approach, addressing various aspects of cybersecurity to create a resilient defense posture. The key components of a comprehensive cybersecurity strategy include risk management, robust security policies, proactive threat intelligence, advanced technology solutions, user education and awareness, incident response planning, continuous monitoring, regulatory compliance, and collaboration with stakeholders.

Risk management forms the foundation of a comprehensive cybersecurity strategy. This component involves the systematic identification, assessment, and prioritization of potential risks to an organization's digital assets. By understanding the landscape of threats and vulnerabilities, organizations can make informed decisions about where to allocate resources for the most effective defense. Risk management also involves establishing risk tolerance levels and implementing measures to mitigate or transfer identified risks. A dynamic risk management process ensures that cybersecurity strategies remain adaptive to emerging threats and evolving business requirements.

Robust security policies are critical components of an effective cybersecurity strategy. These policies define the rules and guidelines for securing an organization's information systems, networks, and data. Security policies cover various aspects, including access controls, data encryption, password management, and acceptable use of technology resources. Well-defined policies set clear expectations for employees and stakeholders, fostering a culture of security within the organization. Regular updates and enforcement of security policies ensure that they remain aligned with the organization's risk appetite and evolving cybersecurity requirements.

Proactive threat intelligence is a crucial element in staying ahead of emerging cyber threats. Organizations need to actively gather, analyze, and utilize intelligence on potential threats and vulnerabilities relevant to their industry and business model. Threat intelligence enables organizations to understand the tactics, techniques, and procedures employed by adversaries, allowing for the development of targeted defense strategies. By integrating threat intelligence feeds, organizations can enhance their ability to detect and respond to emerging threats before they result in security incidents.

Advanced technology solutions play a pivotal role in a comprehensive cybersecurity strategy. These solutions encompass a range of tools and technologies designed to detect, prevent, and respond to cyber threats. This includes antivirus software, intrusion detection systems, firewalls, encryption tools, and security information and event management (SIEM) systems. Employing cutting-edge technologies, such as artificial intelligence and machine learning, enhances the ability to identify and mitigate threats in real-time. The integration of these solutions forms a layered defense approach, providing multiple lines of defense against different attack vectors. User education and awareness are critical components in mitigating the human factor in cybersecurity risks. Organizations must invest in comprehensive training programs to educate employees about cybersecurity best practices, the identification of phishing attempts, and the importance of secure behaviors. Building a security-conscious culture involves promoting a shared responsibility among users, encouraging them to be vigilant, report suspicious activities, and adhere to security policies. Ongoing awareness campaigns help reinforce security principles and empower users to play an active role in the defense against social engineering attacks and other human-centric threats.

Incident response planning is a crucial proactive measure within a comprehensive cybersecurity strategy. Organizations should establish well-defined incident response plans that outline the steps to be taken in the event of a security incident. These plans include roles and responsibilities, communication protocols, and procedures for containment, eradication, and recovery. Regular testing and simulation exercises ensure that incident response teams are well-prepared to handle security incidents effectively. Incident response planning is essential for minimizing the impact of security breaches, reducing downtime, and maintaining business continuity.

Continuous monitoring is an integral component to detect and respond to security incidents promptly. Organizations must implement robust monitoring solutions that provide real-time visibility into network and system activities. Continuous monitoring involves the analysis of logs, network traffic, and user behavior to identify anomalous activities indicative of potential security threats. Automated tools, such as SIEM systems, enhance the efficiency of continuous monitoring by correlating data and generating alerts for suspicious activities. Continuous monitoring is essential for early detection, rapid response, and the prevention of security incidents from escalating.

Regulatory compliance is a key consideration in a comprehensive cybersecurity strategy, especially for organizations operating within regulated industries. Compliance with industry-specific regulations and standards ensures that organizations meet legal requirements related to the protection of sensitive information and the implementation of security controls. Compliance efforts involve regular audits, documentation of security practices, and adherence to frameworks such as the NIST Cybersecurity Framework or ISO/IEC 27001. Aligning cybersecurity strategies with regulatory requirements not only helps organizations avoid legal consequences but also contributes to overall risk management.

Collaboration with stakeholders is vital for a comprehensive cybersecurity strategy. Organizations must engage with internal and external stakeholders, including employees, customers, partners, and regulatory bodies. Internally, fostering a collaborative approach involves breaking down silos between IT and other departments to ensure that cybersecurity considerations are integrated into all aspects of the business. Externally, organizations should collaborate with industry peers, share threat intelligence, and participate in forums or information-sharing groups. Collaboration enhances collective defense capabilities and helps organizations stay informed about emerging threats.

In conclusion, a comprehensive cybersecurity strategy integrates multiple components to create a robust defense posture against evolving cyber threats. From risk management and security policies to proactive threat intelligence, advanced technology solutions, user education, and incident response planning, each component plays a crucial role in establishing an effective cybersecurity framework. Continuous monitoring, regulatory compliance, and collaboration with stakeholders further enhance an organization's ability to adapt

SECURE HORIZONS: AN INTRODUCTION TO
CYBERSECURITY   63

to the dynamic threat landscape. A well-rounded cybersecurity strategy is essential for safeguarding digital assets, maintaining business continuity, and building resilience in the face of an ever-evolving cybersecurity landscape.

Address the integration of prevention, detection, and response mechanisms.

The integration of prevention, detection, and response mechanisms is a fundamental approach within cybersecurity strategies, designed to create a layered defense that addresses the dynamic and multifaceted nature of cyber threats. This integrated approach recognizes that a singular focus on prevention is insufficient in today's sophisticated threat landscape; instead, organizations need a comprehensive strategy that combines proactive measures, continuous monitoring, and effective response capabilities to protect their digital assets.

Preventive measures constitute the first line of defense in the integration of cybersecurity mechanisms. These measures aim to stop potential threats before they can manifest into security incidents. Common preventive strategies include implementing robust access controls, enforcing strong authentication mechanisms, deploying firewalls, and regularly updating and patching software to address known vulnerabilities. Prevention is about establishing a fortified perimeter and minimizing the attack surface to reduce the likelihood of successful cyberattacks. While preventive measures are crucial, they are not foolproof, and cyber threats continue to evolve, necessitating the integration of additional layers in the cybersecurity strategy.

Detection mechanisms are essential for identifying and alerting organizations to potential security incidents. Continuous monitoring, network traffic analysis, and the use of security information and event management (SIEM) systems contribute to effective detection. Advanced threat detection technologies, such as intrusion detection and prevention systems (IDPS) and anomaly detection, play a pivotal role in identifying unusual or suspicious activities that may indicate a security threat. The integration of detection mechanisms enables organizations to move beyond a reliance on preventive measures alone, providing real-time insights into ongoing activities that may require further investigation.

The third crucial component in the integration of cybersecurity mechanisms is the capability to respond effectively to identified threats. Response mechanisms involve a coordinated and timely reaction to mitigate the impact of a security incident, contain the threat, and restore normal operations. Incident response plans, which outline predefined steps and roles for addressing security incidents, form the foundation of this component. The response phase includes activities such as isolating affected systems, eradicating the threat, recovering data, and implementing improvements based on lessons learned. The integration of response mechanisms ensures that organizations are not only able to detect threats promptly but also possess the capability to mitigate and recover from security incidents efficiently.

The integration of prevention, detection, and response mechanisms emphasizes the importance of a proactive and adaptive cybersecurity posture. The traditional model of relying solely on preventive measures has become insufficient in the face of advanced and persistent threats. Prevention serves as the initial barrier, but detection is recognized as the bridge between prevention and response, identifying threats that may bypass preventive measures or occur within the organizational perimeter. Response mechanisms complete the triad by providing the necessary actions to address and recover from security incidents effectively.

Integration begins with the acknowledgment that no cybersecurity strategy can guarantee absolute prevention. Even with robust preventive measures in place, the reality is that determined adversaries may find ways to infiltrate networks or exploit vulnerabilities. Therefore, organizations must shift from a mindset centered solely on preventing breaches to one that encompasses the ability to detect and respond to incidents in a timely and effective manner.

Effective integration involves aligning prevention, detection, and response mechanisms to create a cohesive and synergistic defense strategy. For example, the insights gained from detection mechanisms, such as SIEM systems or anomaly detection, should inform and refine preventive measures. If a new threat vector is identified through detection, organizations can update their access controls, apply patches, or adjust security policies to proactively address the emerging threat. This continuous feedback loop ensures that the organization adapts its preventive measures based on the evolving threat landscape.

Additionally, the integration of response mechanisms with prevention and detection ensures a seamless transition from identifying a security incident to taking decisive action. Incident response plans should be well-coordinated with the organization's preventive and detection measures, allowing for rapid and effective responses. The response phase may involve isolating affected systems to prevent lateral movement, eradicating malware or unauthorized access, and restoring affected systems to normal operation. The integration ensures that response actions are aligned with the organization's broader cybersecurity strategy and risk management objectives.

Automation plays a significant role in the integration of cybersecurity mechanisms, particularly in the realms of detection and response. Automated threat detection tools can analyze vast amounts of data in real-time, identifying patterns or anomalies that may indicate a security threat. Automated response mechanisms can execute predefined actions, such as isolating compromised systems or blocking malicious activities, without the need for manual intervention. Automation enhances the speed and efficiency of both detection and response, allowing organizations to respond promptly to emerging threats and reduce the dwell time of attackers within their networks. Integration extends beyond technology to encompass the human element within cybersecurity strategies. Employee training and awareness programs are integral components of a well-rounded cybersecurity strategy, fostering a security-conscious culture throughout the organization. Employees play a crucial role in both the prevention and detection phases, and their ability to recognize and report suspicious activities contributes significantly to overall cybersecurity resilience. In the response phase, well-trained personnel can follow incident response plans effectively, minimizing the impact of security incidents and facilitating a swift recovery.

The integration of cybersecurity mechanisms is not a one-time effort but an ongoing and iterative process. It requires continuous assessment and refinement based on the evolving threat landscape, technological advancements, and organizational changes. Regular testing of preventive, detection, and response measures through simulated exercises and penetration testing ensures that the integrated cybersecurity strategy remains effective and adaptive to emerging threats.

In conclusion, the integration of prevention, detection, and response mechanisms is paramount for building a robust and adaptive cybersecurity strategy. Prevention establishes the initial barrier, detection identifies ongoing threats, and response ensures a timely and effective reaction to security incidents. The synergy between these components, supported by automation and employee awareness, creates a comprehensive defense posture that can withstand the challenges of the ever-evolving cyber threat landscape. Organizations that recognize the importance of integration and continually refine their approach are better equipped to navigate the complexities of cybersecurity and protect their digital assets against a diverse range of cyber threats.

EXPLORE THE SIGNIFICANCE of security policies in a cyber defense framework.
Security policies play a foundational and critical role in a cyber defense framework, serving as the guiding principles and standards that shape an organization's approach to safeguarding its digital assets, sensitive information, and overall information technology (IT) infrastructure. These policies form the cornerstone of a comprehensive cybersecurity strategy, providing a framework for establishing, maintaining, and continuously improving the security posture of an organization. The significance of security policies extends beyond mere documentation; they are instrumental in creating a culture of security, promoting consistency, ensuring regulatory compliance, and providing a basis for effective risk management within the dynamic and evolving landscape of cyber threats.

One of the primary roles of security policies is to define the rules and guidelines that govern the secure use of an organization's IT resources. These policies articulate the acceptable and expected behaviors of users, administrators, and other stakeholders in the context of information security. For example, access control policies outline who has access to what resources, password policies dictate the requirements for creating and managing passwords, and acceptable use policies establish the boundaries for the appropriate use of IT systems and networks. By clearly defining these expectations, security policies provide a blueprint for mitigating common security risks associated with user behavior, unauthorized access, and other potential vulnerabilities.

Security policies also contribute significantly to the establishment of a security-conscious culture within an organization. When employees, contractors, and other stakeholders understand the importance of security policies, they are more likely to adopt secure practices in their day-to-day activities. This cultural shift is crucial in fostering a collective responsibility for cybersecurity, where individuals recognize their role in protecting the organization's digital assets. Security awareness programs, often based on the principles outlined in security policies, reinforce the significance of secure behaviors and empower users to be active participants in the defense against cyber threats.

In the context of risk management, security policies provide a structured and systematic approach to identifying, assessing, and mitigating potential risks. Risk management policies, a subset of security policies, outline the processes and methodologies for evaluating the impact and likelihood of identified risks. These policies guide organizations in making informed decisions about risk acceptance, risk mitigation, or risk transfer strategies. By integrating risk management principles into security policies, organizations can align their cybersecurity efforts with overall business objectives, industry regulations, and risk tolerance levels. This ensures that security measures are proportionate to the specific risks faced by the organization.

Regulatory compliance is a significant driver for the development and adherence to security policies. Many industries and jurisdictions have specific regulations and standards that mandate the implementation of certain security controls and practices. Security policies serve as a tool for organizations to document their commitment to compliance, outlining how they meet the requirements imposed by regulations such as the General Data Protection Regulation (GDPR), Health Insurance Portability and Accountability Act (HIPAA), or Payment Card Industry Data Security Standard (PCI DSS). Adhering to these regulations not only helps organizations avoid legal consequences but also establishes a foundation for building trust with customers, partners, and regulatory authorities.

The complexity of today's IT environments requires organizations to manage a diverse array of technologies, systems, and applications. Security policies provide a unifying framework that ensures consistency in the application of security controls across this diverse landscape. Whether it is configuring firewalls, implementing encryption, or managing software updates, security policies offer a standardized set of guidelines that help organizations maintain a consistent and effective security posture. This consistency is crucial in preventing security gaps and ensuring that security measures are applied uniformly, reducing the likelihood of oversights or inconsistencies that might be exploited by cyber adversaries.

Security policies are dynamic documents that should evolve alongside the rapidly changing threat landscape and technological advancements. The continuous improvement aspect of security policies is vital in addressing emerging threats and adapting to new challenges. Regular reviews, updates, and revisions ensure that security policies remain relevant, effective, and aligned with the organization's risk appetite and strategic objectives. This adaptability is essential for organizations to stay ahead of evolving cyber threats and technologies, ensuring that security policies provide meaningful guidance in the face of emerging risks.

The development and implementation of security policies involve a collaborative effort that engages stakeholders across the organization. Security policies are not solely the responsibility of the IT department; they require input from legal, human resources, compliance, and other relevant departments. Engaging various stakeholders ensures that security policies address the organization's holistic needs, considering legal requirements, human factors, and industry best practices. Collaborative policy development fosters a sense of ownership and awareness among stakeholders, leading to a more effective and widely embraced security posture.

Security policies are instrumental in incident response and management. Incident response policies outline the steps to be taken in the event of a security incident, guiding organizations through the identification, containment, eradication, recovery, and lessons learned phases. These policies establish roles and responsibilities, communication protocols, and coordination mechanisms that enhance an organization's ability to respond effectively to security incidents. By integrating incident response policies into the broader framework of security policies, organizations ensure a cohesive and well-coordinated approach to handling security breaches and minimizing their impact.

The significance of security policies is particularly pronounced in the context of technological advancements such as cloud computing, Internet of Things (IoT), and artificial intelligence. Security policies guide organizations in navigating the unique security challenges presented by these technologies. For example, cloud security policies address considerations such as data encryption, access controls, and service provider responsibilities in the cloud environment. Policies related to IoT devices outline how to secure and manage the proliferation of interconnected devices. By integrating these considerations into security policies, organizations can embrace technological innovations while maintaining a robust security posture.

In conclusion, security policies form an integral and multifaceted component of a cyber defense framework. They provide the foundational principles that guide organizations in establishing and maintaining a secure IT environment. From defining acceptable behaviors and fostering a security-conscious culture to addressing risk management, regulatory compliance, and incident response, security policies play a pivotal role in shaping the cybersecurity posture of organizations. Their significance extends beyond documentation, influencing organizational culture, aligning with regulatory requirements, and providing a framework for addressing the dynamic challenges of the modern cyber threat landscape. Organizations that recognize and prioritize the significance of security policies are better equipped to build resilience, protect sensitive information, and navigate the complexities of the evolving cybersecurity landscape.

Discuss compliance requirements and their role in cybersecurity.

Compliance requirements play a pivotal role in the realm of cybersecurity, serving as a framework for organizations to establish, implement, and maintain effective security measures. These requirements, often dictated by laws, regulations, and industry standards, are designed to safeguard sensitive information, protect individual privacy, and ensure the overall integrity and reliability of information technology systems. The role of compliance in cybersecurity extends beyond a mere checkbox exercise; it is an integral aspect of risk management, governance, and building trust with stakeholders.

In many industries, specific laws and regulations mandate the implementation of cybersecurity measures to protect sensitive data and ensure the privacy of individuals. The healthcare sector, for example, is subject to regulations such as the Health Insurance Portability and Accountability Act (HIPAA) in the United States, which mandates the secure handling of patient information. Similarly, the financial industry adheres to regulations like the Payment Card Industry Data Security Standard (PCI DSS), which outlines requirements for securing payment card data. Compliance with these regulations is not optional; failure to adhere can result in severe legal consequences, financial penalties, and reputational damage.

Compliance requirements also play a crucial role in shaping governance structures within organizations. Governance, risk management, and compliance (GRC) frameworks integrate these three elements to ensure that an organization operates ethically, manages risks effectively, and complies with applicable laws and regulations. Compliance requirements provide a structured foundation for GRC initiatives, guiding organizations in establishing policies, procedures, and controls that align with legal and regulatory expectations. This alignment fosters transparency and accountability, enhancing the organization's ability to manage cybersecurity risks in a systematic and controlled manner.

Industry-specific standards and frameworks contribute significantly to the role of compliance in cybersecurity. Standards such as ISO/IEC 27001 provide a comprehensive set of guidelines for establishing and maintaining an information security management system (ISMS). Adherence to such standards not only enhances an organization's cybersecurity posture but also demonstrates a commitment to best practices in information security. The adoption of widely recognized frameworks enables organizations to benchmark their security measures against industry peers, fostering a culture of continuous improvement in cybersecurity practices.

Compliance requirements serve as a catalyst for organizations to assess and manage cybersecurity risks effectively. Risk management is an integral component of compliance, as organizations are required to identify, assess, and mitigate risks that could compromise the confidentiality, integrity, or availability of sensitive information. Compliance requirements guide organizations in conducting risk assessments, implementing appropriate controls, and regularly reviewing and updating their cybersecurity measures to address evolving threats. The systematic approach to risk management embedded in compliance enhances an organization's resilience against cyber threats.

The role of compliance in cybersecurity extends to the protection of consumer and stakeholder interests. Individuals and entities entrust organizations with their sensitive information, and compliance requirements ensure that organizations implement adequate safeguards to protect this information. For example, the European Union's General Data Protection Regulation (GDPR) empowers individuals with greater control over their personal data and imposes strict requirements on organizations to ensure its lawful and secure processing. Compliance with such regulations enhances trust be-

tween organizations and their customers, partners, and other stakeholders.

In addition to legal and regulatory requirements, contractual
obligations and industry best practices often contribute to the compliance landscape. Organizations entering into contracts with clients
or business partners may be obligated to adhere to specific cybersecurity standards outlined in contractual agreements. These contractual obligations may mirror or exceed regulatory requirements,
reflecting a commitment to robust cybersecurity practices. Following industry best practices, such as those outlined by cybersecurity
frameworks or consortiums, can also contribute to compliance by
providing organizations with guidelines that go beyond minimum
legal requirements, enhancing the overall security posture.

The role of compliance in cybersecurity is particularly significant
in the context of data breaches and incident response. Many jurisdictions have breach notification laws that require organizations to notify individuals and authorities in the event of a data breach. Compliance with these laws involves not only preventing breaches but also having robust incident response plans in place to detect, contain,
and recover from security incidents. The integration of compliance
requirements into incident response planning ensures that organizations are prepared to meet legal obligations and mitigate the impact
of security incidents on affected individuals.

While compliance requirements provide a structured framework
for cybersecurity, organizations must recognize that compliance
alone does not guarantee immunity from cyber threats. Cyber adversaries are sophisticated and continually evolving, and compliance
standards may not always keep pace with emerging threats. Therefore, organizations are encouraged to adopt a risk-based approach
that goes beyond the minimum requirements stipulated by compliance frameworks. This approach involves continually assessing and

adapting cybersecurity measures based on the organization's specific risk landscape, industry trends, and emerging threats.

The role of compliance in cybersecurity also extends to the boardroom, where executives and leadership teams are responsible for ensuring organizational adherence to legal and regulatory requirements. Cybersecurity is increasingly recognized as a critical aspect of corporate governance, and boards of directors are expected to actively oversee and understand the organization's cybersecurity posture. Compliance reports, risk assessments, and regular updates on cybersecurity measures contribute to informed decision-making at the executive level, fostering a culture of accountability and responsibility for cybersecurity within the organization.

The global nature of cyber threats and the interconnectedness of organizations necessitate a harmonized approach to cybersecurity compliance. International standards and frameworks, such as ISO/ IEC 27001 and NIST Cybersecurity Framework, provide organizations with a globally recognized foundation for cybersecurity practices. Harmonization of cybersecurity compliance efforts enables organizations to operate seamlessly across jurisdictions, facilitates information sharing and collaboration, and ensures a consistent level of security measures globally.

In conclusion, compliance requirements play a multifaceted and integral role in the field of cybersecurity. They provide a structured framework for organizations to establish and maintain effective security measures, ensuring the protection of sensitive information, adherence to legal and regulatory expectations, and the fostering of trust with stakeholders. Compliance is not merely a checklist exercise; it serves as a catalyst for effective governance, risk management, and continuous improvement in cybersecurity practices. Organizations that understand the role of compliance in cybersecurity are better equipped to navigate the complexities of the evolving threat landscape, build resilience against cyber threats, and demonstrate a commitment to the responsible stewardship of sensitive information.

Examine best practices for securing networks.

Securing networks is a complex and crucial aspect of modern cybersecurity, considering the ever-evolving threat landscape and the central role networks play in enabling communication and data exchange. Best practices for securing networks encompass a comprehensive set of strategies and measures aimed at mitigating vulnerabilities, preventing unauthorized access, and ensuring the confidentiality, integrity, and availability of information. This examination delves into key best practices for securing networks, addressing both the technical and human elements of network security.

A fundamental best practice for securing networks involves implementing robust access controls. Access controls dictate who can access what resources within the network, and they are essential for preventing unauthorized users from gaining entry. Role-based access controls (RBAC) are particularly effective, assigning specific permissions to users based on their roles and responsibilities. Regular reviews and audits of access controls help organizations ensure that access permissions align with employees' current roles and responsibilities, minimizing the risk of unauthorized access.

Encryption plays a pivotal role in network security, especially in protecting data in transit. Transport Layer Security (TLS) and its predecessor, Secure Sockets Layer (SSL), are cryptographic protocols that provide secure communication over a computer network. Implementing end-to-end encryption ensures that data is encrypted during transmission, making it difficult for unauthorized parties to intercept or manipulate the information. This is particularly crucial for securing sensitive information such as login credentials, financial transactions, and confidential communications.

Network segmentation is another best practice that enhances security by dividing a network into segments or subnetworks. This limits the lateral movement of attackers in the event of a breach, preventing them from easily accessing critical systems or sensitive data. Network segmentation also helps contain and isolate security incidents, minimizing the potential impact on the entire network. Organizations can use firewalls and routers to enforce segmentation and control the flow of traffic between different segments.

Implementing strong and unique passwords is a basic yet critical best practice for securing network access. Weak or easily guessable passwords are a common entry point for attackers. Password policies should enforce complexity requirements, regular password changes, and the use of multi-factor authentication (MFA) to add an extra layer of security. Educating users about the importance of strong passwords and the risks associated with password reuse further strengthens this aspect of network security.

Regular software patching and updates are essential best practices for securing networks. Software vulnerabilities are often exploited by attackers to gain unauthorized access or execute malicious code. Organizations must establish a systematic approach to patch management, ensuring that operating systems, applications, and network devices are promptly updated with the latest security patches. Automated patching tools can streamline this process, reducing the window of vulnerability and enhancing overall network security.

Intrusion Detection Systems (IDS) and Intrusion Prevention Systems (IPS) are critical components for identifying and mitigating potential security threats within a network. IDS monitors network traffic for suspicious activities or patterns, generating alerts when potential threats are detected. IPS goes a step further by actively blocking or mitigating identified threats. Deploying these systems provides organizations with real-time visibility into network activities, allowing for swift response to potential security incidents.

Network monitoring is an ongoing best practice that involves the continuous observation and analysis of network traffic. Effective monitoring can detect anomalies, identify potential security threats, and provide insights into network performance. Security Information and Event Management (SIEM) systems aggregate and analyze log data from various network devices, enabling organizations to correlate events and detect patterns indicative of malicious activities. Continuous monitoring supports proactive threat detection and incident response, helping organizations stay ahead of evolving cyber threats.

Firewalls are essential network security devices that control incoming and outgoing network traffic based on predetermined security rules. Firewalls act as a barrier between a trusted internal network and untrusted external networks, such as the internet. By inspecting and filtering traffic, firewalls prevent unauthorized access and protect against various types of cyber threats, including malware and unauthorized access attempts. Organizations should configure firewalls to deny all unnecessary traffic and allow only essential services, implementing the principle of least privilege.

Network hygiene involves removing or disabling unnecessary services, protocols, and features that may introduce security vulnerabilities. Unneeded services create additional attack surfaces, providing potential entry points for attackers. Regularly reviewing and cleaning up network configurations ensure that only essential services are active, reducing the overall risk of exploitation. This best practice aligns with the cybersecurity principle of minimizing the attack surface to enhance network security.

User education and awareness are integral components of network security best practices. Despite technical safeguards, human factors remain a significant source of security incidents. Educating users about phishing threats, social engineering tactics, and safe online behaviors helps create a security-conscious culture within the organization. Regular training sessions and simulated phishing exercises can reinforce awareness, empowering users to recognize and report potential security threats.

Secure configuration management is a best practice that involves maintaining and enforcing secure configurations for network devices and systems. This includes routers, switches, servers, and other network components. Secure configurations align with industry best practices and security baselines, reducing the likelihood of misconfigurations that could be exploited by attackers. Automated configuration management tools help organizations maintain consistency and enforce secure configurations across the network.

Regular vulnerability assessments and penetration testing are crucial best practices for identifying and addressing potential weaknesses in network security. Vulnerability assessments involve scanning network devices and systems to identify known vulnerabilities. Penetration testing takes a more proactive approach, simulating real-world attacks to identify and exploit potential weaknesses. Both practices help organizations prioritize remediation efforts, strengthen security controls, and enhance overall network resilience.

Incident response planning is a proactive best practice that ensures organizations are well-prepared to handle security incidents when they occur. Incident response plans outline the steps to be taken in the event of a security incident, including the roles and responsibilities of the incident response team, communication protocols, and procedures for containing and mitigating the incident. Regular testing and simulation exercises help validate the effectiveness of incident response plans and improve the organization's readiness to respond to security incidents.

Network forensics is a best practice that involves the collection, analysis, and preservation of network-related evidence in the aftermath of a security incident. Network forensics enables organizations to understand the scope and impact of a security breach, identify the tactics used by attackers, and support legal or regulatory investigations. Implementing network forensics capabilities enhances an organization's ability to learn from incidents, improve security measures, and prevent similar incidents in the future.

Collaboration and information sharing within the cybersecurity community contribute to the collective defense against evolving threats. Threat intelligence feeds, forums, and information-sharing platforms enable organizations to stay informed about the latest threats, vulnerabilities, and attack techniques. Participating in collaborative initiatives helps organizations leverage the insights and experiences of the broader cybersecurity community, enhancing their ability to proactively defend against emerging threats.

In conclusion, securing networks requires a multifaceted approach that addresses both technical and human aspects of cybersecurity. The best practices outlined above provide a foundational framework for organizations seeking to establish and maintain robust network security. From access controls and encryption to continuous monitoring, incident response planning, and collaboration within the cybersecurity community, these practices collectively contribute to creating a resilient and secure network environment. As cyber threats continue to evolve, organizations that prioritize and implement these best practices are better positioned to protect their networks, sensitive information, and overall cybersecurity posture.

Discuss the implementation of firewalls, intrusion detection systems, and other protective measures.

The implementation of firewalls, intrusion detection systems (IDS), and other protective measures is critical in establishing a robust defense against a wide array of cyber threats. These protective measures constitute essential components of network security, working collaboratively to safeguard digital assets, prevent unauthorized access, and detect and respond to potential security incidents.

Firewalls serve as the first line of defense in network security by controlling the flow of traffic between trusted internal networks and untrusted external networks, such as the internet. Firewalls operate based on predefined security rules that dictate which network packets are allowed or denied. Stateful inspection firewalls, for instance, monitor the state of active connections and make decisions based on the context of the traffic. Implementing firewalls is crucial in preventing unauthorized access, blocking malicious content, and mitigating various cyber threats, including malware, phishing attempts, and unauthorized access attempts.

Intrusion Detection Systems (IDS) complement firewalls by actively monitoring network and system activities for signs of malicious behavior or security policy violations. IDS operate in two primary modes: signature-based and anomaly-based. Signature-based IDS identify known patterns of malicious activity by comparing network traffic against a database of predefined signatures. On the other hand, anomaly-based IDS detect deviations from normal behavior by establishing a baseline of typical network activity and raising alerts when anomalies are detected. The integration of IDS enhances the organization's ability to detect sophisticated threats that may evade traditional security measures.

The deployment of intrusion prevention systems (IPS) builds upon the capabilities of IDS by actively taking measures to prevent detected threats. IPS operate in real-time to block or mitigate malicious activities, providing a proactive layer of defense. By dynamically updating security policies based on the intelligence gathered from IDS and other threat sources, IPS can automatically respond to emerging threats. This real-time responsiveness is crucial in minimizing the impact of security incidents, preventing unauthorized access, and protecting sensitive information from compromise.

Secure access controls form a fundamental aspect of protective measures within network security. These controls dictate who can access what resources within the network, and they are instrumental in preventing unauthorized access and privilege escalation. Role-based access controls (RBAC) are commonly employed, assigning specific permissions to users based on their roles and responsibilities. Implementing the principle of least privilege ensures that users only have access to the resources necessary for their tasks, reducing the potential attack surface and minimizing the impact of security incidents.

Virtual Private Networks (VPNs) play a crucial role in securing communications over networks, especially in the context of remote access and the use of public networks. VPNs create encrypted tunnels that protect the confidentiality and integrity of data in transit. Remote users connecting to corporate networks, for instance, can use VPNs to securely access resources while ensuring that sensitive information remains protected from eavesdropping or interception. The implementation of VPNs extends the perimeter of secure communication beyond physical office boundaries, enabling secure connectivity for remote workers.

Next-generation firewalls (NGFW) represent an evolution of traditional firewalls, incorporating advanced features and capabilities to address the evolving threat landscape. NGFW integrate traditional firewall functionalities with additional security features such as intrusion prevention, application-layer filtering, and deep packet inspection. This holistic approach enables NGFW to provide more granular control over network traffic, identify and block sophisticated threats, and enhance overall security posture. The implementation of NGFW reflects a proactive stance in adapting to the complexities of modern cyber threats.

Network segmentation is a protective measure that involves dividing a network into segments or subnetworks, each with its own security controls and access policies. Network segmentation limits the lateral movement of attackers within the network, preventing them from easily accessing critical systems or sensitive data. By isolating segments, organizations can contain security incidents, minimize the potential impact of breaches, and enhance overall network resilence. The use of firewalls or routers to enforce segmentation controls contributes to a defense-in-depth strategy, creating barriers that impede unauthorized access.

Security Information and Event Management (SIEM) systems represent a vital component in the implementation of protective measures. SIEM systems aggregate and analyze log data from various network devices, servers, and applications to provide real-time insights into security events. These systems enable organizations to correlate events, detect patterns indicative of malicious activities, and generate alerts for further investigation. The implementation of SIEM enhances situational awareness, supports incident response efforts, and contributes to compliance with regulatory requirements by providing a centralized platform for monitoring and managing security events.

Endpoint protection, including antivirus software, endpoint detection and response (EDR) solutions, and mobile device management (MDM) tools, is essential in extending protective measures to end-user devices. Endpoints, including desktops, laptops, and mobile devices, are common targets for cyber threats. Antivirus software detects and removes known malware, while EDR solutions provide advanced threat detection and response capabilities. MDM tools allow organizations to enforce security policies on mobile devices, ensuring that these devices do not become vulnerable entry points into the network.

Security awareness training for employees is a protective measure that addresses the human element of cybersecurity. Despite robust technical defenses, human factors remain a significant source of security incidents, often arising from social engineering attacks such as phishing. Security awareness training educates employees about common cyber threats, safe online practices, and the importance of adhering to security policies. This proactive approach empowers employees to recognize and report potential security threats, contributing to a culture of security within the organization.

The implementation of protective measures also involves regular security audits and vulnerability assessments. Security audits evaluate the effectiveness of existing security controls, policies, and procedures, ensuring compliance with security standards and regulatory requirements. Vulnerability assessments involve scanning systems and networks for known vulnerabilities, identifying potential weaknesses that could be exploited by attackers. These assessments provide organizations with insights into their security posture, prioritize remediation efforts, and support continuous improvement in cybersecurity measures.

Advanced threat intelligence feeds play a pivotal role in enhancing the effectiveness of protective measures. Threat intelligence provides organizations with timely and relevant information about emerging threats, vulnerabilities, and attack techniques. By integrating threat intelligence into security operations, organizations can proactively update security controls, adjust security policies, and prepare for potential threats. Collaboration with threat intelligence-sharing communities further enriches the organization's ability to anticipate and defend against evolving cyber threats.

The implementation of a comprehensive incident response plan is a crucial protective measure that ensures organizations are well-prepared to handle security incidents effectively. Incident response plans outline the steps to be taken in the event of a security incident, including the roles and responsibilities of the incident response team, communication protocols, and procedures for containing and mitigating the incident. Regular testing and simulation exercises help validate the effectiveness of incident response plans, ensuring a coordinated and swift response to security incidents.

Biometric authentication represents an advanced protective measure that leverages unique biological characteristics such as fingerprints, retina scans, or facial recognition to authenticate users. Biometric authentication enhances the security of access controls by providing a more robust and tamper-resistant method of verifying user identities. While not a panacea, biometric authentication adds an additional layer of protection, particularly in scenarios where high-assurance authentication is required.

Honeypots and deception technologies contribute to the implementation of protective measures by actively deceiving attackers and diverting their attention away from critical assets. Honeypots are decoy systems designed to attract and lure attackers, providing organizations with insights into their tactics and techniques. Deception technologies extend this concept by creating a deceptive layer within the network, presenting false information to attackers and creating confusion. The use of these technologies enhances threat detection capabilities and allows organizations to gather intelligence on potential adversaries.

The implementation of Security Orchestration, Automation, and Response (SOAR) solutions streamlines and enhances the effectiveness of protective measures by automating repetitive security tasks, orchestrating responses to security incidents, and providing a centralized platform for managing security operations. SOAR solutions integrate with existing security tools, enabling organizations to respond rapidly to threats, minimize manual intervention, and improve overall incident response efficiency.

In conclusion, the implementation of firewalls, intrusion detection systems, and other protective measures is a multifaceted and dynamic process aimed at fortifying network security. These measures collectively contribute to creating a layered defense strategy that addresses diverse cyber threats. From traditional firewalls and IDS to advanced technologies such as SOAR and biometric authentication, organizations must adopt a holistic approach to cybersecurity. This approach considers the interconnected nature of protective measures, their adaptability to evolving threats, and their ability to safeguard digital assets, critical systems, and sensitive information in the complex and dynamic landscape of cybersecurity.

Detail the importance of having a well-defined incident response plan.

The importance of having a well-defined incident response plan (IRP) in cybersecurity cannot be overstated, as it serves as a cornerstone for effectively managing and mitigating the impact of security incidents. An incident response plan is a comprehensive and structured set of guidelines, procedures, and actions that an organization follows when facing a cybersecurity incident, ensuring a coordinated, timely, and organized response. In an increasingly complex and dynamic threat landscape, organizations must recognize the critical role that a well-crafted incident response plan plays in minimizing damage, restoring normal operations, and preserving the overall integrity and trustworthiness of the information technology infrastructure.

First and foremost, an incident response plan establishes a systematic approach to handling security incidents. By defining clear roles, responsibilities, and communication channels, the plan ensures that every member of the incident response team understands their specific duties during an incident. This level of clarity is vital, particularly during high-pressure situations, where swift and decisive action is required to contain and remediate the incident. The plan acts as a blueprint, providing a step-by-step guide that allows the team to follow a predefined process, reducing the likelihood of errors and ensuring a more efficient response.

One of the fundamental aspects of an incident response plan is its role in minimizing the dwell time of an adversary within the organization's network. Dwell time refers to the duration between the initial compromise and the detection and containment of the security incident. A well-defined plan aims to shorten this dwell time by facilitating early detection, rapid response, and efficient containment measures. By reducing dwell time, organizations can limit the potential damage caused by the incident, prevent lateral movement by attackers, and safeguard sensitive information from exfiltration.

The incident response plan is instrumental in facilitating a swift and effective response to security incidents, regardless of their nature or complexity. Whether dealing with a malware infection, a data breach, a denial-of-service attack, or any other cybersecurity incident, the plan provides a structured framework for the incident response team to follow. This includes steps for identifying the incident, classifying its severity, containing its impact, eradicating the threat, and recovering affected systems. The plan's predefined procedures and workflows streamline these processes, ensuring a well-coordinated response that minimizes disruption and accelerates recovery efforts.

Effective communication is a linchpin in incident response, and a well-defined plan establishes communication protocols that are crucial during a security incident. The plan outlines who needs to be informed, how information should be disseminated, and the frequency of updates to stakeholders. Clear communication channels within the incident response team, as well as with external entities such as legal teams, public relations, and law enforcement, ensure that everyone involved is well-informed and can contribute effectively to the resolution of the incident. Transparent and timely communication is essential not only for managing the incident but also for maintaining trust with internal and external stakeholders.

Preparation and practice are integral components of incident response, and a well-defined plan provides the foundation for conducting regular drills and simulations. Incident response exercises allow the team to test the effectiveness of the plan, identify areas for improvement, and enhance the overall preparedness of the organization. Simulating different types of incidents helps the team develop muscle memory, refine response procedures, and improve coordination. These exercises also provide an opportunity to train new team members, ensuring that the entire incident response team is well-versed in executing the plan when a real incident occurs.

Legal and regulatory compliance is a critical consideration for organizations facing a security incident, and a well-defined incident response plan helps navigate these complex landscapes. The plan includes provisions for adhering to applicable laws and regulations governing data breaches and cybersecurity incidents. By outlining the steps for notifying regulatory bodies, affected individuals, and other relevant parties, the plan ensures that the organization meets its legal obligations. Compliance with regulatory requirements not only helps mitigate legal repercussions but also contributes to maintaining the organization's reputation and standing in the eyes of regulators, customers, and the public.

In the aftermath of a security incident, organizations must conduct thorough post-incident analysis and documentation. This retrospective examination, often referred to as a post-incident review or lessons learned, is essential for refining and improving the incident response plan. The plan should include provisions for documenting the incident, analyzing the root causes, assessing the effectiveness of response actions, and identifying areas for enhancement. This feedback loop ensures that the incident response plan remains a living document, evolving to address emerging threats, technological changes, and lessons gleaned from previous incidents.

The importance of a well-defined incident response plan extends beyond technical considerations to encompass the organization's overall resilience and reputation. Effective incident response is a key component of risk management, and the plan contributes to the organization's ability to identify, assess, and mitigate cybersecurity risks. By demonstrating a commitment to proactive incident response, organizations build resilience against evolving cyber threats and enhance their capacity to recover swiftly from security incidents. A robust incident response capability also bolsters the organization's reputation, assuring customers, partners, and stakeholders that the organization is prepared to address and overcome cybersecurity challenges.

Public relations and communication strategies are integral elements of incident response, especially when dealing with incidents that may impact the organization's public image. A well-defined plan includes provisions for managing public relations during and after a security incident. It outlines how to communicate with the media, customers, and the public, balancing transparency with the need to protect sensitive information. The plan guides the organization in crafting clear and accurate messages, managing public expectations, and mitigating reputational damage. Effective public relations, as facilitated by the incident response plan, is essential for maintaining trust and credibility in the wake of a cybersecurity incident.

Cybersecurity incidents often involve complex technical investigations to determine the scope and impact of the breach. A well-defined incident response plan addresses the technical aspects of investigations, outlining procedures for collecting and preserving digital evidence. This includes forensic analysis of affected systems, network traffic, and logs to understand the tactics, techniques, and procedures employed by the attackers. By incorporating forensic procedures into the plan, organizations enhance their ability to attribute the incident, gather intelligence, and share relevant information with law enforcement, if necessary.

The continuous evolution of the cyber threat landscape requires organizations to stay adaptive and agile in their incident response capabilities. A well-defined incident response plan is not a static document but a dynamic framework that undergoes regular updates to reflect emerging threats, changes in the organization's infrastructure, and lessons learned from previous incidents. Regular reviews and updates ensure that the plan remains aligned with the organization's risk profile, technological environment, and industry-specific considerations. This adaptability is crucial for maintaining the plan's relevance and effectiveness in the face of an ever-changing cybersecurity landscape.

In conclusion, the importance of having a well-defined incident response plan in cybersecurity cannot be overstated. It is a strategic asset that empowers organizations to respond effectively to security incidents, minimize damage, and protect sensitive information. The plan provides a structured framework for incident response teams, facilitating a coordinated and efficient response. Beyond its technical aspects, the plan addresses legal, regulatory, public relations, and forensic considerations, contributing to the organization's overall resilience and reputation. A living document, the incident response plan evolves through regular testing, drills, and post-incident reviews, ensuring that it remains a robust and adaptive tool in the face of evolving cyber threats.

Provide a step-by-step guide to developing and implementing an effective response strategy.

Developing and implementing an effective response strategy is a crucial undertaking for organizations seeking to fortify their cybersecurity posture and minimize the impact of potential security incidents. This step-by-step guide provides a comprehensive overview of the key considerations and actions involved in creating a robust response strategy.

The first step in developing an effective response strategy is to establish a dedicated incident response team (IRT). This team should be composed of individuals with diverse skills, including cybersecurity experts, IT professionals, legal advisors, and communication specialists. Designate specific roles and responsibilities within the team, ensuring clarity on who will lead the response efforts, coordinate communication, conduct technical analysis, and liaise with external entities. The team should be well-trained, regularly updated on emerging threats, and capable of swift and coordinated action during a security incident.

Once the incident response team is formed, the next step is to conduct a thorough risk assessment. Identify and assess potential risks to the organization's information systems, data assets, and critical infrastructure. This assessment should consider external threats, internal vulnerabilities, and the potential impact of different types of security incidents. By understanding the organization's risk landscape, the incident response team can prioritize efforts and tailor the response strategy to address the most significant and likely threats.

Following the risk assessment, the organization should define an incident. Clearly articulate what constitutes a security incident for your organization, encompassing various scenarios such as data breaches, malware infections, denial-of-service attacks, and unauthorized access attempts. Establishing a precise definition ensures that the incident response team can quickly recognize and categorize incidents, enabling a timely and effective response.

Developing an incident response plan (IRP) is a pivotal step in the process. The IRP should be a comprehensive document that outlines the procedures, workflows, and communication protocols to be followed during a security incident. Include predefined steps for incident identification, classification, containment, eradication, recovery, and post-incident analysis. The plan should be dynamic and adaptable, reflecting the organization's evolving risk landscape and incorporating lessons learned from previous incidents.

Training and awareness are critical components of a successful response strategy. Ensure that all members of the incident response team undergo regular training sessions and simulations to familiarize themselves with the IRP and practice responding to different types of incidents. Additionally, extend training efforts to relevant staff across the organization to enhance overall cybersecurity awareness.

Educate employees on recognizing potential security threats, reporting incidents promptly, and following established procedures for incident response.

Integration with existing cybersecurity measures is essential for a cohesive response strategy. Ensure that the incident response plan aligns with other security frameworks, policies, and controls in place within the organization. Integrate incident response activities with security information and event management (SIEM) systems, intrusion detection systems (IDS), and other security tools to enhance detection capabilities and automate certain response actions.

Establishing communication protocols is a key aspect of incident response. Define internal and external communication channels, specifying who needs to be informed during different phases of an incident. This includes communication within the incident response team, coordination with executive leadership, legal teams, public relations, and external entities such as law enforcement or regulatory bodies. Clear and timely communication is vital for managing the incident effectively and maintaining trust with stakeholders.

Developing relationships with external entities is crucial for a comprehensive response strategy. Collaborate with law enforcement agencies, regulatory bodies, incident response organizations, and industry peers. Establish communication channels, share threat intelligence, and participate in information-sharing initiatives. Collaborative efforts enhance the organization's ability to respond to sophisticated threats, receive timely alerts about emerging risks, and contribute to the collective defense against cyber adversaries.

The development of incident response playbooks further refines the response strategy. Playbooks are specific sets of procedures tailored to address common types of incidents or specific threat scenarios. They provide detailed guidance on responding to incidents with well-defined patterns, reducing decision-making time during high-pressure situations. Playbooks can be developed for various incident categories, such as ransomware attacks, data breaches, or advanced persistent threats (APTs).

Conducting regular tabletop exercises and simulations is a proactive step to validate and enhance the response strategy. Simulate different types of incidents, allowing the incident response team to practice their roles, refine procedures, and test the effectiveness of the IRP. These exercises also provide an opportunity to identify areas for improvement, update response playbooks, and ensure that the entire team is well-prepared to respond to real incidents.

In the event of an actual security incident, the first action is to promptly identify and classify the incident. Leverage the organization's monitoring and detection capabilities, such as SIEM systems and IDS, to identify anomalous activities. Classify the incident based on its severity, impact, and nature, aligning it with the predefined categories in the incident response plan. Rapid identification and classification lay the foundation for an effective response.

Containment follows the identification and classification of the incident. The goal is to prevent further damage, limit the impact on affected systems, and isolate the incident to prevent its spread. Containment measures may include isolating affected systems from the network, blocking malicious communication channels, or implementing access controls to prevent unauthorized access. The incident response team should act decisively to implement containment measures based on the predefined procedures in the IRP.

Once containment is achieved, the next step is to eradicate the threat. Eradication involves identifying and removing the root cause of the incident from the affected systems. This may involve patching vulnerabilities, removing malware, closing security gaps, and implementing corrective measures to prevent a recurrence of the incident. Eradication efforts should be thorough and well-documented to ensure a comprehensive resolution.

Recovery focuses on restoring affected systems and services to normal operation. The incident response team works to rebuild, restore, and validate the integrity of affected systems, ensuring that they are free from compromise and functioning as intended. Recovery efforts may involve restoring data from backups, applying patches, and conducting system validations. The goal is to minimize downtime, restore business continuity, and mitigate the overall impact on the organization's operations.

Post-incident analysis is a critical phase in the response strategy. Conduct a thorough examination of the incident, analyzing the root causes, tactics employed by the attackers, and the effectiveness of response actions. Document lessons learned, identify areas for improvement in the incident response plan, and update response playbooks based on the insights gained. This retrospective analysis contributes to the organization's continuous improvement and adaptive response capabilities.

Communication during and after the incident is paramount. Keep stakeholders informed about the incident, its impact, and the organization's response efforts. Develop clear and accurate messages for internal and external audiences, balancing transparency with the need to protect sensitive information. Maintain open lines of communication with executive leadership, legal teams, public relations, and affected parties. Effective communication is essential for managing the public relations aspect of the incident and maintaining trust with stakeholders.

Legal and regulatory considerations play a significant role in the aftermath of a security incident. Ensure compliance with applicable laws and regulations governing data breaches, privacy, and cybersecurity incidents. Promptly notify regulatory bodies, affected individuals, and other relevant parties in accordance with legal requirements. Collaborate with legal advisors to navigate the legal implications of the incident and support any subsequent investigations or legal proceedings.

Documentation and reporting are crucial for accountability and regulatory compliance. Thoroughly document all aspects of the incident response process, including actions taken, timelines, decisions made, and lessons learned. Maintain a detailed incident report that can serve as a valuable resource for internal reviews, regulatory inquiries, and legal proceedings. Accurate and comprehensive documentation enhances the organization's ability to demonstrate due diligence and compliance with legal and regulatory requirements.

Continuous improvement is the final step in the response strategy. Regularly review and update the incident response plan based on insights gained from post-incident analysis, changes in the threat landscape, and emerging technologies. Conduct periodic training sessions and tabletop exercises to keep the incident response team well-prepared and adaptive to evolving threats. Foster a culture of continuous improvement and learning within the organization's cybersecurity practices.

In conclusion, developing and implementing an effective response strategy is a comprehensive and ongoing process that requires meticulous planning, coordination, and adaptability. By establishing a dedicated incident response team, conducting risk assessments, developing an incident response plan, and integrating with existing cybersecurity measures, organizations can create a solid foundation for response efforts. Training, collaboration with external entities, and the development of incident response playbooks further refine the strategy. During an actual incident, prompt identification, classification, containment, eradication, recovery, and post-incident analysis form the core of the response efforts. Clear communication, legal compliance, documentation, and continuous improvement contribute to the organization's overall resilience and ability to respond effectively to the dynamic landscape of cybersecurity threats.

Chapter 3: Unraveling Encryption: Shielding Your Data

E xplain the basics of encryption and its role in securing data. Encryption is a fundamental aspect of modern cybersecurity, playing a pivotal role in safeguarding sensitive data from unauthorized access and potential exploitation. At its core, encryption is a process of transforming information into an unreadable format using a cryptographic algorithm and a key. This conversion ensures that even if unauthorized parties gain access to the encrypted data, they cannot decipher its meaning without the corresponding decryption key. The primary objective of encryption is to provide confidentiality, integrity, and authenticity to digital information, forming a crucial component of information security frameworks across various domains.

Confidentiality is one of the primary objectives of encryption, ensuring that only authorized individuals or systems can access and comprehend the protected data. This is achieved through the use of encryption algorithms that convert plaintext, or readable data, into ciphertext, which is unintelligible without the appropriate decryption key. By employing strong encryption techniques, organizations can prevent unauthorized access and eavesdropping, maintaining the privacy and confidentiality of sensitive information. In the context of communication channels, encryption ensures that the data transmitted remains confidential, mitigating the risk of interception by malicious entities.

Integrity is another critical aspect of data security addressed by encryption. It ensures that the information remains unchanged and unaltered during storage, transmission, or processing. By applying cryptographic hash functions or digital signatures, encryption provides a means to verify the integrity of the data. Hash functions generate fixed-size hash codes unique to the content of the data, enabling users to detect any modifications or tampering. Digital signatures, on the other hand, involve the use of asymmetric key pairs to sign and verify the authenticity of the sender, assuring the recipient that the data has not been compromised.

Authentication, closely related to integrity, is the process of verifying the identity of parties involved in a communication or data exchange. Encryption contributes to authentication through the use of digital certificates and digital signatures. Digital certificates, issued by trusted entities known as certificate authorities, validate the authenticity of a user or system by confirming their possession of a private key corresponding to a public key in the certificate. Digital signatures, created using asymmetric cryptography, verify the origin of a message and ensure that it has not been altered during transmission. This authentication mechanism is crucial in preventing unauthorized entities from posing as legitimate users.

Encryption can be broadly categorized into two main types: symmetric and asymmetric encryption. Symmetric encryption, also known as secret-key encryption, employs a single key for both encryption and decryption processes. The challenge with symmetric encryption lies in securely distributing and managing the key among communicating parties, as any compromise of the key could jeopardize the confidentiality of the data. Despite this challenge, symmetric encryption is computationally efficient and is often used for securing bulk data.

Asymmetric encryption, or public-key encryption, utilizes a pair of keys – a public key for encryption and a private key for decryption. The public key is shared openly, while the private key is kept confidential. This approach addresses the key distribution issue encountered in symmetric encryption, as the public key can be freely distributed without compromising the security of the data. Asymmetric encryption is commonly used for securing communication channels, establishing secure connections, and facilitating digital signatures for authentication.

The process of encryption involves converting plaintext into ciphertext using an algorithm and a key. The algorithm serves as the mathematical function that transforms the data, while the key acts as the parameter for the algorithm, influencing the specific transformation applied. The strength of encryption relies on the complexity of the algorithm and the length and randomness of the key. Advanced Encryption Standard (AES) is a widely adopted symmetric encryption algorithm, known for its security and efficiency. Asymmetric encryption commonly employs algorithms such as RSA (Rivest-Shamir-Adleman) and Elliptic Curve Cryptography (ECC).

Key management is a critical aspect of encryption, encompassing the generation, distribution, storage, and disposal of cryptographic keys. In symmetric encryption, the challenge lies in securely distributing and managing the shared secret key among communicating parties. This process often involves the use of key distribution protocols and mechanisms to establish secure channels for key exchange. Asymmetric encryption, while mitigating some key distribution challenges, introduces the need for managing key pairs, safeguarding private keys, and establishing trust in the public keys through digital certificates issued by certificate authorities.

The effectiveness of encryption relies not only on the strength of the cryptographic algorithms and keys but also on the implementation of secure protocols and practices. Secure communication protocols, such as SSL/TLS for web traffic and IPSec for network communication, leverage encryption to establish secure channels. The proper implementation of these protocols ensures end-to-end encryption, safeguarding data as it traverses networks and communication channels. Additionally, secure key storage and management practices are vital to prevent unauthorized access to encryption keys, which could compromise the security of encrypted data.

Encryption is widely applied in various domains to protect sensitive information and secure digital communication. In the realm of e-commerce, for example, encryption is integral to ensuring the confidentiality of financial transactions and the protection of customers' personal data. Online banking relies on secure communication channels established through encryption to prevent unauthorized access and financial fraud. Similarly, healthcare organizations utilize encryption to safeguard electronic health records, ensuring patient privacy and compliance with data protection regulations.

The proliferation of mobile devices and the increasing dependence on cloud services have amplified the importance of encryption in safeguarding data at rest and in transit. Mobile device encryption ensures that the data stored on smartphones and tablets remains secure, even if the device is lost or stolen. Cloud providers implement encryption to protect customer data stored in their servers, addressing concerns about data breaches and unauthorized access. Encryption plays a crucial role in building trust in cloud services, enabling organizations to leverage the benefits of cloud computing without compromising the security of their data.

In the context of government and defense, encryption is a cornerstone of national security. Military communications, intelligence operations, and classified information rely on encryption to prevent adversaries from intercepting and deciphering sensitive data. Governments often mandate the use of encryption standards and protocols to ensure the security of their communication infrastructure and protect national interests.

While encryption provides robust protection against unauthorized access, it is not immune to evolving threats. Quantum computing, with its potential to break certain encryption algorithms, poses a future challenge to the security landscape. To address this, researchers are exploring quantum-resistant cryptographic algorithms that can withstand the computational power of quantum computers. Continuous advancements in cybersecurity are essential to stay ahead of emerging threats and ensure the long-term efficacy of encryption in securing digital information.

In conclusion, encryption serves as a cornerstone of modern cybersecurity, addressing the imperatives of confidentiality, integrity, and authenticity in the digital realm. Its role in securing data spans across various domains, from financial transactions and healthcare to government communications and cloud computing. Encryption provides a robust defense against unauthorized access and eavesdropping, ensuring the privacy and security of sensitive information. As technology evolves, the ongoing refinement of cryptographic algorithms and key management practices is essential to stay ahead of potential threats and challenges, preserving the efficacy of encryption in an ever-changing digital landscape.

Explore different encryption algorithms and their applications.

Encryption algorithms are fundamental tools in the field of cybersecurity, playing a crucial role in securing digital data across various applications and domains. One of the most widely used symmetric encryption algorithms is the Advanced Encryption Standard (AES). AES operates on fixed-size blocks of data and supports key lengths of 128, 192, or 256 bits. Known for its efficiency and security, AES is employed in securing a multitude of applications, including data at rest, file encryption, and communication channels. Its widespread adoption makes it a cornerstone in ensuring the confidentiality of sensitive information in both civilian and military contexts.

In contrast to symmetric encryption, asymmetric encryption, or public-key cryptography, utilizes a pair of keys for encryption and decryption. The RSA algorithm, named after its inventors Ron Rivest, Adi Shamir, and Leonard Adleman, is a prominent example of an asymmetric encryption algorithm. RSA relies on the mathematical complexity of factoring large composite numbers, making it secure against classical computing attacks. It is commonly used in securing communication channels, digital signatures for authentication, and key exchange protocols. Despite its security, RSA's computational intensity has led to the exploration of alternative algorithms, especially in resource-constrained environments.

Elliptic Curve Cryptography (ECC) is another asymmetric encryption algorithm gaining prominence, particularly in mobile and Internet of Things (IoT) applications. ECC leverages the mathematical properties of elliptic curves over finite fields to achieve the same level of security as traditional asymmetric algorithms with shorter key lengths, resulting in reduced computational overhead and improved efficiency. Its suitability for environments with limited resources makes ECC an attractive choice for securing communication in devices where power consumption and processing capacity are critical considerations.

In the realm of secure communication over the internet, the Transport Layer Security (TLS) protocol plays a pivotal role. TLS incorporates both symmetric and asymmetric encryption algorithms to establish secure connections between clients and servers. The RSA algorithm, as well as its elliptic curve counterparts, is often used in the key exchange phase of TLS, while symmetric encryption, commonly with AES, is employed for the bulk data transfer. TLS ensures the confidentiality, integrity, and authenticity of data exchanged over the internet, forming the foundation for secure online transactions, web browsing, and communication.

Hash functions, while not encryption algorithms in the traditional sense, are integral to data security and integrity. The SHA-2 (Secure Hash Algorithm 2) family, including variants such as SHA-256 and SHA-3, is widely employed for generating fixed-size hash codes from variable-sized data. Hash functions are utilized in various applications, including password hashing, digital signatures, and data integrity verification. The one-way nature of hash functions ensures that it is computationally infeasible to reverse the process, providing a means to verify the integrity of data without exposing the original content.

In the context of securing email communications, Pretty Good Privacy (PGP) and its open-source counterpart GNU Privacy Guard (GPG) use a combination of symmetric and asymmetric encryption. PGP and GPG employ the RSA algorithm for key pair generation and management, while symmetric encryption is utilized to secure the actual content of the email. This hybrid approach allows for efficient encryption of large volumes of data with the security assurances provided by asymmetric encryption for key exchange and integrity verification.

In the field of disk encryption, where the protection of data at rest is paramount, algorithms such as AES and Twofish are commonly employed. Full Disk Encryption (FDE) solutions use symmetric encryption to secure the entire contents of a storage device, ensuring that data remains confidential even if the physical device is lost or stolen. These algorithms operate transparently to the user, with decryption occurring on-the-fly as data is read from the disk. FDE is a critical component in securing sensitive information on laptops, desktops, and other storage devices.

Blockchain technology, the underlying structure of cryptocurrencies like Bitcoin, relies on cryptographic principles for security.

The SHA-256 hash function is a fundamental component of the Bitcoin protocol, used to create the unique identifier (hash) for each block in the blockchain. Additionally, elliptic curve cryptography is employed in Bitcoin for key pair generation and digital signatures to secure transactions. The decentralized and tamper-resistant nature of blockchain relies on these cryptographic algorithms to maintain the integrity and security of the distributed ledger.

In the realm of mobile device security, where resource constraints are a significant consideration, Lightweight Cryptography (LWC) algorithms come into play. LWC focuses on designing cryptographic primitives that offer a balance between security and efficiency, making them suitable for deployment in devices with limited processing power and memory. These algorithms, such as the SIMON and SPECK family of block ciphers, cater to the specific needs of lightweight devices, including IoT devices, smart cards, and low-power sensors.

Post-Quantum Cryptography (PQC) is an emerging field driven by the potential threat posed by quantum computers to existing encryption algorithms. Quantum computers, with their ability to perform certain calculations exponentially faster than classical computers, could compromise the security of widely used encryption schemes, such as RSA and ECC. PQC aims to develop cryptographic algorithms that remain secure in the presence of quantum computers. Lattice-based cryptography, hash-based cryptography, and code-based cryptography are among the promising approaches explored in the quest for post-quantum security.

In conclusion, encryption algorithms play a diverse and critical role in securing digital information across a spectrum of applications. From the widely adopted AES for symmetric encryption in data protection to RSA and ECC for secure communication and key exchange, these algorithms form the backbone of modern cybersecurity. Hash functions ensure data integrity, while hybrid approaches like

PGP/GPG secure email communications. The evolving landscape of cryptography incorporates lightweight algorithms for resource-constrained environments and explores post-quantum cryptography to address potential future threats. As technology continues to advance, the ongoing development and deployment of robust encryption algorithms remain essential for maintaining the security and privacy of digital data in an ever-changing digital landscape.

Discuss secure communication protocols (e.g., SSL/TLS) and their importance.

Secure communication protocols, exemplified by the widely adopted SSL/TLS (Secure Sockets Layer/Transport Layer Security), play a pivotal role in safeguarding sensitive data exchanged over networks, particularly the internet. The importance of these protocols lies in their ability to establish encrypted connections between communicating parties, ensuring the confidentiality, integrity, and authenticity of the transmitted information. SSL, introduced by Netscape in the 1990s, laid the foundation for secure web communication, and its successor TLS has become the de facto standard for securing a broad range of online transactions and interactions.

One of the primary functions of secure communication protocols is to encrypt data in transit, mitigating the risk of eavesdropping and unauthorized access. When users engage in online activities such as accessing websites, submitting forms, or conducting financial transactions, the data exchanged between their devices and servers often traverses multiple networks. SSL/TLS employs encryption algorithms, commonly including symmetric ciphers like Advanced Encryption Standard (AES), to transform plaintext data into ciphertext, making it indecipherable to potential eavesdroppers. This cryptographic protection ensures that sensitive information, such as login credentials or payment details, remains confidential during transmission.

Data integrity is another critical aspect addressed by secure communication protocols. In transit, data packets may be susceptible to alterations or tampering, either intentionally or as a result of network issues. SSL/TLS employs cryptographic hash functions to generate checksums, known as message digests, for transmitted data. These digests act as fingerprints, allowing the recipient to verify the integrity of the received data by comparing the computed checksum with the original. Any unauthorized modification to the data would result in a mismatch, signaling a potential security breach.

The establishment of a secure connection involves a process known as the handshake, wherein the communicating parties negotiate the parameters for encryption and authentication. During this phase, SSL/TLS employs asymmetric encryption algorithms, such as RSA or Elliptic Curve Cryptography (ECC), to exchange cryptographic keys securely. The server presents its digital certificate, a key component of the public-key infrastructure, to the client to authenticate its identity. This certificate, issued by a trusted third party known as a certificate authority, validates the legitimacy of the server, instilling confidence in the user that they are interacting with the intended recipient.

Public-key cryptography, integral to the handshake process, also plays a role in establishing the authenticity of the client through client certificates. While less common than server certificates, client certificates enable the server to verify the identity of the connecting client, adding an extra layer of mutual authentication. This two-way authentication process ensures that both parties involved in the communication can trust each other's identity, reducing the risk of man-in-the-middle attacks and unauthorized access.

The secure communication protocols like SSL/TLS operate at different layers of the OSI (Open Systems Interconnection) model. While SSL operated primarily at the application layer, TLS operates at the transport layer, providing a more comprehensive and versatile security solution. This enables TLS to secure a wide array of applications beyond the web, including email communication (SMTP, IMAP, POP), file transfer (FTP), and virtual private networks (VPN). The flexibility of TLS in adapting to various communication scenarios contributes to its widespread adoption across diverse digital applications.

The evolution of secure communication protocols, particularly the transition from SSL to TLS, reflects an ongoing commitment to addressing vulnerabilities and enhancing security. Over the years, multiple versions of TLS have been released, each introducing improvements in cryptographic algorithms, key exchange methods, and overall security features. As cryptographic standards evolve and vulnerabilities are discovered, the development and deployment of updated versions become imperative to stay ahead of potential threats and ensure the continued efficacy of secure communication.

SSL/TLS also plays a crucial role in securing online financial transactions, such as e-commerce purchases and online banking. The Payment Card Industry Data Security Standard (PCI DSS), a set of security standards designed to ensure the protection of credit card data, mandates the use of secure communication protocols. When users enter their credit card information on an e-commerce website or access their online banking account, SSL/TLS ensures that this sensitive data is encrypted during transmission, safeguarding it from interception and unauthorized access.

The adoption of SSL/TLS in securing web traffic is underscored by its role in search engine optimization (SEO). Search engines prioritize websites that prioritize user security, and SSL/TLS plays a significant role in this regard. Websites that implement HTTPS (Hypertext Transfer Protocol Secure), the secure version of HTTP facilitated by SSL/TLS, receive favorable rankings in search engine results. This incentivizes website owners to adopt SSL/TLS not only for security reasons but also to enhance their online visibility and credibility.

In recent years, SSL/TLS has faced challenges related to vulnerabilities and attacks. One notable example is the POODLE (Padding Oracle On Downgraded Legacy Encryption) attack, which exploited weaknesses in SSL 3.0. Subsequently, industry experts recommended the deprecation of SSL in favor of TLS. The ongoing maintenance and updating of secure communication protocols are essential to address emerging threats and vulnerabilities, ensuring the resilience of these protocols against evolving attack vectors.

Beyond traditional web applications, the emergence of Web Services and Application Programming Interfaces (APIs) has expanded the scope of secure communication protocols. APIs facilitate the integration of different software systems, enabling them to communicate and share data. Secure communication protocols such as TLS are crucial in protecting the confidentiality and integrity of data exchanged between systems, whether it be for financial transactions, data synchronization, or third-party integrations. The secure exchange of data between APIs ensures that sensitive information remains protected in an increasingly interconnected digital ecosystem.

In conclusion, secure communication protocols, exemplified by SSL/TLS, form the bedrock of online security, providing a framework for encrypting, authenticating, and ensuring the integrity of data exchanged over networks. These protocols play a pivotal role in safeguarding sensitive information during online activities, including web browsing, financial transactions, and communication. The handshake process, public-key cryptography, and the use of digital certificates contribute to the establishment of trust between communicating parties. The versatility of SSL/TLS in securing a broad spectrum of applications, coupled with its adaptability to evolving cryptographic standards, underscores its enduring importance in the ever-changing landscape of digital security. The ongoing commitment to addressing vulnerabilities and evolving security standards is crucial to maintaining the efficacy of secure communication protocols in the face of emerging threats.

Explore the use of VPNs for secure data transmission.

Virtual Private Networks (VPNs) have become integral tools for ensuring secure data transmission in an era marked by increased reliance on digital communication and remote connectivity. The fundamental purpose of a VPN is to create a secure, encrypted tunnel over a public network, typically the internet, allowing users to transmit data between their devices and a private network as if they were directly connected to it. This encryption serves as a protective shield, ensuring the confidentiality and integrity of the transmitted data, and is particularly crucial in scenarios where sensitive information is exchanged over untrusted networks.

One of the primary use cases for VPNs is in the realm of remote access. As organizations increasingly adopt remote work models, employees need secure access to the corporate network from various locations. VPNs provide a secure conduit for remote workers to connect to the corporate network, encrypting the data exchanged between their devices and the internal network. This not only safeguards sensitive corporate information from potential eavesdropping on public networks but also ensures that remote employees can access resources as if they were physically present in the office.

In the context of business operations, site-to-site VPNs offer a secure means of connecting geographically distributed offices or branches. These VPNs establish encrypted communication channels between the local networks of different office locations, allowing seamless data exchange. This is particularly beneficial for organizations with a global presence or multiple branches, as it enables secure and efficient interoffice communication. Site-to-site VPNs contribute to the creation of a unified, secure network infrastructure, facilitating collaboration and resource sharing across disparate geo-graphical locations.

VPN usage extends beyond the corporate sphere to the broader context of internet privacy and security. In an age where online privacy is increasingly under scrutiny, individuals have turned to VPNs as a means of safeguarding their personal information from potential threats and surveillance. By routing their internet traffic through a VPN server, users can obscure their IP addresses and encrypt their online activities. This not only protects against potential cyber threats but also enhances privacy by preventing internet service providers, advertisers, and other entities from monitoring and tracking user behavior.

In regions where internet censorship and content restrictions are prevalent, VPNs serve as valuable tools for circumventing such limitations. By connecting to a VPN server located in a different geographic region, users can effectively bypass restrictions imposed by governments or organizations, accessing content that may be otherwise inaccessible. This has significant implications for freedom of information and expression, enabling users to navigate the internet without being subject to arbitrary restrictions on content.

Encryption is a foundational element of VPN technology, and the choice of encryption protocols significantly influences the security of data transmission. Commonly used VPN encryption protocols include the Internet Key Exchange version 2 (IKEv2), Point-to-Point Tunneling Protocol (PPTP), Layer 2 Tunneling Protocol (L2TP), and OpenVPN. IKEv2 is known for its strong security features and efficient reconnection capabilities, making it suitable for mobile devices that may experience connectivity interruptions. PPTP, while less secure, is still employed for its compatibility with various platforms. L2TP provides a secure tunneling protocol but often in combination with the IPsec (Internet Protocol Security) protocol for enhanced security. OpenVPN is an open-source and highly configurable protocol, offering a good balance between security and performance.

While VPNs offer robust security features, it is essential to recognize that the choice of protocol and encryption strength can impact performance. Strong encryption algorithms, such as those used in modern VPN protocols, can introduce computational overhead, potentially leading to a reduction in data transmission speed. This trade-off between security and performance is a consideration for users, especially those engaged in bandwidth-intensive activities, such as video streaming or online gaming.

Security vulnerabilities, such as those related to outdated encryption protocols or misconfigurations, can pose risks to VPN users. The potential for security breaches underscores the importance of regularly updating and patching VPN software to address vulnerabilities and ensure the adoption of the latest security standards. Additionally, the selection of a reputable VPN service provider is crucial, as the provider's infrastructure, logging policies, and commitment to user privacy directly impact the overall security of the VPN service.

Beyond encryption, VPNs often employ additional security measures, including the use of authentication protocols such as username and password, digital certificates, or multi-factor authentication. These measures contribute to the establishment of a secure connection by verifying the identity of the user or device attempting to access the VPN. Multi-factor authentication, in particular, adds an extra layer of security by requiring users to provide multiple forms of identification, such as a password and a one-time code sent to their mobile device.

The rise of mobile computing and the proliferation of mobile devices have fueled the demand for VPN solutions tailored to the unique challenges of the mobile environment. Mobile VPNs are designed to provide secure connectivity for users on the go, ensuring that their data remains protected when accessing public Wi-Fi networks or other potentially insecure connections. These VPNs are optimized for mobile platforms, addressing issues such as seamless handovers between different network types (Wi-Fi to cellular, for example) and efficient use of resources to minimize the impact on battery life.

While VPNs offer a robust solution for secure data transmission, it is essential to acknowledge that they are not immune to potential risks and limitations. The effectiveness of a VPN relies on the trustworthiness of the VPN service provider. Users must carefully evaluate the privacy policies, logging practices, and jurisdiction of the provider to ensure that their data is handled in a manner consistent with their expectations. Additionally, the concept of the "VPN trust model" emphasizes the importance of trust in the VPN service provider, as users essentially entrust the provider with the responsibility of handling their internet traffic.

The growing importance of VPNs in ensuring secure data transmission is underscored by their adoption in various sectors, ranging from business and government to individual users seeking online privacy. As the digital landscape continues to evolve, and the need for secure remote access and data protection becomes increasingly critical, the role of VPNs is likely to expand. The ongoing development of VPN technologies, coupled with an emphasis on user education regarding best practices and potential risks, will contribute to the continued relevance and effectiveness of VPNs in securing digital communication. In a world where data privacy and security are paramount concerns, VPNs stand as indispensable tools, providing a secure conduit for the seamless and confidential transmission of data across the vast and interconnected expanse of the internet.

Detail the importance of encrypting data at rest.

Encrypting data at rest is a critical practice in contemporary cybersecurity, serving as a fundamental layer of defense against unauthorized access, data breaches, and potential exploitation. At rest, data resides on storage devices such as hard drives, solid-state drives, or other media, presenting a vulnerability if left unprotected. The importance of encrypting data at rest lies in its ability to safeguard sensitive information, ensuring that even if physical or logical security measures are bypassed, the data remains indecipherable to unauthorized parties.

Confidentiality, one of the pillars of information security, is a paramount consideration in the context of encrypting data at rest. By applying encryption to stored data, organizations and individuals can mitigate the risk of unauthorized access. This is particularly crucial in scenarios where storage devices may be lost, stolen, or accessed by malicious actors. The use of robust encryption algorithms transforms plaintext data into ciphertext, rendering it unreadable without the corresponding decryption key. As a result, even if an unauthorized individual gains physical access to the storage medium, they would be unable to comprehend the information without the appropriate decryption credentials.

The protection of sensitive information is especially critical in sectors dealing with highly confidential data, such as healthcare, finance, and government. In healthcare, for instance, patient records contain sensitive medical information that is subject to stringent privacy regulations. Encrypting this data at rest ensures compliance with data protection laws, such as the Health Insurance Portability and Accountability Act (HIPAA) in the United States. Similarly, in the financial sector, encrypting data at rest is essential to safeguard customer financial records, account details, and transaction histories, reducing the risk of identity theft and financial fraud. Government entities also rely on encryption to secure classified and sensitive information stored on various systems.

The regulatory landscape underscores the significance of encrypting data at rest, with many industry-specific and data protection regulations mandating its implementation. The General Data Protection Regulation (GDPR) in the European Union, for example, emphasizes the need for organizations to implement appropriate security measures to protect personal data. Encrypting data at rest is explicitly mentioned as a recommended practice to ensure the confidentiality and integrity of personal information. Failure to comply with such regulations can result in severe penalties, fines, and reputational damage, highlighting the legal and compliance-driven imperative for organizations to adopt robust encryption practices.

Data breaches have become an unfortunately common occurrence, impacting organizations across sectors and compromising the personal information of millions of individuals. Encrypting data at rest serves as a crucial line of defense against the potential fallout of a data breach. In the event that a storage device is compromised, the encrypted data remains incomprehensible without the decryption key. This layer of protection limits the impact of a breach, as even if an adversary gains access to the encrypted data, they would face the formidable challenge of deciphering the information, which is computationally infeasible without the proper cryptographic key.

The importance of encrypting data at rest extends beyond traditional computing environments to encompass emerging technologies such as cloud computing. With the increasing adoption of cloud storage services, organizations entrust their data to third-party providers, necessitating additional measures to secure information stored in the cloud. Encrypting data at rest in the cloud ensures that even if a breach or unauthorized access occurs within the cloud infrastructure, the encrypted data remains unreadable. Cloud service providers often offer encryption features, allowing organizations to leverage encryption keys and maintain control over their data security.

Encryption of data at rest aligns with the broader concept of defense-in-depth, emphasizing the implementation of multiple layers of security to protect against various threats. While network security and access controls are crucial components of a comprehensive security strategy, encrypting data at rest serves as the last line of defense, ensuring that even if perimeter defenses are breached, the data itself remains resilient to exploitation. This multi-layered approach reduces the risk of unauthorized access and data leakage, enhancing the overall security posture of an organization's information assets.

The preservation of data integrity is another key aspect of encrypting data at rest. While encryption primarily focuses on confidentiality, the cryptographic processes involved also contribute to ensuring the integrity of the data. Hash functions, often employed in conjunction with encryption algorithms, generate fixed-size hash codes unique to the content of the data. These hash codes act as fingerprints, enabling users to detect any unauthorized modifications or tampering of the encrypted data. By verifying the integrity of the data at rest through cryptographic means, organizations can maintain the trustworthiness and reliability of their stored information.

The proliferation of mobile devices and the increasing reliance on external storage devices further underscore the importance of encrypting data at rest. Mobile phones, tablets, and external hard drives often store sensitive information, making them potential targets for theft or loss. Encrypting data on these devices safeguards against unauthorized access, ensuring that if a device is misplaced or stolen, the data remains protected. Mobile device management (MDM) solutions often include features for enforcing encryption on devices used in enterprise settings, emphasizing the importance of extending data protection practices to the mobile environment.

Organizations with a commitment to data privacy and security recognize that encryption is not a one-time implementation but an ongoing process that requires regular updates and adherence to best practices. As computing power advances, encryption algorithms may face vulnerabilities, and the need for stronger encryption standards becomes apparent. Staying abreast of advancements in cryptography and adopting the latest encryption protocols is essential to maintain the effectiveness of data protection measures. Regularly updating cryptographic keys and reevaluating encryption strategies contribute to the resilience of data encryption practices over time.

In conclusion, encrypting data at rest is a cornerstone of modern cybersecurity, addressing the imperative of safeguarding sensitive information from unauthorized access, data breaches, and potential exploitation. The practice ensures the confidentiality, integrity, and compliance of stored data, offering a crucial layer of defense against a range of threats. From regulatory requirements and legal mandates to the protection of personal and financial information, the importance of encrypting data at rest spans across industries and sectors. As technology continues to evolve, the ongoing commitment to robust encryption practices remains essential to navigating the dynamic landscape of information security and preserving the trust placed in organizations to protect valuable data assets.

Discuss techniques for securing data stored on various devices and platforms.

Securing data stored on various devices and platforms is a multifaceted challenge in the dynamic landscape of cybersecurity. It requires a comprehensive approach that encompasses a variety of techniques to safeguard information from unauthorized access, data breaches, and potential exploitation. One fundamental aspect of securing data is the use of encryption. Encrypting data at rest ensures that even if physical or logical security measures are bypassed, the stored information remains indecipherable to unauthorized parties. Techniques such as full disk encryption (FDE) and file-level encryption are commonly employed to protect data on devices like laptops, desktops, and external storage drives. Full disk encryption encrypts the entire contents of a storage device, making it inaccessible without the appropriate decryption key, while file-level encryption allows for the selective encryption of specific files or folders.

Access controls play a crucial role in securing data on various devices and platforms. Implementing strong authentication mechanisms, such as passwords, biometrics, or multi-factor authentication, helps ensure that only authorized users can access sensitive information. Role-based access control (RBAC) is another effective technique that restricts access based on the user's role within an organization. By assigning specific permissions and privileges to users based on their roles, RBAC minimizes the risk of unauthorized access and limits the potential impact of security incidents. Additionally, organizations often leverage identity and access management (IAM) solutions to centralize and automate user provisioning, de-provisioning, and authentication processes, enhancing overall data security.

Data masking or obfuscation is a technique employed to protect sensitive information by replacing, encrypting, or scrambling original data with fictional or pseudonymous data. This is particularly relevant when dealing with databases or environments where developers or testers need access to data for application development or testing purposes. Data masking helps prevent exposure of sensitive information during these processes, reducing the risk of inadvertent data leaks or unauthorized access. Techniques like tokenization, which replaces sensitive data with tokens, and anonymization, which removes personally identifiable information, are commonly used forms of data masking.

Secure coding practices are essential for preventing vulnerabilities and ensuring the integrity of software applications that handle sensitive data. Techniques such as input validation, output encoding, and parameterized queries help mitigate common security risks such as SQL injection and cross-site scripting (XSS) attacks. Employing secure coding frameworks and conducting regular code reviews contribute to the identification and remediation of potential security flaws. Furthermore, organizations often conduct penetration testing, where ethical hackers attempt to identify and exploit vulnerabilities in applications, to assess the resilience of their software against real-world threats and enhance overall security.

In the context of mobile devices, where data is often stored locally and accessed remotely, implementing robust mobile device management (MDM) solutions is imperative. MDM allows organizations to enforce security policies on mobile devices, including the enforcement of encryption, the configuration of access controls, and the ability to remotely wipe or lock devices in case of loss or theft. Mobile application management (MAM) complements MDM by focusing on securing the data and applications themselves, ensuring that sensitive information remains protected even if the device is compromised. Techniques like containerization, which isolates corporate data from personal data on the device, contribute to a more secure mobile computing environment.

Cloud computing has transformed the way organizations store and access data, introducing new challenges and opportunities for data security. Cloud security techniques involve a combination of encryption, access controls, and auditing mechanisms. Implementing encryption for data both in transit and at rest in the cloud ensures that data remains protected from interception and unauthorized access. Cloud access security brokers (CASBs) are tools that provide visibility and control over data transferred between on-premises devices and cloud services. These brokers enforce security policies, monitor user activities, and detect anomalies to prevent unauthorized access to sensitive information in cloud environments.

Regular data backups are a critical component of data security, serving as a recovery mechanism in the event of data loss due to hardware failures, malware attacks, or other unforeseen incidents. Backing up data to secure, isolated locations helps prevent the loss of critical information and facilitates quick recovery. Techniques such as automated backup schedules and versioning ensure that organizations have access to the most recent and historical copies of their data. Additionally, organizations often conduct disaster recovery planning and testing to validate the effectiveness of their backup and recovery processes, ensuring business continuity in the face of unforeseen events.

Endpoint security is essential for protecting data stored on individual devices such as laptops, desktops, and servers. Antivirus and anti-malware solutions help detect and prevent malicious software that could compromise the security of stored data. Endpoint detection and response (EDR) solutions go beyond traditional antivirus tools by providing real-time monitoring, threat detection, and response capabilities. Implementing device encryption, securing firmware and operating systems, and enforcing endpoint security policies contribute to a robust defense against potential threats and vulnerabilities.

Data classification is a technique that involves categorizing data based on its sensitivity, importance, and regulatory implications. By assigning labels to different types of data, organizations can tailor security controls and access permissions accordingly. Highly sensitive or confidential data may require stronger encryption, stricter access controls, and additional monitoring compared to less critical information. Data loss prevention (DLP) solutions complement data classification by monitoring and preventing the unauthorized transmission or exfiltration of sensitive data, both within the organization and through external channels.

Network security techniques play a vital role in securing data during transmission and communication. Implementing virtual private networks (VPNs) creates encrypted tunnels over public networks, ensuring the confidentiality and integrity of data in transit. Firewalls, intrusion detection systems (IDS), and intrusion prevention systems (IPS) contribute to safeguarding data by monitoring network traffic, detecting anomalies, and preventing unauthorized access or malicious activities. Secure socket layer (SSL) and transport layer security (TLS) protocols are used to encrypt data exchanged between clients and servers over the internet, securing online transactions and communications.

Auditing and monitoring techniques are essential for maintaining visibility into data access, changes, and potential security incidents. Security information and event management (SIEM) solutions aggregate and analyze log data from various sources, helping organizations identify and respond to security events in real-time. Regular security audits, including file integrity checks and access reviews, assist in identifying and remedying potential security gaps. User and entity behavior analytics (UEBA) solutions analyze patterns of user behavior to detect abnormal activities and potential security threats, enhancing overall data security.

Incident response and preparedness are critical components of a robust data security strategy. Developing and regularly testing an incident response plan ensures that organizations are well-prepared to respond effectively to security incidents. This includes identifying and containing security breaches, investigating the root causes, and implementing remediation measures. Post-incident analysis and documentation contribute to continuous improvement and resilience against future security threats. Communication plans, involving timely and transparent communication with stakeholders, help manage the fallout of security incidents and maintain trust in the organization's commitment to data security.

In conclusion, securing data stored on various devices and platforms demands a comprehensive and dynamic approach that encompasses a multitude of techniques. From encryption and access controls to secure coding practices, mobile device management, and cloud security measures, organizations must adopt a layered and adaptive strategy to address the evolving landscape of cybersecurity threats. The importance of securing data extends across industries, regulatory frameworks, and technological advancements, emphasizing the need for continuous vigilance and improvement. As technology continues to evolve, organizations must stay proactive in implementing the latest security techniques and best practices to safeguard their valuable data assets from the ever-present and evolving threat landscape.

Explore the critical role of key management in maintaining the integrity of encryption.

Key management plays a critical and foundational role in maintaining the integrity of encryption systems, serving as the linchpin that ensures the confidentiality, authenticity, and integrity of sensitive information in various digital communication and storage environments. At its core, encryption involves the transformation of plaintext data into ciphertext using cryptographic algorithms and keys. The security of this process hinges on the robustness and proper management of encryption keys throughout their lifecycle.

The lifecycle of an encryption key encompasses key generation, distribution, storage, usage, and retirement. Each stage requires careful attention to detail to prevent vulnerabilities and unauthorized access. Key generation sets the initial tone for security; weak or predictable keys can undermine the entire encryption system. Randomness and entropy are crucial factors in generating strong keys, and the use of well-established cryptographic algorithms is essential to withstand sophisticated attacks.

Distribution of encryption keys poses another critical challenge. Safely transmitting keys to authorized parties while preventing interception by adversaries is a delicate balancing act. Secure key exchange protocols, such as Diffie-Hellman, facilitate this process, ensuring that only the intended recipients possess the necessary keys for decryption. Additionally, the use of key management protocols, like the Key Management Interoperability Protocol (KMIP), streamlines key distribution across different systems and platforms, enhancing interoperability and security.

The secure storage of encryption keys is imperative to prevent unauthorized access and potential compromise. Physical security measures, such as hardware security modules (HSMs), safeguard keys from theft or tampering. Moreover, cryptographic key storage practices, such as key wrapping and secure key vaults, add an additional layer of protection against unauthorized access. Regularly auditing and monitoring key storage systems help detect any anomalies or potential security breaches promptly.

Effective key usage policies dictate how encryption keys are employed during data encryption and decryption processes. Access controls and proper user authentication mechanisms ensure that only authorized individuals or systems can utilize encryption keys. Implementing strong access management practices, including role-based access control (RBAC) and multifactor authentication (MFA), adds layers of defense against unauthorized key usage. Regularly rotating keys and implementing session key management practices further mitigate risks associated with long-term key usage.

Key revocation and retirement strategies are crucial components of key management, ensuring that compromised or outdated keys do not compromise the overall security of encrypted data. Establishing clear processes for key revocation and updating key status in a timely manner is vital. Additionally, cryptographic agility, the ability to transition to new encryption algorithms or key lengths, allows organizations to adapt to emerging threats and technology advancements without compromising security.

Interoperability and standardization in key management are essential for organizations operating in diverse technology landscapes. Standards like the Advanced Encryption Standard (AES) and KMIP facilitate the integration of encryption solutions from different vendors, promoting a cohesive and secure ecosystem. Ensuring that cryptographic protocols adhere to industry standards enhances the resilience and trustworthiness of encryption systems.

Key management challenges are further accentuated in cloud environments, where data is often distributed across various locations and services. Cloud service providers typically offer key management services, allowing users to centralize and delegate key management responsibilities. However, organizations must carefully evaluate and configure these services to align with their specific security requirements, taking into account factors such as data residency, compliance, and access controls.

Despite the importance of key management, it is often a neglected aspect of cryptographic implementations. Poor key management practices can lead to catastrophic security breaches, as demonstrated by historical incidents where compromised keys resulted in unauthorized access to sensitive data. The advent of quantum computing poses an additional threat, as quantum computers have the potential to break widely-used encryption algorithms, emphasizing the need for quantum-resistant key management strategies.

In conclusion, the critical role of key management in maintaining the integrity of encryption cannot be overstated. A well-designed and meticulously executed key management strategy is essential for safeguarding sensitive information in the digital age. From key generation to retirement, each phase of the key lifecycle demands attention to detail, adherence to standards, and a proactive approach to evolving security threats. As technology continues to advance, organizations must prioritize robust key management practices to ensure the continued effectiveness of encryption in protecting data from unauthorized access and manipulation.

Discuss best practices for key generation, storage, and distribution.

Best practices for key generation, storage, and distribution are paramount in ensuring the security and effectiveness of encryption systems. Key generation, as the foundational step in the encryption process, demands meticulous attention to detail. Strong cryptographic keys should be generated using secure algorithms that provide a high level of entropy, making it computationally infeasible for adversaries to predict or brute-force the keys. Cryptographic libraries and pseudorandom number generators (PRNGs) should be carefully selected and regularly updated to mitigate vulnerabilities. Additionally, organizations should adopt key length recommendations based on current cryptographic standards to resist emerging threats and advances in computational power. Rigorous testing and validation procedures during key generation are essential to identify any weaknesses in the process and to guarantee the production of robust encryption keys.

Equally critical is the secure storage of encryption keys. Protecting keys from unauthorized access, tampering, or theft is fundamental to maintaining the integrity of encrypted data. Hardware Security Modules (HSMs) provide a dedicated, tamper-resistant environment for key storage, offering a physical barrier against attacks. Encryption keys stored in software-based solutions should be safeguarded using strong access controls, encryption at rest, and secure key vaults. Regularly auditing and monitoring key storage systems can help detect anomalies or potential security breaches promptly. Moreover, organizations should implement key backup and recovery mechanisms to prevent data loss in the event of hardware failure or other unforeseen circumstances, ensuring the continued availability of critical encryption keys.

Efficient key distribution is another key aspect of a robust encryption strategy. Securely transmitting keys to authorized parties while preventing interception by adversaries requires the implementation of strong key exchange protocols. Protocols like the Diffie-Hellman key exchange algorithm enable secure key negotiation over insecure communication channels. Public Key Infrastructure (PKI) provides a framework for secure key distribution by utilizing digital certificates to authenticate the identity of communication parties. Additionally, the Key Management Interoperability Protocol (KMIP) facilitates standardized key exchange and management across different systems and platforms, enhancing interoperability and simplifying the complexities of key distribution in diverse environments. Organizations should prioritize the secure transmission of keys, employing encryption and authentication mechanisms to safeguard keys in transit and prevent man-in-the-middle attacks.

Adopting effective key usage policies is imperative to control and monitor how encryption keys are employed during data encryption and decryption processes. Access controls and user authentication mechanisms should be implemented to ensure that only authorized individuals or systems can utilize encryption keys. Role-based access control (RBAC) and multifactor authentication (MFA) add additional layers of defense against unauthorized key usage. Regularly rotating keys and implementing session key management practices further mitigate risks associated with long-term key usage. It is essential to strike a balance between providing access to authorized users and limiting exposure to potential attackers, and organizations should continuously evaluate and update their key usage policies to align with evolving security requirements and industry best practices.

The revocation and retirement of encryption keys are critical components of key management that often get overlooked. Establishing clear processes for key revocation in the event of a compromise or other security incident is essential to prevent unauthorized access. Updating key status in a timely manner ensures that compromised or outdated keys do not compromise the overall security of encrypted data. Cryptographic agility, the ability to transition to new encryption algorithms or key lengths, allows organizations to adapt to emerging threats and technology advancements without compromising security. Effective key retirement processes should include the secure deletion or archival of retired keys to prevent unintended access and minimize the risk of unauthorized decryption.

Interoperability and standardization play a vital role in key management, particularly when dealing with diverse technology landscapes. Adhering to well-established standards, such as the Advanced Encryption Standard (AES) for symmetric encryption or the RSA algorithm for public-key cryptography, enhances the resilience and trustworthiness of encryption systems. Standardized protocols like KMIP facilitate the integration of encryption solutions from different vendors, promoting a cohesive and secure ecosystem. Organizations should prioritize compatibility with industry standards to ensure seamless interoperability and avoid potential pitfalls associated with proprietary or non-standardized key management approaches.

In cloud environments, where data is often distributed across various locations and services, key management practices become even more crucial. Cloud service providers typically offer key management services, allowing users to centralize and delegate key management responsibilities. However, organizations must carefully evaluate and configure these services to align with their specific security requirements, taking into account factors such as data residency, compliance, and access controls. Employing encryption key management as a service (KMSaaS) can streamline key management in the cloud, providing a centralized and scalable solution for securing cryptographic keys.

Despite the implementation of best practices, it is essential for organizations to continuously monitor and update their key management strategies. Regular security audits, vulnerability assessments, and compliance checks help identify and rectify any weaknesses or deviations from established best practices. As technology evolves, so do the threats, and organizations must remain vigilant in adapting their key management practices to address emerging challenges and stay ahead of potential security risks. In conclusion, a comprehensive and well-executed approach to key generation, storage, and distribution is crucial for the overall security and resilience of encryption systems, ensuring the protection of sensitive information in an increasingly interconnected and digitized world.

Provide insights into emerging trends in encryption technology.

Emerging trends in encryption technology reflect the evolving landscape of digital security, driven by technological advancements, regulatory changes, and the growing sophistication of cyber threats. Quantum-resistant encryption stands out as a prominent trend, propelled by the looming threat of quantum computers capable of breaking widely used encryption algorithms. As quantum computing continues to progress, there is a heightened focus on developing encryption methods that can withstand quantum attacks. Post-quantum cryptography, including lattice-based cryptography, hash-based cryptography, and multivariate polynomial cryptography, is gaining attention as a potential solution to secure data against quantum threats, ensuring the long-term integrity of encrypted communications.

The integration of homomorphic encryption represents another noteworthy trend in encryption technology. Homomorphic encryption enables computations on encrypted data without the need for decryption, preserving data privacy throughout the processing lifecycle. This capability is particularly relevant in scenarios where sensitive information needs to be analyzed or processed by third-party entities without exposing the underlying data. As advancements in homomorphic encryption continue, industries such as healthcare, finance, and collaborative research are exploring its applications for secure and privacy-preserving data analysis, opening up new possibilities for secure data sharing and collaboration.

Blockchain technology, popularized by cryptocurrencies like Bitcoin, is influencing encryption trends by providing a decentralized and tamper-resistant framework for secure transactions. The use of blockchain in encryption applications, known as blockchain-based encryption, offers enhanced transparency, immutability, and traceability. Integrating blockchain with encryption technologies can be advantageous in scenarios where trust and integrity verification are paramount, such as supply chain management, secure communication, and data provenance. The synergy between blockchain and encryption is expected to play a pivotal role in reshaping the landscape of secure and verifiable data transactions.

The advent of confidential computing is transforming how encryption is implemented in cloud environments. Confidential computing environments, facilitated by technologies like Intel's Software Guard Extensions (SGX) and AMD's Secure Encrypted Virtualization (SEV), allow for the execution of code and processing of data in a secure enclave, isolated from the underlying infrastructure. This ensures that even cloud service providers cannot access sensitive data during processing. As organizations increasingly migrate to the cloud, confidential computing provides a robust solution for protecting data confidentiality and integrity in multi-tenant cloud environments.

The rise of zero-trust security models is influencing encryption strategies to adapt to a perimeterless security paradigm. Zero-trust architectures operate under the assumption that no entity, whether internal or external, should be inherently trusted. This approach mandates strong authentication, continuous monitoring, and robust encryption at every layer of the network and data infrastructure. Encryption plays a crucial role in securing data both in transit and at rest within a zero-trust framework, providing an additional layer of protection against unauthorized access and data breaches in dynamic and distributed computing environments.

Another emerging trend is the evolution of encryption key management solutions. As organizations grapple with the complexities of managing an increasing number of encryption keys across diverse environments, key management solutions are evolving to provide centralized, scalable, and interoperable approaches. Cloud-based key management services, often referred to as Key Management as a Service (KMaaS), are gaining popularity, offering organizations the flexibility to manage encryption keys in a centralized manner while benefiting from the scalability and accessibility of cloud services. Additionally, the integration of automation and artificial intelligence into key management processes is streamlining key lifecycle management, enhancing security, and reducing the risk of human error.

The growing importance of data privacy regulations, such as the General Data Protection Regulation (GDPR) and the California Consumer Privacy Act (CCPA), is influencing encryption trends. Organizations are increasingly adopting encryption as a fundamental component of their compliance strategies to protect sensitive data and ensure regulatory compliance. End-to-end encryption for communication platforms and applications is becoming more prevalent, providing users with a heightened level of privacy and control over their personal information. This trend reflects a broader societal shift toward prioritizing individual privacy rights and the need for robust data protection mechanisms.

In response to the escalating threat landscape, the integration of artificial intelligence (AI) and machine learning (ML) into encryption solutions is gaining traction. AI and ML technologies enhance the detection of anomalous activities, predict potential security threats, and automate responses in real-time. Applied to encryption, these technologies can optimize key management, identify patterns indicative of cyber attacks, and enhance the overall efficacy of security measures. The synergy between AI/ML and encryption is empowering organizations to proactively defend against evolving cyber threats and ensure the resilience of their encrypted communication and data storage systems.

The evolution of encryption technology is closely tied to the broader landscape of cybersecurity. The rise of encrypted traffic analysis tools and techniques is addressing the challenge of inspecting encrypted traffic for potential security threats without compromising user privacy. Innovations in this space include the development of techniques that preserve the confidentiality of user data while enabling the identification and mitigation of malicious activities within encrypted communications. As encryption becomes more pervasive, finding a balance between privacy and security will continue to be a focal point of research and development efforts.

In conclusion, the landscape of encryption technology is undergoing a dynamic transformation, driven by a convergence of factors such as quantum computing threats, the need for privacy-preserving technologies, advancements in confidential computing, and the proliferation of data privacy regulations. The trends outlined, including quantum-resistant encryption, homomorphic encryption, blockchain-based encryption, confidential computing, zero-trust security models, evolving key management solutions, compliance-driven encryption, AI/ML integration, and encrypted traffic analysis, collectively shape the trajectory of encryption in addressing contemporary challenges and safeguarding digital assets in an increasingly interconnected and data-driven world. As organizations navigate these trends, a proactive and adaptive approach to encryption technology is essential to stay ahead of emerging threats and embrace the opportunities presented by evolving security paradigms.

Discuss the challenges and opportunities posed by quantum computing on current encryption methods.

Quantum computing presents both significant challenges and intriguing opportunities that reverberate across the landscape of current encryption methods. At the heart of the challenge lies the potential for quantum computers to break widely used cryptographic algorithms, posing a formidable threat to the security of encrypted communications and data. The most prominent risk comes from Shor's algorithm, a quantum algorithm that can efficiently factor large numbers, challenging the security of widely employed public-key cryptography schemes like RSA and ECC. As quantum computers advance, the ability to factor large numbers exponentially faster than classical computers could render existing encryption methods obsolete, jeopardizing the confidentiality and integrity of sensitive information that relies on these cryptographic protocols.

The vulnerabilities introduced by quantum computing demand a proactive response from the field of cryptography, leading to the exploration of post-quantum cryptography as a potential solution. This burgeoning field seeks cryptographic algorithms that can resist attacks from both classical and quantum computers, providing a level of security that remains robust even in the face of quantum advancements. Lattice-based cryptography, hash-based cryptography, code-based cryptography, and multivariate polynomial cryptography are among the promising approaches under consideration. The aim is to develop encryption methods that can withstand quantum attacks, ensuring the continued confidentiality and integrity of encrypted data in a post-quantum era.

The race to develop and standardize post-quantum cryptographic algorithms is accompanied by challenges such as the need for thorough scrutiny of candidate algorithms, the establishment of a standardized selection process, and the integration of post-quantum algorithms into existing cryptographic infrastructures. The transition to post-quantum cryptography involves a delicate balance between maintaining interoperability with current systems and preparing for the quantum future, requiring careful planning, collaboration, and adherence to evolving industry standards. Organizations need to stay vigilant, monitoring developments in quantum computing and adjusting their cryptographic strategies accordingly to ensure a smooth transition to post-quantum security.

Beyond the challenges posed by quantum computing, there are opportunities for innovation and exploration in the realm of quantum-safe cryptography. Quantum key distribution (QKD) stands out as a promising avenue that leverages the principles of quantum mechanics to secure communication channels. QKD uses the quantum properties of particles, such as photons, to enable the exchange of cryptographic keys in a way that is theoretically immune to interception or eavesdropping. While QKD is still in the experimental stage and faces practical challenges in deployment, it represents a potential paradigm shift in securing communication channels against both classical and quantum threats. The development of practical and scalable QKD solutions could usher in a new era of quantum-safe communication.

Additionally, quantum-resistant algorithms, designed to withstand attacks from both classical and quantum computers, offer an opportunity to enhance the security of existing systems before the advent of large-scale quantum computing. Cryptographic agility, the ability to transition to new encryption algorithms or key lengths, is a key consideration in preparing for the quantum threat. Organizations can adopt a forward-looking approach by incorporating quantum-resistant algorithms into their cryptographic protocols, ensuring that their systems remain secure in the face of evolving technological landscapes.

As the quantum computing landscape unfolds, the potential impact on current encryption methods extends beyond algorithmic vulnerabilities. Quantum computers could also compromise the security of stored data encrypted with currently prevalent symmetric encryption algorithms. Grover's algorithm, a quantum algorithm designed for searching an unsorted database, has the potential to reduce the security of symmetric key lengths by half. To counter this threat, organizations may need to adjust their key management practices, such as doubling key lengths, to maintain the same level of security. Quantum-resistant symmetric encryption algorithms are also under exploration to address the challenges posed by Grover's algorithm.

The integration of quantum-resistant cryptography into existing systems and protocols introduces a transition phase during which organizations must manage a hybrid cryptographic environment. This phase involves supporting both classical and quantum-resistant algorithms, ensuring backward compatibility with existing systems while gradually adopting quantum-safe alternatives. The complexity of this transition underscores the need for careful planning and a phased approach to updating cryptographic protocols, taking into account factors such as system dependencies, resource constraints, and the potential impact on performance.

While quantum computing introduces formidable challenges to the security of current encryption methods, it also fosters collaboration and innovation within the global cryptographic community. Standardization bodies, such as the National Institute of Standards and Technology (NIST), are actively engaged in soliciting, evaluating, and standardizing post-quantum cryptographic algorithms. This collaborative effort involves researchers, academics, and industry experts worldwide, fostering a collective response to the quantum threat. The open and transparent nature of the selection process contributes to the robustness and credibility of the chosen post-quantum algorithms, reflecting a commitment to the security and resilience of cryptographic systems in the face of quantum advancements.

In conclusion, the advent of quantum computing introduces unprecedented challenges to current encryption methods, particularly those reliant on classical cryptographic algorithms. Shor's algorithm and Grover's algorithm pose specific threats to public-key and symmetric-key cryptography, respectively, necessitating a paradigm shift in cryptographic strategies. The ongoing exploration of post-quantum cryptography, quantum key distribution, and quantum-resistant algorithms presents opportunities for innovation and reinforces the importance of cryptographic agility. Organizations must navigate the complex landscape of quantum computing, preparing for a future where the security of encrypted data hinges on cryptographic methods that can withstand the computational power of quantum computers. As the field evolves, the collaboration between researchers, industry, and standardization bodies becomes pivotal in shaping a secure and quantum-resistant cryptographic future.

Chapter 4: Navigating Threat Landscapes: Cybersecurity Threats and Trends

D iscuss the ever-evolving nature of cybersecurity threats.
The ever-evolving nature of cybersecurity threats is a dynamic and relentless challenge that constantly reshapes the landscape of digital security. Cyber adversaries, driven by financial motives, geopolitical interests, or simply a desire for disruption, continually adapt their tactics to exploit vulnerabilities and stay one step ahead of defensive measures. The breadth and sophistication of these threats have expanded exponentially over the years, encompassing a diverse array of attack vectors, techniques, and motivations.

One prominent facet of this evolution is the rise of advanced persistent threats (APTs), which are complex, long-term cyber campaigns orchestrated by well-funded and organized adversaries. APTs often target specific organizations or entities with the aim of exfiltrating sensitive information, conducting cyber-espionage, or compromising critical infrastructure. These campaigns involve meticulous planning, reconnaissance, and the use of sophisticated malware to achieve their objectives. The ongoing evolution of APTs underscores the need for organizations to adopt proactive and adaptive security measures that go beyond traditional defense mechanisms.

Malware, a pervasive and multifaceted cybersecurity threat, continues to evolve in sophistication and diversity. From the early days of viruses and worms, the landscape has expanded to include ransomware, polymorphic malware, fileless malware, and other variants that constantly challenge traditional antivirus solutions. Ransomware attacks, in particular, have become more targeted and lucrative for cybercriminals, with ransom demands escalating and tactics becoming more strategic. The ability of malware to mutate and evade detection emphasizes the importance of robust endpoint protection, threat intelligence, and user education to mitigate the impact of these persistent threats.

Social engineering, a deceptive manipulation of human psychology, remains a prevalent and effective tactic in cyberattacks. Phishing attacks, spear-phishing, and business email compromise (BEC) are examples of social engineering techniques that exploit human vulnerabilities to gain unauthorized access or extract sensitive information. Cybercriminals continuously refine their social engineering tactics, leveraging psychological manipulation, personalization, and contextually relevant content to deceive even the most vigilant individuals. The need for comprehensive cybersecurity awareness training, combined with advanced email filtering and authentication mechanisms, is essential to counter the ever-evolving threat landscape of social engineering attacks.

Supply chain attacks have emerged as a significant and sophisticated cybersecurity threat, targeting organizations through vulnerabilities in their interconnected networks of suppliers and service providers. Adversaries exploit the trust established within these supply chains to infiltrate and compromise the target organization. The SolarWinds incident is a notable example of a supply chain attack that affected numerous government and private sector entities. As organizations increasingly rely on interconnected ecosystems, the need for robust supply chain security practices, continuous monitoring, and threat intelligence sharing becomes imperative to detect and prevent such attacks.

The proliferation of Internet of Things (IoT) devices introduces a new dimension to the cybersecurity threat landscape. The inherent vulnerabilities in many IoT devices, coupled with the widespread adoption of these devices in homes, businesses, and critical infrastructure, create a vast attack surface for cyber adversaries. Mirai and other botnet attacks targeting IoT devices have demonstrated the potential for large-scale disruption and the exploitation of insecure IoT ecosystems for malicious purposes. The integration of security-by-design principles, regular firmware updates, and network segmentation are essential strategies to mitigate the risks associated with the growing prevalence of IoT-related threats.

Cybersecurity threats are increasingly intertwined with geopolitical tensions and state-sponsored activities. Nation-state actors engage in cyber-espionage, cyber-attacks, and cyber-warfare to achieve political, economic, or military objectives. The Stuxnet worm, attributed to state-sponsored actors, was a watershed moment that highlighted the potential for cyber operations to impact physical infrastructure. The blurred lines between cybercrime and state-sponsored cyber activities create a complex and challenging landscape, where attribution becomes difficult, and the motivations behind cyber operations are multifaceted. The need for international cooperation, norms, and agreements in cyberspace is essential to establish a framework for responsible state behavior and mitigate the risks associated with geopolitical cyber threats.

The advent of cloud computing and the widespread adoption of remote work have introduced new attack vectors and expanded the attack surface for cyber adversaries. Cloud security misconfigurations, data breaches, and unauthorized access to cloud environments are increasingly common cybersecurity concerns. The shift to remote work, accelerated by the global pandemic, has amplified the risks associated with phishing attacks, insecure home networks, and the use of personal devices for work-related activities. Organizations need to prioritize cloud security best practices, implement robust identity and access management controls, and provide secure remote access solutions to address the evolving challenges posed by the dynamic nature of modern work environments.

Cryptocurrency-related threats have also gained prominence, driven by the increasing use of cryptocurrencies for both legitimate and illicit purposes. Cryptocurrency exchanges, wallets, and transactions are targeted by cybercriminals seeking financial gains through theft, fraud, or ransom demands. The anonymity and decentralization inherent in cryptocurrency transactions present challenges for law enforcement and regulatory authorities. As the adoption of cryptocurrencies continues to grow, addressing the cybersecurity risks associated with these digital assets becomes crucial, requiring a combination of technological solutions, regulatory frameworks, and international cooperation.

Artificial intelligence (AI) and machine learning (ML) are being leveraged by both cyber defenders and adversaries, introducing a new layer of complexity to the cybersecurity landscape. While AI and ML technologies offer the potential to enhance threat detection, automate response mechanisms, and analyze vast datasets for patterns indicative of cyber threats, they are also susceptible to adversarial attacks. Cybercriminals can exploit vulnerabilities in AI algorithms to evade detection, launch targeted attacks, or manipulate security systems. The cat-and-mouse game between AI-driven cyber defenses and AI-enhanced cyber threats underscores the need for continuous innovation, research, and the ethical use of AI in cybersecurity.

In conclusion, the ever-evolving nature of cybersecurity threats reflects the relentless innovation and adaptability of cyber adversaries. From sophisticated APTs and malware variants to social engineering tactics, supply chain attacks, IoT vulnerabilities, geopolitical cyber activities, cloud-related risks, cryptocurrency threats, and the integration of AI/ML in cyber operations, the threat landscape is dynamic and multifaceted. Organizations and cybersecurity professionals must adopt a proactive and adaptive mindset, staying abreast of emerging threats, leveraging advanced technologies, and implementing comprehensive security strategies that address the evolving challenges of the digital era. International cooperation, information sharing, and a commitment to cybersecurity best practices are essential components of a resilient defense against the ever-changing and increasingly sophisticated array of cyber threats.

Highlight the challenges posed by emerging technologies.

The rapid pace of technological advancement has ushered in a new era of innovation, but it also brings forth a myriad of challenges that demand careful consideration and proactive solutions. One significant challenge posed by emerging technologies is the escalating concern over privacy and data security. The widespread adoption of Internet of Things (IoT) devices, smart homes, and connected ecosystems raises apprehensions about the potential misuse of personal data. The continuous collection, processing, and sharing of sensitive information in these interconnected environments amplify the risk of unauthorized access, data breaches, and privacy violations. Striking a balance between the benefits of technological innovation and safeguarding individual privacy becomes increasingly complex as the boundaries of data usage blur.

Artificial intelligence (AI) and machine learning (ML) technologies, while holding immense potential for transformative applications, present challenges related to ethical considerations and bias. The algorithms powering AI systems are only as unbiased as the data they are trained on, and if historical data carries inherent biases, the resulting AI models may perpetuate and even amplify those biases. This raises concerns about fairness, accountability, and transparency in decision-making processes. Efforts to address these challenges involve developing ethical frameworks for AI deployment, implementing robust data governance practices, and promoting diversity in the teams responsible for designing and training AI systems.

The advent of 5G technology brings both promises and challenges, particularly in the realm of cybersecurity. The ultra-fast speeds and low latency offered by 5G networks enable the proliferation of connected devices and the expansion of the IoT landscape. However, the increased attack surface, coupled with the complexity of securing the vast array of devices connected to 5G networks, introduces new cybersecurity risks. Threats such as device vulnerabilities, network slicing vulnerabilities, and the potential for large-scale disruptions underscore the importance of designing resilient and secure 5G infrastructures. Cybersecurity strategies must evolve to address the unique challenges posed by the increased connectivity and complexity inherent in 5G networks.

The rise of quantum computing introduces a paradigm shift in the field of cryptography, challenging the security of widely used encryption methods. Quantum computers have the potential to break existing cryptographic algorithms, rendering current encryption techniques obsolete. This necessitates the development and adoption of quantum-resistant cryptographic algorithms to ensure the continued confidentiality and integrity of sensitive information in the face of quantum threats. Preparing for the era of quantum computing requires a concerted effort to integrate quantum-safe encryption methods into existing systems and protocols, emphasizing the importance of cryptographic agility in the ever-changing landscape of cybersecurity.

Automation and robotics, while streamlining processes and increasing efficiency, raise concerns about the impact on employment and the workforce. The integration of robotic process automation (RPA) and autonomous systems in various industries can lead to job displacement and shifts in the skills demanded by the job market. Navigating the ethical implications of workforce automation, upskilling the workforce to adapt to changing job requirements, and addressing issues of job displacement are critical considerations in ensuring a smooth transition to an automated future while mitigating societal and economic challenges.

Biotechnology advancements, including gene editing technologies like CRISPR-Cas9, pose ethical dilemmas and biosafety concerns. The ability to modify the human genome raises questions about the potential for unintended consequences, the creation of designer babies, and the potential misuse of biotechnological tools. The ethical implications of gene editing extend beyond human applications to agriculture, where genetically modified organisms (GMOs) raise concerns about environmental impact, biodiversity, and the long-term sustainability of food systems. Balancing the potential benefits of biotechnological innovations with ethical considerations and robust regulatory frameworks is essential to navigate the challenges associated with the rapid progress in biotechnology.

The intersection of technology and mental health introduces both opportunities and challenges. The pervasive use of social media, online platforms, and digital devices has reshaped communication and interaction patterns, but it also raises concerns about the impact on mental well-being. Issues such as cyberbullying, social media addiction, and the negative psychological effects of constant connectivity demand attention. Striking a balance between leveraging technology to promote mental health awareness and support while addressing the adverse effects of technology on mental well-being requires a holistic approach that involves collaboration among technology developers, mental health professionals, and policymakers.

In the realm of space exploration and satellite technology, the proliferation of satellites and space debris raises sustainability and environmental concerns. The increasing number of satellites in low Earth orbit (LEO) and the potential for collisions among these satellites pose risks to space infrastructure and the generation of space debris that could impact future space missions. Sustainable space practices, responsible satellite deployment, and international cooperation on space debris mitigation become imperative to ensure the long-term viability of space activities.

The ethical considerations surrounding the use of emerging technologies in surveillance and facial recognition systems present challenges to privacy and civil liberties. The widespread deployment of surveillance technologies, coupled with the ability to analyze vast amounts of visual data, raises concerns about mass surveillance, unwarranted intrusions into personal privacy, and the potential for abuse. Establishing clear regulatory frameworks, ethical guidelines, and oversight mechanisms is crucial to safeguard individual rights and prevent the misuse of surveillance technologies.

Amid the ongoing advancements in healthcare technologies, the integration of electronic health records (EHRs), telemedicine, and wearable health devices introduces challenges related to data security and patient privacy. Ensuring the confidentiality and integrity of health information, protecting against cyber threats targeting healthcare systems, and addressing ethical concerns surrounding the use of patient data for research purposes are critical considerations. Striking a balance between harnessing the benefits of healthcare technologies for improved patient outcomes and safeguarding the privacy and security of sensitive health data is essential for the responsible adoption of emerging technologies in the healthcare sector.

In conclusion, the challenges posed by emerging technologies span a broad spectrum, encompassing ethical considerations, privacy concerns, cybersecurity risks, societal impacts, and environmental sustainability. Navigating this complex landscape requires a multidisciplinary approach that involves collaboration among technology developers, policymakers, ethicists, cybersecurity experts, and the wider society. Establishing robust regulatory frameworks, ethical guidelines, and international cooperation mechanisms is essential to harness the opportunities presented by emerging technologies while mitigating the associated challenges. As we navigate the ever-evolving terrain of technological innovation, a thoughtful and proactive approach is imperative to ensure that emerging technologies contribute positively to the betterment of society while addressing the multifaceted challenges they introduce.

Define APTs and their sophisticated strategies.

Advanced Persistent Threats (APTs) represent a category of cyber threats characterized by their advanced, targeted, and persistent nature. APTs are orchestrated by well-funded and organized adversaries, often nation-states or sophisticated cybercriminal groups, with specific objectives such as cyber-espionage, data theft, or the compromise of critical infrastructure. A key characteristic of APTs is their long-term and persistent engagement with a targeted entity, distinguishing them from more opportunistic and short-lived cyber-attacks. APT actors employ a combination of advanced tactics, techniques, and procedures (TTPs) to infiltrate and maintain unauthorized access to their targets, often remaining undetected for extended periods.

The strategies employed by APTs are multifaceted and adaptive, reflecting the sophistication of these adversaries. One of the primary elements of APT strategies is meticulous reconnaissance and intelligence gathering. APT actors invest significant resources in understanding their targets, collecting information about the target's infrastructure, personnel, vulnerabilities, and security mechanisms. This reconnaissance phase enables APTs to tailor their attack vectors and increase the likelihood of successful infiltration.

Social engineering is a fundamental component of APT strategies, exploiting human vulnerabilities to gain a foothold within the target organization. APT actors employ techniques such as spear-phishing, where highly targeted and personalized emails are crafted to deceive specific individuals within the organization. These emails may contain malicious attachments or links, aiming to exploit trust and trick recipients into executing malicious code or revealing sensitive information. The sophistication of APT social engineering lies in the careful curation of messages that align with the target's context and may appear legitimate, making them challenging to detect.

APT actors leverage advanced malware to achieve their objectives, often developing custom-designed tools or modifying existing malware to evade detection by traditional security measures. Polymorphic malware, which dynamically changes its code to avoid signature-based detection, is frequently used by APTs. Additionally, APTs deploy fileless malware, which operates in memory without leaving a footprint on the target's system, making it harder to detect and analyze. The use of malware by APTs is not only for initial compromise but also for establishing persistence within the target environment, allowing continued access and data exfiltration.

Once inside the target network, APTs employ lateral movement techniques to navigate and escalate privileges. This involves compromising additional systems within the network, moving laterally to find valuable information, and gaining higher-level access to critical resources. APTs often exploit vulnerabilities in software, misconfigurations, or weak access controls to escalate privileges and extend their reach within the targeted organization. This phase of the attack demonstrates the adaptability and persistence of APTs in navigating complex network architectures.

To maintain stealth and avoid detection, APTs employ sophisticated evasion techniques. This includes the use of encryption to conceal communications, obfuscation of malicious code to bypass signature-based detection, and the manipulation of timestamps to blend in with normal network traffic. APT actors are adept at monitoring the target's security measures and adapting their tactics to circumvent evolving defenses. The use of zero-day exploits, targeting vulnerabilities unknown to the software vendor or the public, is another strategy employed by APTs to maximize the effectiveness of their attacks.

APT campaigns often involve the exfiltration of sensitive data, and APT actors prioritize methods that allow them to quietly transfer stolen information without raising alarms. Secure communication channels, such as command-and-control servers hosted on compromised infrastructure, are utilized to transmit data outside the target network. APTs may also leverage steganography, hiding data within seemingly innocuous files or communications, to obfuscate their activities and avoid detection during data exfiltration.

Attribution, or the identification of APT actors, is a complex challenge due to the use of false flags, proxy servers, and other tactics to mask their true origins. APT actors often go to great lengths to make their activities appear as if they are originating from a different source, making it difficult for investigators to definitively attribute an attack to a specific entity. The use of digital forensics, threat intelligence, and collaboration among cybersecurity researchers and law enforcement agencies is essential to piece together the puzzle of APT attribution.

In summary, APTs employ highly sophisticated and targeted strategies that involve meticulous reconnaissance, social engineering, advanced malware, lateral movement, evasion techniques, and data exfiltration. The persistence and adaptability of APTs make them formidable adversaries, often requiring a combination of advanced technologies, threat intelligence, and human expertise to detect, mitigate, and attribute their activities. As APTs continue to evolve, organizations must adopt proactive cybersecurity measures, stay informed about emerging threats, and collaborate with the broader cybersecurity community to defend against these persistent and sophisticated cyber threats.

Explore notable examples of APTs in recent cybersecurity history.

In recent cybersecurity history, Advanced Persistent Threats (APTs) have emerged as sophisticated and persistent cyber threats, often orchestrated by well-funded and highly skilled adversaries. One prominent example is the Stuxnet worm, discovered in 2010, which was designed to target supervisory control and data acquisition (SCADA) systems, particularly those used in Iran's nuclear facilities. Stuxnet was groundbreaking due to its complexity and the use of multiple zero-day vulnerabilities, showcasing a level of sophistication indicative of a nation-state-sponsored APT.

Another notable APT is the Equation Group, believed to be associated with the U.S. National Security Agency (NSA). Active for over a decade, Equation Group developed a range of advanced cyber weapons, including the infamous malware dubbed "DoublePulsar" and "EternalBlue." These tools were later leaked and repurposed by other threat actors, most notably in the WannaCry ransomware attack of 2017, highlighting the potential consequences of APTs' unintended collateral damage.

The APT28 group, also known as Fancy Bear, gained notoriety for its alleged ties to the Russian government and involvement in various cyber espionage campaigns. Notable incidents include the targeting of the Democratic National Committee (DNC) during the 2016 U.S. presidential election, where sensitive emails were exfiltrated and subsequently leaked. This incident underscored the potential geopolitical implications of APTs, as cyber operations became intertwined with traditional statecraft.

Chinese-sponsored APTs, such as APT1 (or Comment Crew), have been implicated in cyber espionage activities targeting a wide range of industries, including aerospace, energy, and telecommunications. APT1's activities were extensively documented in the Mandiant APT1 report, which provided insights into the group's modus operandi and the extent of its cyber operations. These revelations heightened awareness of the persistent and organized nature of state-sponsored cyber threats emanating from China.

DarkTequila, a sophisticated APT discovered in 2018, targeted financial institutions primarily in Latin America. Known for its ability to avoid detection and its multi-stage infection process, Dark-Tequila aimed to steal financial information and login credentials. Its stealthy nature and focus on the financial sector highlighted the evolving tactics employed by APTs to achieve their objectives.

APT groups associated with North Korea, such as Lazarus, gained attention for their involvement in cybercrime, financial theft, and politically motivated attacks. Lazarus was linked to the infamous Sony Pictures hack in 2014, where sensitive data was leaked and destructive malware was employed. Subsequently, North Korean APTs targeted cryptocurrency exchanges, deploying tactics such as spear-phishing and malware to steal funds, emphasizing their adaptability and evolving capabilities.

In the realm of supply chain attacks, the SolarWinds incident in 2020 demonstrated the impact of a highly sophisticated APT campaign. Believed to be the work of APT29, also known as Cozy Bear, the attack involved compromising the software supply chain to distribute a malicious update to SolarWinds' Orion platform. This enabled the threat actors to gain access to numerous organizations, including several U.S. government agencies, highlighting the potential for APTs to exploit trusted channels for widespread infiltration.

The rise of APTs underscores the need for robust cybersecurity measures, threat intelligence, and international cooperation to mitigate the risks posed by these persistent and well-resourced adversaries. As APTs continue to evolve, staying vigilant and proactive in the face of these advanced threats remains paramount to safeguarding critical infrastructure, sensitive data, and geopolitical stability in the digital age.

Uncover the various forms of social engineering used in cyber-attacks.

Social engineering, a manipulative technique that exploits human psychology to gain access to sensitive information or perform unauthorized actions, manifests in various forms within cyber-attacks. Phishing, one of the most prevalent social engineering tactics, involves deceiving individuals into revealing confidential information by posing as a trustworthy entity. This can take the form of emails, messages, or websites that mimic legitimate sources, tricking users into divulging passwords, financial details, or other personal data. Spear phishing, a more targeted approach, tailors these deceptive communications to specific individuals or organizations, often leveraging personal information to enhance credibility and increase the chances of success.

Pretexting is another form of social engineering that involves creating a fabricated scenario to manipulate individuals into divulging information or performing actions they might not otherwise undertake. The attacker adopts a false identity or pretext to establish trust and credibility, often relying on detailed and convincing stories to exploit human kindness or curiosity. By convincing the target that the request is legitimate, the attacker can extract valuable information or access.

Quizzes, surveys, or seemingly innocent requests for information are employed in the guise of social media quizzes or online contests, exploiting individuals' willingness to share personal details willingly. This type of social engineering leverages the natural inclination to participate in seemingly harmless activities, with the collected information used for identity theft, account compromise, or other malicious purposes. The allure of entertainment or curiosity prompts users to provide information that can later be exploited.

Impersonation, or masquerading as a trusted entity, is a social engineering technique commonly used in cyber-attacks. Attackers may impersonate authoritative figures, such as IT support personnel, to convince individuals to share passwords or perform actions that compromise security. In business email compromise (BEC) attacks, threat actors often impersonate executives or high-ranking officials to manipulate employees into transferring funds or disclosing sensitive corporate information.

Baiting involves enticing individuals with the promise of something desirable, such as free software, movies, or other downloads, to trick them into downloading malicious software or divulging sensitive information. Often conducted through physical mediums like infected USB drives left in public places or online platforms, baiting exploits human curiosity and the desire for freebies, leading to unwitting compromise.

In the context of social engineering, the manipulation of human emotions plays a crucial role. Fear, for instance, is leveraged in scareware attacks where individuals are presented with alarming messages about nonexistent security threats, compelling them to download malicious software or pay for unnecessary services. By capitalizing on the urgency of the situation, attackers exploit the natural instinct to resolve perceived threats quickly.

Tailgating, or piggybacking, involves an attacker physically following an authorized person into a restricted area without proper authentication. This form of social engineering exploits the human tendency to be polite or helpful, as individuals may hold doors open for others without verifying their credentials. Once inside, the attacker can gain unauthorized access to sensitive information or systems.

Pharming is a social engineering technique that involves redirecting users from legitimate websites to fraudulent ones without their knowledge. This is often accomplished by exploiting vulnerabilities in DNS servers or by utilizing malware. Users are directed to fake websites where they unwittingly enter sensitive information, thinking they are interacting with a trusted platform. Pharming attacks are particularly insidious as they undermine the trust users place in familiar online environments.

Vishing, a combination of "voice" and "phishing," involves using phone calls to deceive individuals into divulging sensitive information. Attackers may impersonate legitimate entities, such as banks or government agencies, to create a sense of urgency or importance. By manipulating emotions and creating a false sense of trust, vishing attacks exploit the human tendency to respond to authoritative voices, leading to the disclosure of confidential information.

In conclusion, social engineering encompasses a wide array of manipulative tactics that exploit human psychology to compromise security. From phishing and pretexting to impersonation and baiting, these techniques prey on human emotions, trust, and natural inclinations. Understanding the diverse forms of social engineering is crucial for individuals and organizations to bolster their cybersecurity defenses and mitigate the risks posed by these insidious tactics. Education, awareness, and the implementation of robust security measures are essential in navigating the ever-evolving landscape of social engineering threats in the digital age.

Provide guidance on recognizing and mitigating social engineering threats.

Recognizing and mitigating social engineering threats is paramount in safeguarding individuals and organizations from manipulative cyber-attacks. A crucial aspect of defense lies in fostering awareness and education. Individuals should be trained to recognize common social engineering tactics, such as phishing emails or suspicious phone calls. Awareness campaigns that simulate real-world scenarios can help users develop a critical eye and a heightened sense of skepticism when confronted with unexpected requests for sensitive information.

Organizations must prioritize cybersecurity training for employees, emphasizing the importance of verifying the legitimacy of requests, especially those involving sensitive data or financial transactions. Regularly updating employees on the latest social engineering techniques and tactics ensures that they remain informed and vigilant against evolving threats. Encouraging a culture of open communication where employees feel comfortable reporting suspicious activities helps create a collaborative defense against social engineering.

Implementing robust email security measures is fundamental in mitigating social engineering threats, as email remains a common vector for phishing attacks. Advanced email filtering systems can identify and block malicious emails, reducing the likelihood of successful phishing attempts. Additionally, organizations can deploy email authentication protocols like DMARC (Domain-based Message Authentication, Reporting, and Conformance) to prevent attackers from using spoofed email addresses, enhancing email trustworthiness.

Multi-factor authentication (MFA) is a powerful tool in mitigating social engineering threats by adding an extra layer of verification beyond passwords. Even if attackers manage to obtain login credentials through social engineering, MFA requires an additional authentication step, such as a code sent to a registered device, to access an account. This significantly enhances security and mitigates the risk of unauthorized access, even in the event of compromised credentials.

Regularly updating and patching software is essential for addressing vulnerabilities that social engineering attacks may exploit. Keeping systems and applications up-to-date ensures that known vulnerabilities are patched, reducing the attack surface available to malicious actors. Cybercriminals often target outdated software with known vulnerabilities, and a proactive approach to software maintenance can effectively thwart their efforts.

Endpoint protection solutions, including antivirus and anti-malware software, play a crucial role in mitigating social engineering threats. These tools can detect and block malicious software, preventing its execution on endpoints. Additionally, behavior-based analysis can identify suspicious activities indicative of social engineering attacks, providing an additional layer of defense against evolving threats.

Implementing a comprehensive cybersecurity policy that includes guidelines for handling sensitive information and responding to potential social engineering threats is essential. Clear and well-communicated policies empower employees to make informed decisions and establish a framework for responding to security incidents. Regularly reviewing and updating these policies ensures they remain relevant in the face of evolving social engineering tactics.

Regular security audits and vulnerability assessments can help organizations identify and address potential weaknesses in their security posture. By proactively seeking out vulnerabilities and addressing them before they can be exploited, organizations can significantly reduce the risk of falling victim to social engineering attacks. This includes assessing both technical vulnerabilities and potential gaps in human-centric security measures.

Creating a reporting and incident response framework is crucial for effectively addressing social engineering threats. Employees should be encouraged to report any suspicious activities promptly, and organizations should have a well-defined process for investigating and responding to reported incidents. This not only facilitates a swift response to potential threats but also provides valuable insights for improving security measures and training programs.

Collaboration and information-sharing within the cybersecurity community are essential for staying ahead of social engineering threats. Participating in threat intelligence sharing platforms and industry-specific forums allows organizations to benefit from collective knowledge and insights. Being aware of emerging social engineering tactics and the experiences of other organizations enhances preparedness and enables a proactive defense against evolving threats.

In conclusion, recognizing and mitigating social engineering threats require a multifaceted and proactive approach. Educating individuals, implementing technical safeguards, fostering a culture of security, and maintaining up-to-date security policies collectively contribute to a robust defense against social engineering attacks. As cyber threats continue to evolve, a holistic and adaptive cybersecurity strategy remains crucial in navigating the complex landscape of social engineering in the digital age.

Investigate the prevalence and impact of ransomware attacks.

The prevalence and impact of ransomware attacks have reached alarming levels in recent years, posing significant threats to individuals, businesses, and critical infrastructure. Ransomware, a form of malicious software designed to block access to a computer system or files until a sum of money is paid, has evolved into a lucrative criminal enterprise. The widespread adoption of digital technologies, coupled with the increasing sophistication of ransomware tactics, has fueled a surge in incidents, leaving organizations grappling with the far-reaching consequences.

Ransomware attacks often start with a user unknowingly downloading or executing malicious code, typically delivered through phishing emails, compromised websites, or malicious software downloads. Once inside a system, the ransomware encrypts files, rendering them inaccessible to the rightful owner. The attackers then demand a ransom, usually in cryptocurrency, in exchange for providing the decryption key. This method allows cybercriminals to operate with a degree of anonymity, complicating law enforcement efforts to track and apprehend perpetrators.

The prevalence of ransomware attacks has surged globally, affecting a diverse range of entities. Small and medium-sized enterprises (SMEs) are often targeted due to their potentially weaker cybersecurity defenses and limited resources for robust protection measures. However, larger enterprises, critical infrastructure, healthcare institutions, and even government agencies have not been immune to the pervasive threat of ransomware. Attackers often leverage automated tools and exploit vulnerabilities to cast a wide net, seeking vulnerable systems across various sectors.

One of the most infamous ransomware strains is WannaCry, which made headlines in 2017 by infecting hundreds of thousands of computers worldwide. Exploiting a vulnerability in the Windows operating system, WannaCry spread rapidly, affecting organizations such as the National Health Service (NHS) in the United Kingdom, disrupting healthcare services and highlighting the potentially life-threatening consequences of ransomware attacks.

The impact of ransomware extends far beyond the immediate financial cost of paying a ransom. The disruption caused by encrypted files can paralyze essential business operations, leading to significant downtime and financial losses. In the case of critical infrastructure, such as energy grids or transportation systems, the consequences of ransomware attacks can be severe, posing risks to public safety and national security. The healthcare sector, in particular, has been a prime target, with ransomware attacks on hospitals and medical facilities compromising patient care, data integrity, and even, in some cases, leading to tragic outcomes.

Beyond the financial toll and operational disruptions, the reputational damage inflicted by ransomware attacks can be long-lasting. Organizations that fall victim to such incidents often experience a loss of trust from clients, partners, and the public. The perception of inadequate cybersecurity measures can tarnish an entity's image and erode confidence in its ability to safeguard sensitive information.

The rise of ransomware-as-a-service (RaaS) has further democratized cybercrime, enabling even less technically proficient individuals to launch ransomware attacks. Criminals can now purchase or rent ransomware tools on the dark web, reducing barriers to entry into the world of cyber extortion. This commodification has led to a proliferation of ransomware variants, each with its own tactics and targeting strategies, making it challenging for cybersecurity professionals to keep pace with the evolving threat landscape.

Law enforcement agencies and cybersecurity experts consistently advise against paying ransoms, as there is no guarantee that the attackers will provide the decryption key, and paying only fuels the profitability of ransomware operations. However, some organizations, faced with the urgency of restoring operations, may opt to pay the ransom as a last resort. This ethical dilemma underscores the need for a collective and coordinated effort to combat ransomware, involving enhanced cybersecurity measures, international cooperation, and a commitment to holding cybercriminals accountable.

As ransomware attacks continue to evolve in sophistication, defenders must adopt a multi-faceted approach to mitigate the risks effectively. This includes implementing robust cybersecurity practices, regularly updating and patching software, conducting comprehensive employee training to recognize and avoid phishing attempts, and deploying advanced endpoint protection solutions. Collaborative efforts between public and private sectors, information sharing, and the development of international norms for responding to cyber threats are essential components of a resilient defense against the pervasive and damaging impact of ransomware attacks.

Discuss preventive measures and effective response strategies.

Preventing and effectively responding to cybersecurity threats require a comprehensive and strategic approach that encompasses both technical measures and human awareness. The landscape of cyber threats is constantly evolving, necessitating adaptive and proactive strategies to safeguard individuals, organizations, and critical infrastructure. A key component of preventive measures is the implementation of robust cybersecurity protocols. This includes the regular updating and patching of software to address known vulnerabilities, as cybercriminals often exploit outdated systems. Organizations should establish a strong perimeter defense with firewalls, intrusion detection systems, and secure network configurations to prevent unauthorized access.

Multi-factor authentication (MFA) is a critical preventive measure that adds an extra layer of security beyond traditional password protection. By requiring users to authenticate their identity through multiple means, such as a password and a one-time code sent to a registered device, MFA significantly reduces the risk of unauthorized access even if login credentials are compromised. Encouraging the use of strong, unique passwords and implementing password management tools can further enhance the security of user accounts.

Regular security awareness training for employees is essential in building a human firewall against cyber threats. Training programs should educate individuals about common social engineering tactics, such as phishing and pretexting, and provide practical guidance on how to recognize and avoid falling victim to these manipulative techniques. Simulated phishing exercises can be instrumental in gauging the effectiveness of training and reinforcing a culture of cybersecurity awareness within an organization.

Endpoint protection solutions, including antivirus and anti-malware software, play a crucial role in preventing malicious software from compromising individual devices. These tools should be kept up-to-date to detect and block emerging threats effectively. Additionally, the use of advanced endpoint detection and response (EDR) solutions can provide real-time visibility into endpoint activities, enabling rapid response to potential security incidents.

Regular security audits and vulnerability assessments help organizations identify and address weaknesses in their cybersecurity posture. Conducting these assessments proactively allows for the identification and remediation of vulnerabilities before they can be exploited. Penetration testing, where ethical hackers simulate real-world attacks to identify vulnerabilities, is a valuable method for evaluating the resilience of an organization's defenses.

Implementing a robust incident response plan is crucial for minimizing the impact of a cybersecurity incident and ensuring a swift and coordinated response. The incident response plan should define roles and responsibilities, establish communication protocols, and include predefined steps for identifying, containing, eradicating, recovering from, and learning from security incidents. Regular testing and updating of the incident response plan are essential to maintain its effectiveness in the face of evolving cyber threats.

Collaboration and information sharing within the cybersecurity community and across industries are vital for staying ahead of emerging threats. Participating in threat intelligence sharing platforms and industry-specific forums allows organizations to benefit from collective knowledge and insights. Sharing information about new attack vectors, tactics, and indicators of compromise enhances the overall resilience of the cybersecurity ecosystem.

Establishing a robust backup and recovery strategy is a fundamental aspect of both preventive measures and effective response strategies. Regularly backing up critical data and ensuring that backups are stored in a secure, isolated environment enables organizations to recover quickly in the event of a ransomware attack or data loss. Testing the restoration process periodically ensures the viability of backup solutions when needed.

Implementing network segmentation is an effective preventive measure that limits the lateral movement of attackers within a network. By dividing a network into segments with restricted access, organizations can contain the impact of a potential breach, preventing attackers from moving freely across the entire infrastructure. This segmentation strategy hinders the lateral spread of malware and restricts unauthorized access to sensitive systems.

Engaging in threat hunting, an active and iterative process of searching for indicators of compromise within a network, is a proactive measure to detect and mitigate potential threats before they escalate. Threat hunting involves analyzing network and endpoint data to identify anomalous patterns and behaviors that may indicate a security incident. This approach complements traditional security measures by actively seeking out threats that may evade automated detection.

As cyber threats continue to evolve, organizations must adopt a holistic and adaptive approach to cybersecurity. Combining technical measures, such as strong authentication, endpoint protection, and network segmentation, with human-centric strategies, including training and awareness programs, creates a resilient defense against a wide range of cyber threats. Moreover, establishing effective response strategies, such as incident response planning, information sharing, and regular testing, ensures organizations can respond swiftly and effectively to mitigate the impact of security incidents. In a rapidly changing digital landscape, a proactive and collaborative approach is essential for staying ahead of cyber adversaries and safeguarding the integrity of systems and data.

Explore current trends shaping the cybersecurity landscape.

The cybersecurity landscape is continuously evolving, shaped by technological advancements, emerging threats, and changing patterns of digital behavior. One prominent trend is the increasing sophistication of cyber threats, driven by well-funded and organized cybercriminal groups. Advanced Persistent Threats (APTs), often state-sponsored, demonstrate a level of expertise that goes beyond traditional cybercrime, with the ability to conduct long-term, targeted campaigns. These APTs leverage advanced techniques, such as zero-day exploits and complex malware, to infiltrate and persist within networks, posing significant challenges to defenders.

Ransomware attacks continue to be a pervasive and evolving threat, with attackers adopting new tactics to maximize their impact. Notably, there is a shift toward double extortion, where cybercriminals not only encrypt data but also threaten to release sensitive information unless a ransom is paid. This strategy increases the pressure on victims, amplifying the potential consequences of a ransomware attack. Additionally, the rise of ransomware-as-a-service (RaaS) has democratized the ability to launch ransomware attacks, allowing even less technically proficient individuals to participate in this lucrative criminal enterprise.

Supply chain attacks have gained prominence as a favored tactic among cyber adversaries. By targeting software vendors or service providers, attackers can compromise a multitude of downstream organizations through a single breach. The SolarWinds incident in 2020 exemplified the far-reaching impact of a supply chain attack, as malicious actors infiltrated a trusted software supplier to distribute a compromised software update, leading to widespread compromises across various sectors.

The Internet of Things (IoT) presents a growing attack surface, with the proliferation of interconnected devices creating new opportunities for cybercriminals. Insecure IoT devices, often lacking robust security features, become attractive targets for exploitation. Cyber attackers can compromise these devices to gain unauthorized access to networks, launch distributed denial-of-service (DDoS) attacks, or even use them as entry points for broader cyber campaigns.

Cloud security has become a critical focus area as organizations increasingly migrate their infrastructure and services to cloud environments. While cloud providers offer robust security measures, misconfigurations and inadequate access controls can expose sensitive data to unauthorized access. The shared responsibility model emphasizes the need for organizations to actively manage their cloud security posture, ensuring that configurations align with best practices and compliance requirements.

Artificial Intelligence (AI) and machine learning (ML) are being leveraged by both defenders and attackers, marking a new frontier in cybersecurity. AI-driven tools empower security teams to analyze vast datasets, detect anomalies, and automate response actions. However, cybercriminals are also harnessing AI for malicious purposes, such as crafting more convincing phishing emails or evading traditional detection mechanisms. The cat-and-mouse game between AI-driven security solutions and AI-enhanced cyber threats is intensifying.

Zero Trust Architecture has gained traction as a security paradigm, challenging the traditional perimeter-based security model. In a Zero Trust framework, trust is never assumed, and verification is required from anyone trying to access resources, regardless of their location. This approach aligns with the evolving nature of modern work environments, where remote and mobile access is prevalent, and traditional network boundaries are increasingly porous.

The regulatory landscape for cybersecurity is evolving globally, with an increasing emphasis on data protection and privacy. Regulations such as the General Data Protection Regulation (GDPR) in Europe and the California Consumer Privacy Act (CCPA) in the United States impose stringent requirements on organizations regarding the collection, storage, and processing of personal data. Compliance with these regulations not only mitigates legal risks but also underscores the growing societal awareness and expectations surrounding data privacy.

The cybersecurity skills gap remains a persistent challenge, with the demand for skilled professionals outpacing the supply. As cyber threats become more sophisticated, organizations struggle to find and retain talent with the necessary expertise to defend against

evolving attack vectors. This gap highlights the importance of investing in cybersecurity education and workforce development to build
a robust pipeline of skilled professionals.

Nation-state cyber activities continue to shape the geopolitical
landscape, with state-sponsored cyber espionage, influence operations, and disruptive attacks becoming commonplace. The attribution of cyber incidents to specific nation-states is a complex challenge, often involving advanced forensic analysis and intelligence collaboration. The blurring of lines between traditional espionage, cyber warfare, and criminal activities underscores the need for international norms and agreements to govern state behavior in cyberspace.

In conclusion, the current trends shaping the cybersecurity landscape reflect a dynamic and multifaceted environment. From the increasing sophistication of cyber threats to the transformative impact
of technologies like AI and the challenges posed by the evolving
regulatory landscape, organizations face a complex array of challenges. Addressing these challenges requires a holistic and adaptive
approach, encompassing advanced technical solutions, proactive
strategies, and a commitment to collaboration and education. As
the digital landscape continues to evolve, staying ahead of emerging
trends is essential for organizations and cybersecurity professionals
seeking to protect against the ever-changing threat landscape.

**Discuss the impact of technological advancements and
geopolitical factors.**

Technological advancements and geopolitical factors exert profound and interconnected influences on global affairs, shaping the
trajectory of societies, economies, and security landscapes. In the
realm of technology, the advent of artificial intelligence (AI) stands
out as a transformative force with far-reaching implications. AI has
the potential to revolutionize industries, automate processes, and enhance decision-making capabilities. However, the rapid integration
of AI also raises ethical concerns, ranging from job displacement and

privacy issues to the potential weaponization of AI in cyber warfare and autonomous weaponry. The impact of technological advancements extends to the realm of cybersecurity, where the evolution of cyber threats, such as sophisticated malware and ransomware, necessitates the continuous development of advanced defense mechanisms.

Moreover, the proliferation of the Internet of Things (IoT) amplifies the interconnectedness of devices, creating a vast attack surface that can be exploited by malicious actors. While IoT technologies offer unprecedented convenience and efficiency, the security implications pose significant challenges, as insecure devices may be leveraged in large-scale distributed denial-of-service (DDoS) attacks or provide entry points for cyber intrusions. Consequently, the ongoing technological revolution demands vigilant governance, ethical considerations, and robust cybersecurity measures to harness the benefits of innovation while mitigating associated risks.

Geopolitical factors, including the shifting balance of power among nations, geopolitical tensions, and the rise of new global players, further shape the contours of the contemporary world. The dynamics of international relations are increasingly influenced by cyber capabilities, with nation-states engaging in cyber espionage, information warfare, and cyberattacks as tools of statecraft. The attribution of cyber incidents to specific actors poses significant challenges, blurring the lines between state-sponsored activities, criminal enterprises, and hacktivism. As cyberspace becomes an arena for geopolitical competition, establishing norms and rules of engagement in the digital domain becomes imperative to prevent destabilizing escalations and ensure a secure global cyberspace.

The emergence of 5G technology represents a pivotal technological advancement with significant geopolitical implications. As countries vie for leadership in the deployment and standardization of 5G networks, concerns about technological dependence, supply chain security, and the potential for espionage through telecommunications infrastructure have come to the forefront. The race to dominate 5G technology underscores the intertwined nature of technological competition and geopolitical influence, with implications for economic competitiveness, national security, and the overall geopolitical landscape.

In the context of artificial intelligence, the competition for AI dominance has become a focal point of geopolitical rivalry. Nations recognize the strategic importance of AI in areas such as military applications, economic competitiveness, and technological innovation. The development of national AI strategies and investments in research and development are emblematic of the geopolitical competition to lead in the AI-driven future. The ethical dimensions of AI, including bias in algorithms and the impact on employment, further complicate the intersection of technological advancements and geopolitical considerations.

Technological advancements also play a pivotal role in shaping economic structures and global trade patterns. The rise of digital economies, characterized by the dominance of technology giants and the increasing importance of data as a valuable asset, introduces new dynamics into international trade. The digitalization of commerce, finance, and communication has created opportunities for economic growth but also poses challenges related to data governance, privacy, and competition. The geopolitical implications of these shifts are evident in debates over data sovereignty, trade policies, and the regulation of multinational technology companies.

Moreover, the geopolitical landscape is intricately linked with environmental considerations, and technological innovations play a crucial role in addressing global challenges such as climate change. Advancements in renewable energy technologies, sustainable agriculture practices, and climate modeling contribute to the development of solutions aimed at mitigating environmental risks. International collaborations on research and technology transfer become essential in addressing shared environmental concerns, illustrating the interconnected nature of technological progress and geopolitical cooperation.

The interplay between technology and geopolitics extends into space exploration and satellite technologies. The strategic importance of space assets for communication, navigation, and surveillance has heightened geopolitical competition in space. Nations are investing in space programs not only for scientific exploration but also to assert strategic advantages. The militarization of space, satellite-based cyber threats, and the development of anti-satellite capabilities underscore the intricate links between technological advancements and the geopolitics of space.

As nations grapple with the challenges posed by the convergence of technology and geopolitics, international governance frameworks become essential. Collaborative efforts to establish norms, standards, and agreements that govern the responsible use of emerging technologies are crucial for fostering a stable and secure global order. The ethical dimensions of technological advancements, particularly in areas such as AI, genetic engineering, and biotechnology, necessitate a thoughtful and inclusive approach to policymaking that considers the diverse perspectives and interests of the global community.

In conclusion, the impact of technological advancements and geopolitical factors is profound and multifaceted, influencing the way societies function, economies operate, and nations interact on the global stage. The intricate relationship between technology and geopolitics requires careful consideration of ethical, security, and economic implications. Navigating this complex terrain demands a collaborative and forward-looking approach to international governance, one that fosters innovation, addresses shared challenges, and ensures that the benefits of technological progress are equitably distributed across the global community. As the pace of technological change accelerates, the interplay between technology and geopolitics will continue to shape the future trajectory of the world.

Chapter 5: Securing the Human Element: Cyber Hygiene and Awareness

E mphasize the role of individuals in maintaining good cyber hygiene.

The role of individuals in maintaining good cyber hygiene is increasingly crucial in the contemporary digital landscape, where our daily lives are intricately intertwined with technology. Cyber hygiene encompasses a set of practices and habits that individuals can adopt to safeguard their personal information, privacy, and digital well-being. At the core of good cyber hygiene lies the recognition that every individual is a potential target for cyber threats, and proactive measures are essential to mitigate risks and vulnerabilities.

One fundamental aspect of individual cyber hygiene is the adoption of strong and unique passwords. Passwords serve as the first line of defense against unauthorized access, and creating robust passwords is a simple yet effective way to protect sensitive accounts. Individuals should avoid using easily guessable passwords such as "123456" or "password" and opt for a combination of letters, numbers, and symbols. Additionally, using different passwords for various accounts enhances security, as a breach in one account does not compromise others.

Regularly updating passwords is an integral component of good cyber hygiene. With the prevalence of data breaches and leaks, reusing old passwords across multiple accounts poses significant risks. Individuals should consider using password manager tools that generate and securely store complex passwords, reducing the burden of memorizing numerous credentials while enhancing overall security.

Another critical practice in maintaining good cyber hygiene is the careful management of personal information. Individuals should be cautious about sharing sensitive data online and should refrain from oversharing on social media platforms. Cybercriminals often leverage personal information, such as birthdays, addresses, or family details, to craft convincing phishing attacks or gain unauthorized access to accounts. Being mindful of the information shared online helps mitigate the risk of falling victim to social engineering tactics.

Vigilance against phishing attacks is paramount for individuals seeking to maintain good cyber hygiene. Phishing emails, messages, or websites often mimic legitimate entities to deceive individuals into revealing sensitive information. Individuals should scrutinize unexpected emails, especially those requesting personal information or urging urgent action. Verifying the authenticity of communication through official channels or contacting the purported sender directly adds an extra layer of protection against phishing attempts.

Installing and regularly updating antivirus and anti-malware software is a foundational practice in good cyber hygiene. These tools detect and remove malicious software that can compromise the security of devices and personal data. Individuals should ensure that their antivirus software is set to automatically update to guard against emerging threats and vulnerabilities. Additionally, keeping operating systems and software up-to-date with the latest security patches is crucial for addressing known vulnerabilities and enhancing overall system security.

Securing devices with strong authentication methods is integral to good cyber hygiene. Enabling multi-factor authentication (MFA) adds an extra layer of protection beyond passwords, requiring an additional form of verification, such as a code sent to a registered device. MFA significantly enhances the security of online accounts and serves as a deterrent to unauthorized access.

Data backups play a pivotal role in mitigating the impact of ransomware attacks and data loss incidents. Individuals should regularly back up essential files and data to external drives or secure cloud storage. In the event of a cyber incident, having recent backups ensures the ability to restore information without succumbing to ransom demands. Automating the backup process reduces the likelihood of neglecting this critical aspect of cyber hygiene.

Staying informed about the latest cybersecurity threats and trends is an ongoing responsibility for individuals committed to maintaining good cyber hygiene. Cyber threats evolve rapidly, and being aware of emerging risks empowers individuals to adapt their practices accordingly. Following reputable cybersecurity news sources, participating in awareness campaigns, and leveraging available resources contribute to building a well-informed and resilient approach to cybersecurity.

Education and training are indispensable components of individual cyber hygiene. Many individuals may not be aware of the evolving tactics used by cybercriminals or the potential risks associated with certain online behaviors. Cybersecurity awareness programs, whether offered by employers, educational institutions, or online platforms, provide valuable insights into recognizing and mitigating cyber threats. By investing time in learning about cybersecurity best practices, individuals can enhance their digital literacy and contribute to a safer online environment.

The responsible use of personal devices, particularly in the context of Bring Your Own Device (BYOD) policies in workplaces, is another dimension of good cyber hygiene. Individuals should implement security measures on their personal devices, such as smartphones and tablets, including device encryption, biometric authentication, and remote tracking and wiping capabilities. By maintaining the security of personal devices, individuals contribute to overall organizational cybersecurity efforts.

Privacy-conscious online behavior is integral to good cyber hygiene. Reviewing and adjusting privacy settings on social media platforms, web browsers, and online services allows individuals to control the amount of personal information shared with third parties. Being mindful of the permissions granted to apps and services helps mitigate the risk of unauthorized access to sensitive data.

As the boundaries between personal and professional life blur, individuals must extend good cyber hygiene practices to their professional endeavors. In workplaces, employees should adhere to organizational cybersecurity policies, use secure communication channels, and report any suspicious activities promptly. Cybersecurity awareness training for employees fosters a culture of collective responsibility and resilience against cyber threats.

In conclusion, the role of individuals in maintaining good cyber hygiene is pivotal in the face of evolving cyber threats. Adopting strong passwords, practicing cautious data management, remaining vigilant against phishing attempts, utilizing security tools, and staying informed about cybersecurity best practices collectively contribute to individual cyber resilience. As the digital landscape continues to evolve, individuals must recognize their agency in safeguarding personal and collective digital well-being. By embracing good cyber hygiene practices, individuals become active participants in fortifying the digital ecosystem and fostering a safer and more secure online environment for everyone.

Provide practical tips for securing personal and professional digital environments.

Securing personal and professional digital environments is paramount in the contemporary era, where our reliance on digital technologies exposes us to various cyber threats. Practical measures encompass a holistic approach that addresses both personal devices and professional workspaces, emphasizing a proactive stance against evolving cyber risks.

First and foremost, the cornerstone of digital security lies in the use of strong and unique passwords. Adopting complex passwords that combine letters, numbers, and symbols enhances the resilience of accounts against unauthorized access. It is essential to avoid easily guessable passwords, such as "password" or "123456," and refrain from using the same password across multiple accounts. Employing a reputable password manager to generate and securely store complex passwords simplifies the task of managing numerous credentials while bolstering overall security.

Regularly updating passwords is a fundamental practice to thwart potential security breaches. With the increasing frequency of data breaches and leaks, individuals must refrain from reusing old passwords across different platforms. Implementing a routine to change passwords and leveraging two-factor authentication (2FA) whenever possible significantly fortifies the security of personal and professional accounts, as it adds an extra layer of verification beyond passwords.

In both personal and professional contexts, safeguarding personal information is paramount. Users should exercise caution when sharing sensitive data online, be it on social media platforms, e-commerce websites, or other digital services. Cybercriminals often exploit personal information, such as birthdays, addresses, or family details, to craft convincing phishing attacks or gain unauthorized access to accounts. A prudent approach involves minimizing the amount of personal information shared online and adjusting privacy settings to restrict access to sensitive data.

Vigilance against phishing attacks is crucial for securing personal and professional digital environments. Phishing emails, messages, or websites often mimic legitimate entities to deceive individuals into revealing sensitive information. Individuals should cultivate a habit of scrutinizing unexpected emails, especially those requesting personal information or urging urgent action. Verifying the authenticity of communication through official channels or contacting the purported sender directly adds an extra layer of protection against phishing attempts.

In both personal and professional settings, installing and regularly updating antivirus and anti-malware software is fundamental. These security tools detect and remove malicious software that can compromise the security of devices and personal data. Regular updates ensure that antivirus software is equipped to handle emerging threats, while maintaining up-to-date operating systems and software addresses known vulnerabilities, reducing the risk of exploitation by cybercriminals.

Securing personal devices, such as smartphones, tablets, and laptops, is integral to maintaining a safe digital environment. Implementing strong authentication methods, including biometric options and PINs, adds an extra layer of protection to these devices. Device encryption safeguards stored data, preventing unauthorized access in case of loss or theft. Individuals should regularly update the operating systems and applications on their devices to patch security vulnerabilities and ensure optimal protection.

The adoption of multi-factor authentication (MFA) is a powerful measure that enhances the security of personal and professional accounts. By requiring an additional form of verification beyond passwords, MFA significantly reduces the risk of unauthorized access. Whether in personal email accounts, social media platforms, or professional workspaces, enabling MFA serves as a robust defense against account compromise, mitigating the impact of credential-based attacks.

Data backups play a pivotal role in securing personal and professional digital environments. Individuals should regularly back up essential files and data to external drives or secure cloud storage. In case of a hardware failure, ransomware attack, or accidental data loss, having recent backups ensures the ability to restore information without succumbing to ransom demands. Automating the backup process reduces the likelihood of neglecting this critical aspect of digital security.

Privacy-conscious online behavior is integral to securing personal and professional digital environments. Users should be mindful of the permissions granted to applications, websites, and online services, limiting access to only necessary data. Reviewing and adjusting privacy settings on social media platforms and web browsers empowers individuals to control the amount of personal information shared with third parties, reducing the risk of unauthorized data collection.

In a professional setting, organizations should implement and enforce robust cybersecurity policies to protect both company assets and employee data. Employee training and awareness programs contribute to creating a security-conscious culture, ensuring that staff members are well-informed about potential threats and best practices. Workplaces should also consider implementing secure remote access policies, especially in environments where remote work is prevalent, to safeguard sensitive company information.

In a professional digital environment, the use of virtual private networks (VPNs) adds an extra layer of security by encrypting internet connections and protecting data from potential eavesdropping. VPNs are particularly crucial when employees access company resources from public Wi-Fi networks, mitigating the risks associated with unsecured connections.

Regular software updates and patch management are critical elements in securing professional digital environments. Organizations should implement protocols to ensure that all software, including operating systems, applications, and security tools, is regularly updated to address known vulnerabilities. Automated update systems can streamline this process, reducing the likelihood of oversight and minimizing the attack surface available to cybercriminals.

Controlling access to sensitive information is fundamental in professional digital environments. Implementing access controls and user permissions ensures that employees have the necessary access for their roles without exposing the entire organization to unnecessary risks. Regularly reviewing and updating access permissions as job roles change helps maintain a secure and well-organized digital workspace.

In conclusion, securing personal and professional digital environments demands a proactive and multifaceted approach that encompasses various aspects of cybersecurity. From strong password practices and vigilant protection against phishing attempts to the use of security tools, encryption, and data backups, individuals play a pivotal role in fortifying the digital landscape. In professional settings, organizational policies, employee training, and robust security measures collectively contribute to a resilient defense against evolving cyber threats. By adopting and consistently practicing these practical tips, individuals can contribute to creating a safer and more secure digital environment for themselves and their organizations.

Discuss the significance of ongoing training programs for individuals and employees.

Ongoing training programs for individuals and employees are of paramount significance in the rapidly evolving landscape of technology and cybersecurity. The dynamic nature of the digital realm, coupled with the persistent emergence of new cyber threats, underscores the necessity for continuous education and skill development. Individuals, whether in personal or professional capacities, benefit from staying abreast of the latest cybersecurity trends, best practices, and threat vectors. These training programs not only empower individuals to navigate the digital landscape securely but also cultivate a culture of cyber awareness that extends its benefits to workplaces, organizations, and the broader community.

In personal contexts, ongoing training programs play a pivotal role in enhancing digital literacy and fostering responsible online behaviors. Individuals often encounter an array of digital risks, from phishing attacks and malware infections to identity theft and online scams. Continuous training equips them with the knowledge to recognize and respond to these threats effectively. It enables individuals to differentiate between legitimate and malicious online activities, fortifying their defenses against cybercriminals who exploit vulnerabilities through deceptive tactics.

Moreover, ongoing training programs for individuals emphasize the importance of personal data protection and privacy. With the increasing digitization of personal information and the prevalence of online services, individuals need to be cognizant of the risks associated with sharing sensitive data. Training initiatives guide individuals in configuring privacy settings, managing permissions on digital platforms, and adopting secure online practices. By instilling an understanding of the value of personal data and the potential consequences of its compromise, ongoing training empowers individuals to make informed decisions about their digital footprint.

In professional settings, ongoing training programs for employees are instrumental in cultivating a resilient cybersecurity posture for organizations. Cyber threats are constantly evolving, becoming more sophisticated and targeted. Employees, being one of the primary attack vectors, need to be equipped with the knowledge and skills to recognize and thwart cyber threats effectively. Regular training sessions on topics such as phishing awareness, social engineering, and secure password practices help employees become the first line of defense against cyber attacks.

Training programs also play a crucial role in addressing the human factor in cybersecurity incidents. Many security breaches result from unintentional actions by employees, such as clicking on malicious links or falling prey to social engineering tactics. Ongoing training fosters a heightened sense of cyber awareness, encouraging employees to adopt a cautious approach and question the legitimacy of unexpected communications or requests. This proactive mindset reduces the likelihood of falling victim to common cyber scams and phishing attempts.

Furthermore, as remote work becomes increasingly prevalent, ongoing training programs for employees gain added significance. Remote work environments introduce new challenges and security considerations, necessitating training on secure remote access, the use of virtual private networks (VPNs), and the secure handling of company data outside the traditional office setting. Training initiatives tailored to the remote work paradigm contribute to a secure and productive virtual workspace.

The technical landscape evolves rapidly, and ongoing training programs ensure that employees remain well-versed in the latest cybersecurity technologies and defense strategies. These programs cover topics such as endpoint security, network security, and the use of encryption technologies. By keeping employees informed about the implementation and best practices of these technologies, organizations bolster their overall cybersecurity resilience and readiness to face emerging threats.

Beyond technical aspects, ongoing training programs also address compliance and regulatory requirements. Many industries are subject to specific cybersecurity regulations and standards, such as the General Data Protection Regulation (GDPR) or the Health Insurance Portability and Accountability Act (HIPAA). Regular training ensures that employees are aware of these regulatory frameworks, understand their responsibilities in compliance, and can contribute to maintaining a secure and legally compliant organizational environment.

Ongoing training programs contribute to creating a cybersecurity-aware organizational culture. When employees are actively engaged in learning and adopting security best practices, they become stakeholders in the organization's overall security posture. This cultural shift fosters a sense of shared responsibility, where employees perceive themselves as integral contributors to the organization's cybersecurity resilience. A workforce that is well-informed and motivated to prioritize cybersecurity significantly enhances the organization's ability to detect, prevent, and respond to security incidents effectively.

The significance of ongoing training programs is further accentuated in the context of emerging technologies such as artificial intelligence (AI) and the Internet of Things (IoT). As these technologies become integral components of organizational infrastructures, employees need to understand the associated cybersecurity implications. Training programs provide insights into the risks and vulnerabilities associated with AI and IoT, guiding employees in adopting security measures to mitigate potential threats.

Additionally, ongoing training programs facilitate the development of cybersecurity skills and expertise within the workforce. Cybersecurity is a multifaceted field, encompassing areas such as incident response, threat intelligence, penetration testing, and security analysis. Training programs provide employees with the opportunity to deepen their knowledge in specific domains, fostering the growth of in-house expertise. This, in turn, contributes to the organization's ability to proactively address evolving cyber threats and challenges.

The ever-expanding attack surface, fueled by the increasing complexity of IT infrastructures and interconnected systems, necessitates ongoing training programs that address the diverse facets of cybersecurity. From cloud security and mobile device management to secure coding practices and risk management, employees benefit from comprehensive training that aligns with the evolving nature of digital risks. Training initiatives that encompass a wide range of cybersecurity domains ensure that employees are equipped to navigate the complexities of the modern digital landscape.

In conclusion, the significance of ongoing training programs for individuals and employees cannot be overstated in the context of the evolving digital landscape and the persistent threat of cyber attacks. Whether in personal or professional realms, these programs empower individuals with the knowledge, skills, and mindset required to navigate the digital space securely. By fostering a culture of cyber awareness, ongoing training programs contribute to the collective defense against cyber threats, enhancing the resilience of individuals, organizations, and the broader digital community. As the digital landscape continues to evolve, the commitment to ongoing education remains a foundational pillar in the proactive and effective response to the ever-changing dynamics of cybersecurity.

Provide guidance on creating effective cybersecurity awareness initiatives.

Creating effective cybersecurity awareness initiatives is crucial in fostering a culture of vigilance and responsibility among individuals and organizations. These initiatives serve as a proactive defense against the evolving landscape of cyber threats, empowering participants with the knowledge and skills needed to recognize, prevent, and respond to cyber risks. A comprehensive approach to cybersecurity awareness involves strategic planning, engaging content, continuous reinforcement, and a commitment to adapting to emerging threats.

First and foremost, the foundation of a successful cybersecurity awareness initiative lies in a clear and well-defined strategy. Understanding the target audience, their roles, and the specific cybersecurity risks they may encounter is essential. Whether the initiative is aimed at individuals, employees within an organization, or a combination of both, tailoring the content and delivery methods to address the unique needs and challenges of the audience is paramount. The strategy should also consider the organization's risk profile, compliance requirements, and the prevalent cybersecurity landscape to ensure relevance and effectiveness.

Engaging content is a cornerstone of any cybersecurity awareness initiative. To capture the attention and interest of participants, the content should be informative, relatable, and presented in a variety of formats. Incorporating real-world examples, case studies, and scenarios relevant to the audience's context makes the material more relatable and memorable. Utilizing multimedia elements such as videos, infographics, and interactive simulations enhances the overall engagement, catering to different learning styles and preferences. Including practical tips and actionable steps further empowers participants to apply cybersecurity best practices in their daily digital activities.

A key aspect of creating effective cybersecurity awareness initiatives is to foster a continuous learning environment. Cyber threats are dynamic and ever-evolving, necessitating ongoing education to stay ahead of new risks and vulnerabilities. Regularly updating and expanding the content to cover emerging threats, industry trends, and evolving best practices ensures that participants remain well-informed and equipped to navigate the changing cybersecurity landscape. Implementing a schedule of regular training sessions, workshops, or awareness campaigns sustains momentum and reinforces the importance of cybersecurity as a continuous priority.

Effective communication is pivotal in any awareness initiative. Clear, concise, and accessible messaging ensures that participants can easily grasp key concepts and take away actionable insights. Employing a variety of communication channels, including emails, intranet announcements, posters, and social media, helps reach diverse audiences and reinforces key messages through multiple touchpoints. Creating a sense of urgency without inducing panic is essential, emphasizing the collective responsibility of individuals in maintaining a secure digital environment.

Tailoring the messaging to resonate with the audience's motivations and concerns enhances the effectiveness of the cybersecurity awareness initiative. For employees within an organization, emphasizing the connection between cybersecurity practices and the protection of sensitive company information, customer trust, and the overall reputation of the organization can be a compelling motivator. In a personal context, highlighting the impact of cybersecurity on personal privacy, identity protection, and financial security can resonate more deeply with individuals.

Incorporating gamification elements into cybersecurity awareness initiatives adds an element of fun and competition, increasing engagement and knowledge retention. Gamified scenarios, quizzes, or simulations create an interactive and immersive learning experience, allowing participants to apply cybersecurity principles in a risk-free environment. Recognizing and rewarding achievements, whether through badges, certificates, or other incentives, further encourages active participation and reinforces positive behaviors.

Promoting a culture of open communication and feedback is integral to the success of cybersecurity awareness initiatives. Participants should feel comfortable reporting potential security incidents, asking questions, and seeking clarification on cybersecurity matters. Establishing channels for reporting suspicious activities, providing a dedicated cybersecurity helpdesk, or hosting regular Q&A sessions fosters a sense of community and collaboration. Encouraging individuals to share their experiences and insights contributes to a collective understanding of cyber threats and reinforces the notion that cybersecurity is a shared responsibility.

Collaboration with key stakeholders, including IT departments, human resources, and leadership, enhances the effectiveness of cybersecurity awareness initiatives. Involving these stakeholders ensures alignment with organizational goals, facilitates the integration of cybersecurity practices into existing processes, and leverages their expertise in supporting the initiative. Leadership endorsement and active participation in awareness campaigns signal the organizational commitment to cybersecurity, setting a tone for prioritizing security throughout the organization.

Regular assessments and metrics are essential components of measuring the effectiveness of cybersecurity awareness initiatives. Conducting pre- and post-training assessments gauges the improvement in participants' knowledge and awareness levels. Monitoring engagement metrics, such as participation rates, completion rates, and feedback, provides valuable insights into the initiative's impact and areas for improvement. Analyzing security incident trends and correlating them with awareness initiatives helps identify the effectiveness of the training in reducing vulnerabilities and mitigating risks.

Tailoring cybersecurity awareness initiatives to specific industry regulations and compliance requirements is critical, particularly for organizations operating in regulated sectors. Ensuring that the content aligns with the standards set forth by regulatory bodies enhances the organization's ability to demonstrate compliance and reinforces the importance of cybersecurity within the regulatory framework. Integrating compliance-related content into the awareness program helps employees understand the implications of noncompliance and underscores the role of cybersecurity in safeguarding sensitive information.

Fostering a sense of ownership and empowerment is a key objective of cybersecurity awareness initiatives. Individuals should perceive themselves as active contributors to the organization's cybersecurity resilience, recognizing the impact of their actions on overall security. Encouraging a mindset of constant improvement and adaptability helps individuals stay vigilant against emerging threats and encourages the proactive adoption of new security practices. Providing resources for self-directed learning and exploration further empowers individuals to deepen their understanding of cybersecurity principles.

In conclusion, creating effective cybersecurity awareness initiatives demands a holistic and strategic approach that considers the unique needs of the audience, embraces engaging content, fosters continuous learning, and aligns with organizational goals. The dynamic nature of cyber threats necessitates ongoing education and adaptability, emphasizing the importance of regular updates and reinforcement. By promoting a culture of cybersecurity awareness, organizations and individuals can collectively contribute to a safer digital environment, mitigating risks and enhancing overall resilience against cyber threats.

Explore the risks associated with social media use in cybersecurity.

The pervasive use of social media has transformed the way individuals communicate, share information, and connect globally. However, this widespread adoption of social platforms introduces a myriad of risks in the realm of cybersecurity. One of the foremost concerns is the exposure of personal information. Social media users often share a wealth of personal details, ranging from birthdates and locations to employment history and relationship status. Cybercriminals exploit this trove of information for identity theft, social engineering attacks, and targeted phishing campaigns. By aggregating seemingly innocuous data, malicious actors can construct comprehensive profiles, enabling them to craft convincing and highly targeted cyber attacks.

The prevalence of social engineering attacks is significantly heightened by the wealth of personal information available on social media platforms. Cybercriminals adept at social engineering leverage psychological manipulation to deceive individuals into divulging sensitive information or performing actions that compromise security. With the detailed personal data readily available on social media profiles, attackers can customize their approaches, making their messages and requests appear legitimate. Common social engineering tactics include impersonation, where attackers pose as trusted individuals, and pretexting, where they create a fabricated scenario to extract information. Such attacks can have far-reaching consequences, leading to unauthorized access, financial fraud, or even the compromise of sensitive organizational data.

Phishing attacks represent a pervasive and evolving threat vector in the realm of social media cybersecurity. Cybercriminals use social media platforms as fertile ground for launching phishing campaigns, exploiting the trust and familiarity among users. Phishing messages may masquerade as friend requests, direct messages, or notifications, leading users to malicious websites or prompting them to download malicious attachments. Additionally, attackers often leverage the interconnected nature of social networks to amplify the impact of phishing attacks. Once compromised, an individual's account can be used to propagate phishing messages to a wider network of contacts, creating a cascading effect that multiplies the potential victims.

Social media facilitates the rapid spread of misinformation and disinformation, posing significant risks to individuals and organizations alike. Malicious actors exploit the viral nature of social platforms to disseminate false narratives, manipulate public opinion, and orchestrate influence campaigns. Cybersecurity risks arise as false information can be used to deceive users into downloading malware, clicking on malicious links, or participating in harmful activities. Moreover, the spread of misinformation on social media can have broader societal implications, affecting public discourse, elections, and even geopolitical events. Addressing these risks requires a combination of technological solutions, media literacy initiatives, and collaborative efforts to counter the spread of deceptive content.

The integration of third-party applications and services with social media accounts introduces additional vulnerabilities in the cybersecurity landscape. Many users grant permissions to third-party apps without fully understanding the extent of access they provide. Malicious applications can exploit these permissions to harvest user data, including personal details, friend lists, and even private messages. The misuse of such data not only compromises individual privacy but can also have cascading effects, as the compromised accounts may be used to propagate further cyber threats within the user's social network.

The prevalence of fake accounts and automated bots on social media platforms exacerbates cybersecurity risks, enabling a range of malicious activities. Fake accounts may be used for identity theft, impersonation, or the dissemination of propaganda and false information. Automated bots, on the other hand, can amplify the reach of phishing campaigns, manipulate trends, and engage in coordinated cyber attacks. The challenge of distinguishing between genuine users and malicious entities adds complexity to the task of identifying and mitigating these risks. Social media platforms continually grapple with the need to enhance their authentication mechanisms and algorithms to detect and prevent the proliferation of fake accounts and automated bots.

Another significant cybersecurity risk associated with social media is the potential for account hijacking and unauthorized access. Weak or reused passwords, coupled with lax security practices, make social media accounts attractive targets for cybercriminals. Successful account hijacking can lead to a range of malicious activities, including the spread of malware, the theft of sensitive information, or the use of the compromised account for fraudulent schemes. Moreover, the interconnected nature of social networks allows attackers to exploit compromised accounts to target a broader audience, amplifying the impact of their actions.

The rise of geo-tagging and location-sharing features on social media platforms introduces a spatial dimension to cybersecurity risks. Users often share their real-time locations, travel plans, and check-ins, providing a treasure trove of information for cybercriminals. This data can be exploited for physical security threats, such as stalking, burglary, or even corporate espionage. Additionally, the correlation of location data with other personal details can lead to highly targeted attacks, where cybercriminals leverage knowledge of an individual's whereabouts to craft convincing phishing or social engineering attempts.

Social media platforms are not immune to data breaches, and incidents involving the compromise of user data pose significant cybersecurity risks. The vast repositories of personal information stored by social media companies make them attractive targets for cybercriminals seeking to access large datasets. Data breaches on social media platforms can result in the exposure of sensitive user information, including usernames, passwords, email addresses, and, in some cases, even payment details. The fallout from such breaches includes identity theft, financial fraud, and the potential for cybercriminals to leverage the stolen data for further attacks.

The emergence of deepfake technology amplifies cybersecurity risks on social media by enabling the creation of highly realistic and deceptive multimedia content. Deepfakes involve the use of artificial intelligence to manipulate or fabricate audio and video recordings, making it appear as if individuals are saying or doing things they never did. Social media platforms become vectors for the spread of deepfake content, leading to misinformation, reputation damage, and even manipulation of public perception. Detecting and mitigating the impact of deepfakes requires advanced technological solutions and heightened media literacy efforts to empower users to discern between genuine and manipulated content.

The convergence of social media and the Internet of Things (IoT) introduces new dimensions of cybersecurity risks. Smart devices connected to social media accounts may inadvertently expose users to privacy breaches and unauthorized access. Location data from IoT devices, for instance, can be correlated with social media posts to create detailed profiles of an individual's habits and routines. Moreover, compromised IoT devices may serve as entry points for cyber attackers to infiltrate broader networks, posing a systemic risk to both individuals and organizations.

In conclusion, the risks associated with social media use in cybersecurity are multifaceted and continually evolving. From the exposure of personal information and the prevalence of social engineering attacks to phishing campaigns, misinformation, and the challenges posed by fake accounts and deepfakes, the impact of these risks reverberates across personal, organizational, and societal levels. Addressing these challenges requires a comprehensive approach that combines technological solutions, user education, and collaborative efforts between social media platforms, users, and cybersecurity experts. As social media continues to play a central role in the digital landscape, proactive measures are essential to mitigate these risks and foster a safer online environment for individuals and communities.

Offer guidelines for secure social media practices to minimize vulnerabilities.

Guidelines for secure social media practices are crucial in minimizing vulnerabilities and safeguarding personal and organizational information in the digital landscape. These practices encompass a comprehensive approach that addresses various aspects of security, ranging from user behaviors and privacy settings to authentication methods and awareness of emerging threats.

One fundamental aspect of secure social media practices is the management of personal information. Users should exercise caution in sharing sensitive details such as birthdates, addresses, and contact numbers on their profiles. Restricting the visibility of such information to a select audience or utilizing privacy settings to limit access helps mitigate the risk of unauthorized access or misuse. Additionally, refraining from oversharing personal details reduces the likelihood of falling victim to social engineering tactics, where cybercriminals exploit publicly available information to craft convincing phishing attempts or gain unauthorized access.

Strong and unique passwords play a pivotal role in securing social media accounts. Users should adopt robust password practices by creating passwords that combine letters, numbers, and symbols. Avoiding easily guessable passwords, such as "password" or "123456," is crucial. Furthermore, using different passwords for various accounts enhances overall security, as a compromise in one account does not jeopardize others. Regularly updating passwords is integral, particularly in light of the prevalence of data breaches. The use of password manager tools provides a convenient and secure way to generate and store complex passwords, alleviating the burden of memorizing numerous credentials.

Enabling two-factor authentication (2FA) adds an extra layer of protection to social media accounts. By requiring an additional form of verification beyond passwords, 2FA enhances security and reduces the risk of unauthorized access. Users should leverage the available options, such as authentication codes sent via text message or generated by authenticator apps. Activating 2FA not only fortifies individual accounts but also contributes to a collective defense against cyber threats by minimizing the potential for account hijacking and unauthorized access.

Vigilance against phishing attacks is paramount for secure social media practices. Users should be cautious about clicking on links or downloading attachments from unknown or suspicious sources. Phishing messages often mimic legitimate communications, urging users to provide sensitive information or login credentials. Verifying the authenticity of messages through official channels or directly contacting the purported sender adds an additional layer of protection against phishing attempts. Regularly updating awareness about common phishing tactics and staying informed about emerging threats enhances the ability to recognize and thwart phishing attacks.

Maintaining awareness of privacy settings on social media platforms is crucial for controlling the visibility of personal information. Users should regularly review and adjust privacy settings to align with their preferences and comfort levels. This includes managing who can view posts, friend requests, and personal details. Restricting access to a limited audience minimizes the potential for unauthorized individuals to gather information and reduces the risk of social engineering attacks. Social media platforms often update their privacy features, and staying informed about these changes allows users to adapt their settings accordingly.

Securing devices used for social media access is integral to minimizing vulnerabilities. Users should implement security measures such as device encryption, biometric authentication, and regular software updates. These measures protect against unauthorized access to devices and enhance overall device security. Additionally, users should be cautious about accessing social media accounts from public computers or unsecured Wi-Fi networks, as these environments may expose them to increased risks of account compromise and unauthorized access.

Regularly monitoring account activity and settings is a proactive measure for maintaining secure social media practices. Users should review login history, connected devices, and active sessions to identify any suspicious or unauthorized access. Any unfamiliar or suspicious activity should be addressed promptly, either by securing the account through password changes or reporting the incident to the social media platform. Additionally, users should be aware of the permissions granted to third-party applications connected to their social media accounts and regularly review and revoke unnecessary access.

Educating oneself about the specific security features and tools provided by each social media platform is essential for maximizing security. Many platforms offer advanced security settings, such as account recovery options, login alerts, and account activity reviews. Familiarizing oneself with these features empowers users to make informed decisions about their security preferences and enhances their ability to respond to potential security incidents effectively.

The responsible use of location-sharing features on social media platforms is crucial for personal security. Users should exercise discretion when enabling location services, especially for posts and updates. Geo-tagging and location-sharing may inadvertently expose individuals to physical security risks, including stalking or burglary. Disabling location services or being selective about when and where they are activated contributes to a more secure social media experience.

Regularly updating social media applications and ensuring the use of the latest versions is an often-overlooked yet critical practice for secure social media usage. Developers release updates to address security vulnerabilities and enhance the overall resilience of the application. Users should enable automatic updates when available or actively check for updates to ensure that they benefit from the latest security patches and features. This practice minimizes the risk of exploitation by cybercriminals who target outdated software.

Cultivating a skeptical mindset and exercising caution with unsolicited friend requests, messages, or requests for personal information is integral to secure social media practices. Malicious actors often use social engineering tactics to establish connections or exploit trust. Users should verify the legitimacy of requests or messages, especially if they seem unusual or come from unknown individuals.

Being cautious about sharing personal information, even with seemingly familiar contacts, contributes to a more secure online experience.

Taking proactive measures to secure social media practices extends to the responsible handling of account recovery options. Users should set up and maintain up-to-date account recovery information, such as alternative email addresses or phone numbers. This ensures a secure means of regaining access in the event of a compromised account or forgotten credentials. Additionally, users should be wary of fraudulent account recovery requests and follow the established procedures provided by the social media platform.

Social media users should be mindful of the content they share, considering the potential implications on personal and professional life. Oversharing personal details, engaging in controversial discussions, or posting sensitive information can have consequences beyond the digital realm. Employers, colleagues, and even potential adversaries may access and use this information. Adhering to a thoughtful and discerning approach in content sharing contributes to a more secure online presence.

In a professional context, organizations should establish and communicate clear social media policies to employees. These policies should delineate acceptable use, guidelines for representing the organization online, and the protection of sensitive information. Employee training on secure social media practices, including recognizing and reporting potential security threats, is essential. Organizations should foster a culture of cybersecurity awareness to ensure that employees understand the importance of secure social media practices in safeguarding both personal and organizational interests.

Collaboration between social media platforms and users is essential for maintaining a secure online environment. Users should actively report suspicious activities, fake accounts, or potential security vulnerabilities to the respective social media platforms. Platforms, in turn, should prioritize user security, promptly address reported issues, and continuously invest in improving their security infrastructure.

In conclusion, adopting secure social media practices involves a multifaceted approach that encompasses user behaviors, privacy settings, authentication methods, and ongoing awareness of emerging threats. By integrating these guidelines into their online activities, users can significantly minimize vulnerabilities and enhance the overall security of their social media presence. The dynamic nature of the digital landscape demands a proactive and adaptive approach to cybersecurity, empowering individuals to navigate the complexities of social media securely.

Discuss the security implications of using personal devices for work.

The use of personal devices for work, commonly referred to as Bring Your Own Device (BYOD), has become a prevalent trend in the modern workplace, introducing a myriad of security implications that organizations must navigate. While BYOD offers flexibility and convenience, it also poses significant challenges related to data security, privacy, and the overall integrity of corporate networks. One of the foremost concerns is the potential exposure of sensitive corporate information to a variety of risks associated with personal devices. These devices, ranging from smartphones and tablets to laptops, may lack the robust security measures implemented in corporate environments, making them susceptible to malware, data breaches, and unauthorized access.

The diversity of personal devices used for work introduces complexities in managing security across various platforms and operating systems. Unlike corporate-owned devices, personal devices encompass a wide range of makes, models, and configurations. This heterogeneity makes it challenging for organizations to enforce consistent security policies and deploy standardized security measures. The lack of uniformity across personal devices increases the attack surface and poses difficulties in implementing centralized security controls, such as device management, antivirus software, and encryption protocols. This diversity also complicates the task of ensuring that all devices accessing corporate resources comply with security standards.

Authentication and access control represent critical security implications when personal devices are used for work purposes. Unlike corporate devices that are typically integrated into centralized identity management systems, personal devices may rely on less secure authentication methods or outdated operating systems that lack the latest security updates. This raises concerns about the integrity of user authentication and the potential for unauthorized individuals to gain access to sensitive corporate data. Implementing robust access controls, including strong authentication mechanisms and authorization protocols, is imperative to mitigate the risks associated with the use of personal devices in a work context.

The intersection of personal and corporate data on BYOD devices presents privacy concerns that organizations must address to maintain compliance with data protection regulations. Personal devices often store a mix of personal and work-related information, creating a challenge in separating and safeguarding these distinct data sets. Organizations must implement clear policies and technological solutions to delineate between personal and corporate data, ensuring that privacy is preserved for the device owner while also safeguarding sensitive corporate information. The risk of unintentional data leakage or the compromise of personal information during work-related activities necessitates careful consideration of privacy implications.

The potential for data loss or theft is heightened when personal devices are used for work, particularly in scenarios where the devices are lost or stolen. Personal devices may not be equipped with the same level of encryption and remote wipe capabilities commonly found in corporate-owned devices. Consequently, if a personal device containing sensitive corporate data is lost or stolen, there is an increased risk of unauthorized access to confidential information. Organizations must establish and communicate clear procedures for reporting lost or stolen devices, as well as implement measures to remotely wipe corporate data from such devices to prevent unauthorized access.

Endpoint security becomes a paramount concern in the context of BYOD, as personal devices often lack the robust security controls implemented in corporate environments. The risk of malware infections, including viruses, ransomware, and other malicious software, is heightened when personal devices connect to corporate networks or access work-related resources. Organizations must implement comprehensive endpoint security solutions, including antivirus software, firewalls, and intrusion detection systems, to mitigate the risk of malware spreading from personal devices to corporate assets. Regular security audits and monitoring of BYOD devices are crucial to identifying and addressing potential security vulnerabilities promptly.

Network security is another dimension impacted by the use of personal devices for work. Personal devices, often used in a variety of network environments, may connect to unsecured public Wi-Fi networks or other potentially risky environments. This introduces the risk of man-in-the-middle attacks, eavesdropping, and unauthorized access to corporate data transmitted over insecure networks. Organizations should encourage the use of virtual private networks (VPNs) to encrypt data in transit, implement secure Wi-Fi policies, and educate users about the risks associated with connecting to untrusted networks.

The integration of personal devices into corporate networks raises challenges related to monitoring and incident response. Traditional network monitoring tools may not provide sufficient visibility into the activities of personal devices, limiting an organization's ability to detect and respond to security incidents effectively. Implementing robust network monitoring solutions capable of identifying and analyzing the activities of BYOD devices is essential for early detection of potential security threats. Additionally, organizations must establish clear incident response procedures specific to BYOD scenarios, ensuring a swift and coordinated response to security incidents involving personal devices.

Mobile device management (MDM) and mobile application management (MAM) solutions play a crucial role in addressing the security implications of using personal devices for work. MDM solutions enable organizations to enforce security policies, configure devices, and remotely manage settings on personal devices accessing corporate resources. MAM solutions focus on securing the applications and data on the device, allowing organizations to containerize and control work-related apps and information. The deployment of such solutions helps organizations strike a balance between enabling BYOD flexibility and maintaining a secure work environment.

Compliance with regulatory frameworks and industry standards becomes a complex endeavor when personal devices are used for work. Data protection regulations, such as the General Data Protection Regulation (GDPR) and the Health Insurance Portability and Accountability Act (HIPAA), impose stringent requirements on the safeguarding of sensitive information. Ensuring compliance with these regulations necessitates not only technical measures but also robust policies, employee training, and documentation of security practices. Organizations must be diligent in addressing the nuances of data protection laws to avoid legal ramifications and reputational damage resulting from non-compliance.

Employee education and awareness programs are essential components of a comprehensive strategy to address the security implications of BYOD. Many security risks associated with personal devices stem from user behaviors, such as clicking on malicious links, using weak passwords, or neglecting software updates. Educating employees about the risks and best practices for secure device usage empowers them to make informed decisions and adopt behaviors that align with organizational security policies. Training programs should cover topics such as secure authentication, data protection, and the responsible use of personal devices for work-related activities.

The challenge of securing personal devices used for work extends to the realm of software and application security. Personal devices may run outdated operating systems or host unpatched software, creating vulnerabilities that can be exploited by attackers. Organizations must implement policies that encourage users to keep their devices and applications up to date with the latest security patches. Regular security assessments and vulnerability scans of personal devices accessing corporate networks help identify and remediate potential weaknesses, contributing to a more resilient security posture.

Legal considerations related to the use of personal devices for work add an additional layer of complexity. Organizations must navigate issues related to data ownership, consent, and the potential need for legal access to personal devices in the event of investigations or legal disputes. Establishing clear policies and obtaining explicit consent from employees regarding the monitoring and management of their personal devices are essential steps in addressing legal implications. Collaboration with legal experts ensures that organizations strike a balance between protecting corporate interests and respecting the privacy rights of employees using personal devices.

In conclusion, the security implications of using personal devices for work are multifaceted and demand a comprehensive and strategic approach. While BYOD offers benefits in terms of flexibility and employee satisfaction, organizations must proactively address the associated risks to protect sensitive information, maintain regulatory compliance, and ensure the overall integrity of corporate networks. The integration of robust security measures, employee education, and adherence to best practices is imperative for organizations seeking to leverage the advantages of BYOD while mitigating potential vulnerabilities in an evolving and dynamic digital landscape.

Provide recommendations for securing personal devices to enhance overall cybersecurity.

Securing personal devices is a critical aspect of enhancing overall cybersecurity, especially in a landscape where individuals use smartphones, tablets, laptops, and other devices for a myriad of personal and professional activities. Adopting a proactive and comprehensive approach to device security is essential to mitigate the risks associated with cyber threats, unauthorized access, and the potential compromise of sensitive information. One fundamental recommendation is to prioritize strong and unique passwords for personal devices. Passwords serve as the first line of defense against unauthorized access, and using complex combinations of letters, numbers, and symbols significantly enhances security. Avoiding easily guessable passwords, such as "password" or "123456," and periodically updating passwords further strengthens the overall security posture of personal devices.

Enabling and configuring two-factor authentication (2FA) is a crucial step in fortifying the security of personal devices. 2FA adds an additional layer of verification beyond passwords, requiring users to provide a secondary form of identification, such as a code sent to a mobile device or generated by an authenticator app. This extra layer of authentication significantly reduces the risk of unauthorized access, even if passwords are compromised. Users should explore and enable available 2FA options on their devices, taking advantage of this effective security measure to enhance the overall resilience against potential threats.

Regular software updates and patches play a pivotal role in securing personal devices. Operating systems, applications, and firmware should be kept up to date with the latest security patches provided by device manufacturers and software developers. These updates often address vulnerabilities that could be exploited by cybercriminals. Enabling automatic updates ensures that personal devices receive the latest security fixes promptly, reducing the window of exposure to potential threats. Regularly checking for and applying updates, including those for third-party applications, is essential for maintaining a secure and robust digital environment.

Implementing device encryption is a critical recommendation for safeguarding sensitive information stored on personal devices. Encryption converts data into a secure format that can only be accessed with the appropriate decryption key, adding an extra layer of protection against unauthorized access. Most modern devices offer built-in encryption features that users can enable through device settings. Encrypting the storage of personal devices protects the data in case the device is lost, stolen, or accessed by unauthorized individuals. Users should familiarize themselves with the encryption options available on their devices and take steps to activate this crucial security feature.

The use of biometric authentication methods, such as fingerprint recognition or facial recognition, enhances the security of personal devices by adding a unique and physiological layer of verification. Biometric authentication provides a convenient and secure alternative to traditional passwords, reducing the likelihood of unauthorized access. Users should explore the biometric options available on their devices and consider incorporating these features into their security settings. Additionally, it is crucial to ensure that biometric data is securely stored on the device and not easily accessible to potential attackers.

Secure internet connections are essential for protecting personal devices from various cyber threats. Users should be cautious about connecting to public Wi-Fi networks, as these environments may lack adequate security measures, exposing devices to potential risks. When using public Wi-Fi, individuals should consider using virtual private network (VPN) services to encrypt data in transit, preventing eavesdropping and man-in-the-middle attacks. Additionally, users should ensure that their home Wi-Fi networks are secured with strong passwords and encryption protocols to minimize the risk of unauthorized access.

Implementing robust antivirus and antimalware solutions is a cornerstone recommendation for securing personal devices. These security tools provide real-time protection against a wide range of malicious software, including viruses, ransomware, and phishing threats. Users should choose reputable antivirus software from trusted vendors and keep it updated regularly to ensure optimal protection. Regular scans of personal devices help identify and mitigate potential security threats, contributing to a proactive defense against evolving cyber risks. It is imperative to research and select antivirus solutions based on their effectiveness, user reviews, and compatibility with the specific operating system.

Practicing safe browsing habits is an essential recommendation for enhancing the cybersecurity of personal devices. Users should exercise caution when clicking on links, downloading attachments, or visiting unfamiliar websites, as these actions can expose devices to various online threats, including malware and phishing attacks. Avoiding suspicious or unverified websites, verifying the legitimacy of email attachments, and being cautious about unexpected pop-ups contribute to a safer online browsing experience. Utilizing browser security features, such as pop-up blockers and privacy settings, further enhances the overall security of personal devices during online activities.

Regular data backups are a critical recommendation for minimizing the impact of potential data loss or device compromise. Users should establish a routine for backing up essential data, such as documents, photos, and important files, to secure storage locations. Cloud-based backup services or external hard drives offer convenient options for creating backups. In the event of device failure, loss, or a ransomware attack, having recent backups ensures that valuable data can be recovered without significant disruptions. Users should verify the effectiveness of their backup procedures and periodically test the restoration process to guarantee the availability of critical information when needed.

Privacy settings and permissions on personal devices should be carefully reviewed and configured to align with the user's preferences and security requirements. Many applications and services on personal devices request access to various features and information. Users should scrutinize and limit permissions to the minimum necessary for the functionality of each application. Regularly reviewing and adjusting privacy settings ensures that personal information is adequately protected, reducing the risk of data exposure or unauthorized access. Being mindful of the information shared with applications and services contributes to a more secure and privacy-aware digital environment.

Implementing a robust mobile device management (MDM) solution, especially for personal smartphones and tablets used for work-related activities, is a recommended best practice. MDM solutions enable users and organizations to enforce security policies, remotely configure devices, and manage access controls. These solutions provide organizations with the ability to monitor and secure personal devices accessing corporate resources, ensuring compliance with security standards. Users should explore MDM options compatible with their devices and consider integrating these solutions, particularly in scenarios where personal devices are used for work purposes.

Creating a guest or secondary user account on personal devices is a prudent security measure, especially when sharing the device with family members or friends. This practice limits access to sensitive information and applications, reducing the risk of unintended data exposure or modifications. Guest accounts provide a controlled environment for others to use the device without compromising the security of the primary user's data. Users should set up and configure guest accounts based on their device's operating system and regularly review and manage user access to maintain a secure computing environment.

Regular security audits and vulnerability assessments are crucial for identifying and addressing potential weaknesses in personal devices. Users should consider conducting periodic assessments using reputable security tools or consulting with cybersecurity professionals to evaluate the overall security posture of their devices. These assessments can identify vulnerabilities, outdated software, or misconfigurations that could be exploited by cybercriminals. By proactively addressing security issues, individuals can bolster the resilience of their personal devices and reduce the likelihood of falling victim to cyber threats.

Education and awareness play a pivotal role in enhancing overall cybersecurity for personal devices. Staying informed about the latest cyber threats, attack vectors, and best practices empowers users to make informed decisions and adopt behaviors that align with a security-conscious mindset. Users should invest time in learning about common cybersecurity threats, understanding the features and settings of their devices, and staying updated on recommended security practices. Ongoing education ensures that individuals remain vigilant, adaptable, and well-equipped to navigate the evolving landscape of cybersecurity.

Collaboration with reputable cybersecurity resources, forums, and communities provides users with valuable insights, advice, and support for securing personal devices. Engaging with cybersecurity experts, participating in online forums, and staying connected to the broader cybersecurity community fosters a culture of shared knowledge and collective defense. Users can benefit from the experiences and expertise of others, gaining practical tips, recommendations, and real-world insights that contribute to a more resilient and secure digital environment.

In conclusion, securing personal devices is a multifaceted endeavor that requires a combination of technical measures, responsible user behaviors, and ongoing awareness. By implementing strong authentication, keeping software up to date, encrypting data, and adopting proactive security practices, individuals can significantly enhance the cybersecurity of their personal devices. These recommendations, when integrated into a holistic approach, contribute to a more robust defense against cyber threats, ensuring that personal information remains protected and devices operate in a secure digital environment.

Highlight the importance of fostering a cybersecurity-conscious culture.

Fostering a cybersecurity-conscious culture within an organization is paramount in today's interconnected and digitized landscape, where cyber threats constantly evolve in sophistication and frequency. The importance of instilling a cybersecurity-conscious mindset cannot be overstated, as the human element remains a critical factor in the overall resilience of any cybersecurity strategy. Cultivating a culture that prioritizes cybersecurity awareness, proactive measures, and a shared responsibility for digital security empowers individuals at all levels of an organization to become active participants in safeguarding sensitive information, critical systems, and the overall integrity of digital assets.

One of the key aspects underscoring the importance of a cybersecurity-conscious culture is the recognition that cybersecurity is not solely the responsibility of the IT department. While robust technical measures are essential, human behavior plays a pivotal role in either fortifying or compromising cybersecurity defenses. Employees across various departments and roles must understand their roles in maintaining a secure environment and be equipped with the knowledge to recognize potential threats, adhere to security protocols, and report incidents promptly. A culture that fosters collective responsibility instills a sense of ownership and accountability for cybersecurity among all members of the organization.

In the face of increasingly sophisticated cyber threats, raising cybersecurity awareness among employees becomes a cornerstone of a cybersecurity-conscious culture. Individuals need to be informed about the latest threat vectors, phishing tactics, malware trends, and other common attack methods. Regular cybersecurity training and awareness programs provide employees with the knowledge and skills necessary to recognize and respond to potential threats effectively. By cultivating a well-informed workforce, organizations create a human firewall that acts as an additional layer of defense against social engineering attacks and other cyber threats that often exploit human vulnerabilities.

Another critical dimension of fostering a cybersecurity-conscious culture is instilling a sense of vigilance and skepticism among employees. Cybercriminals often leverage social engineering tactics that manipulate individuals into divulging sensitive information or clicking on malicious links. A culture that encourages a healthy level of skepticism, combined with the ability to critically assess the legitimacy of communications, significantly reduces the likelihood of falling victim to phishing attacks and other forms of social engineering. Employees should be empowered to question unexpected requests for sensitive information and to verify the authenticity of communications, even if they appear to come from trusted sources.

Creating a cybersecurity-conscious culture involves aligning organizational values with a commitment to digital security. Leadership plays a pivotal role in setting the tone and priorities for the entire organization. When leaders prioritize and actively participate in cybersecurity initiatives, it sends a clear message about the importance of security as a fundamental aspect of the organization's mission. This commitment should be reflected in resource allocation, strategic planning, and a willingness to invest in the technologies, training, and policies necessary to build a robust cybersecurity posture. By integrating cybersecurity into the organizational ethos, leaders create an environment where security is not viewed as an impediment but as a foundational element supporting the organization's success.

Building a cybersecurity-conscious culture requires effective communication strategies that engage employees and make cybersecurity concepts accessible to all. Complex technical jargon can be a barrier to understanding for non-technical staff. Therefore, organizations should employ clear and concise communication methods, including newsletters, posters, and regular updates, to convey essential cybersecurity information in a digestible manner. Emphasizing the relevance of cybersecurity to employees' daily activities and personal lives fosters a sense of connection and encourages a more active and committed approach to security practices both at work and in personal contexts.

An organization's response to security incidents is a critical reflection of its cybersecurity culture. Establishing clear incident response procedures and communicating them effectively ensures that employees know what steps to take in the event of a security incident. This includes reporting suspicious activities, promptly addressing security concerns, and collaborating with the IT or security team for resolution. A culture that encourages open communication and swift action in response to incidents helps minimize the impact of potential breaches, facilitates a faster recovery process, and reinforces the importance of constant vigilance.

In the era of remote work and increased connectivity, fostering a cybersecurity-conscious culture becomes even more crucial. With the blurring of traditional organizational boundaries, employees ac-

cessing corporate networks from various locations and devices introduce additional challenges. A culture that emphasizes secure remote
work practices, such as the use of virtual private networks (VPNs),
encrypted communication channels, and secure access controls, ensures that employees remain vigilant about cybersecurity regardless
of their physical location. By integrating cybersecurity considerations into remote work policies, organizations adapt to the evolving nature of the digital landscape and enhance their overall security
posture.

The adoption of emerging technologies, such as the Internet of
Things (IoT) and cloud computing, further underscores the importance of a cybersecurity-conscious culture. These technologies introduce new attack surfaces and vulnerabilities that demand heightened
awareness and proactive security measures. Employees should be ed-
ucated about the risks associated with IoT devices and cloud services
and trained on best practices for securing these technologies. Integrating security considerations into the procurement, deployment,
and usage of emerging technologies ensures that the organization
embraces innovation while maintaining a robust security posture.

A cybersecurity-conscious culture extends beyond the confines
of an organization and encompasses collaboration with external
partners and stakeholders. Vendors, contractors, and other third parties that interact with the organization's systems should adhere to
similar cybersecurity standards to prevent potential vulnerabilities
introduced through external connections. Organizations should establish clear cybersecurity expectations for their partners, conduct
regular assessments of third-party security practices, and collaborate
on initiatives that enhance the overall cybersecurity ecosystem.

Regulatory compliance and legal considerations further emphasize the importance of a cybersecurity-conscious culture. Many industries are subject to stringent data protection regulations that
mandate secure handling and storage of sensitive information. Com-

pliance with these regulations requires a commitment to cybersecurity best practices, as well as ongoing efforts to stay abreast of evolving legal requirements. A culture that prioritizes compliance fosters a proactive approach to cybersecurity, reducing the risk of legal consequences and reputational damage resulting from non-compliance.

In conclusion, fostering a cybersecurity-conscious culture is a holistic and ongoing effort that involves the entire organization, from leadership to individual employees. The human factor in cybersecurity is central to building resilience against a dynamic and ever-evolving threat landscape. By instilling a sense of collective responsibility, raising awareness, aligning organizational values with security priorities, and adapting to the changing nature of work, organizations can cultivate a culture that not only enhances cybersecurity but also contributes to the overall success and sustainability of the business in the digital age. The investment in a cybersecurity-conscious culture pays dividends in reducing the likelihood and impact of cyber threats, creating a resilient and adaptive organization prepared to navigate the complexities of the modern digital ecosystem.

Discuss organizational strategies for embedding cybersecurity awareness into everyday practices.

Embedding cybersecurity awareness into everyday practices within an organization requires a comprehensive and strategic approach that integrates awareness initiatives, educational programs, policies, and a culture of shared responsibility. Such strategies are essential to empower employees at all levels to understand, prioritize, and actively contribute to the organization's cybersecurity posture. By fostering a cybersecurity-conscious environment, organizations can mitigate the human factor as a vulnerability and instead leverage it as a critical asset in the ongoing battle against evolving cyber threats.

One fundamental organizational strategy for embedding cybersecurity awareness involves the development and implementation of targeted training programs. These programs should be tailored to the specific needs and roles within the organization, ensuring that employees receive relevant and practical knowledge. Training sessions can cover a range of topics, including recognizing phishing attempts, secure password practices, identifying malicious software, and understanding the importance of data protection. The use of engaging and interactive training methods, such as simulations and real-world scenarios, enhances the effectiveness of these programs, making the learning experience more memorable and applicable to employees' daily activities.

Continuous and regular communication plays a pivotal role in reinforcing cybersecurity awareness within an organization. Employers should establish communication channels that deliver timely updates, insights on emerging threats, and reminders of best practices. Internal newsletters, email bulletins, and intranet platforms can serve as effective mediums to disseminate information. Communicating real-world examples of cybersecurity incidents, lessons learned, and success stories can make the abstract concept of cybersecurity more relatable to employees. Additionally, leveraging these channels to highlight the positive impact of individual contributions to cybersecurity fosters a sense of shared responsibility and motivates employees to actively engage in maintaining a secure environment.

Organizations should develop and disseminate clear cybersecurity policies and guidelines that articulate expectations for employees. These policies should cover a spectrum of topics, including acceptable use of company resources, secure communication practices, data handling procedures, and incident reporting protocols. Making these policies easily accessible and understandable is crucial to ensure that employees are aware of their responsibilities and the organization's expectations regarding cybersecurity. Regular reviews and updates to these policies based on the evolving threat landscape and changes in technology contribute to their relevance and effectiveness in guiding everyday practices.

Implementing a role-based access control system is an organizational strategy that aligns cybersecurity awareness with employees' specific roles and responsibilities. By granting access privileges based on job functions, employees only have access to the resources necessary for their duties, minimizing the risk of unauthorized access or accidental data exposure. Role-based access control not only enhances security but also reinforces the concept that cybersecurity is an integral part of each employee's role. This approach can be coupled with ongoing training to ensure that employees understand the rationale behind access controls and recognize their role in maintaining a secure digital environment.

Organizations can leverage technology to embed cybersecurity awareness into everyday practices. Automated security awareness platforms can deliver targeted content, quizzes, and reminders to employees based on their roles, ensuring that the information remains relevant to their specific responsibilities. These platforms can track employee engagement, monitor progress, and provide insights into areas that may require additional focus. Integrating cybersecurity awareness into existing digital platforms and tools, such as intranet portals or collaboration platforms, ensures that employees encounter cybersecurity information seamlessly in the course of their regular work routines.

Creating a culture of positive reinforcement is a strategic organizational approach that encourages and rewards cybersecurity-conscious behaviors. Recognizing and acknowledging employees who demonstrate exemplary cybersecurity practices, report incidents promptly, or actively engage in training initiatives fosters a sense of accomplishment and reinforces positive behaviors. Establishing a reward system, such as recognition awards, certifications, or other incentives, motivates employees to consistently adhere to cybersecurity best practices. This strategy aligns with the principles of positive reinforcement psychology, creating a workplace environment where cybersecurity awareness becomes an integral aspect of professional growth and success.

Engaging leadership in championing cybersecurity awareness is a key organizational strategy that sets the tone for the entire workforce. When leaders visibly prioritize and actively participate in cybersecurity initiatives, it sends a powerful message about the importance of security within the organizational culture. Leadership engagement can take various forms, including participation in training sessions, communicating the significance of cybersecurity in organizational success, and advocating for the allocation of resources to support cybersecurity initiatives. Leaders should serve as role models for cybersecurity-conscious behaviors, demonstrating a commitment to the principles and practices they expect from employees throughout the organization.

Integrating cybersecurity awareness into the onboarding process for new employees is a strategic organizational approach that ensures a consistent foundation of knowledge. New hires should receive comprehensive training on cybersecurity policies, best practices, and the organization's expectations regarding information security. This orientation process sets the tone for a cybersecurity-conscious culture from the beginning of an employee's tenure. Providing access to relevant resources, mentors, and ongoing support during the onboarding period contributes to the successful integration of cybersecurity awareness into everyday practices for new members of the organization.

Organizations should conduct regular cybersecurity drills and simulations as part of their strategic approach to embedding awareness into everyday practices. Simulating real-world cybersecurity incidents, such as phishing attacks or malware infections, allows employees to apply their knowledge in a controlled environment. These exercises not only reinforce cybersecurity training but also provide valuable insights into areas that may require additional attention or improvement. Conducting drills periodically ensures that employees remain vigilant and prepared to respond effectively to actual security incidents, contributing to a culture of readiness and resilience.

Collaboration with external experts and cybersecurity professionals is a strategic organizational approach that enriches the depth and breadth of cybersecurity awareness initiatives. Partnering with cybersecurity firms, industry experts, or participating in collaborative forums provides employees with insights into the latest threat landscapes, emerging technologies, and best practices. External experts can contribute fresh perspectives, share real-world experiences, and offer specialized training that complements internal awareness efforts. This collaborative approach expands the knowledge base within the organization, ensuring that employees receive diverse and up-to-date information about cybersecurity.

Measuring and assessing the effectiveness of cybersecurity awareness initiatives is a strategic organizational strategy that enables continuous improvement. Organizations should establish key performance indicators (KPIs) to evaluate the impact of awareness programs, such as the percentage of employees completing training, the reduction in security incidents, or the improvement in incident response times. Regular assessments, surveys, and feedback mechanisms provide valuable insights into the strengths and weaknesses of cybersecurity awareness initiatives. This data-driven approach allows organizations to adapt and refine their strategies based on measurable outcomes, ensuring that awareness efforts align with organizational goals and contribute to a sustained culture of cybersecurity.

In conclusion, embedding cybersecurity awareness into everyday practices requires a multifaceted and integrated organizational strategy. By combining targeted training, continuous communication, role-based access controls, technology integration, positive reinforcement, leadership engagement, onboarding practices, simulations, external collaboration, and ongoing measurement, organizations can create a culture where cybersecurity is not an isolated initiative but an intrinsic part of daily routines. This strategic approach ensures that employees at all levels understand their role in maintaining a secure environment, actively contribute to cybersecurity efforts, and collectively strengthen the organization's resilience against evolving cyber threats. In the dynamic landscape of digital security, a proactive and adaptive organizational strategy is crucial to cultivating a cybersecurity-conscious culture that withstands the challenges of the modern threat landscape.

Chapter 6: The Role of Artificial Intelligence in Cybersecurity

E xplore how artificial intelligence is revolutionizing threat detection.

Artificial Intelligence (AI) is revolutionizing threat detection in the field of cybersecurity, reshaping the way organizations identify and respond to malicious activities in the ever-evolving digital landscape. One of the fundamental contributions of AI to threat detection lies in its ability to analyze vast amounts of data at speeds and scales beyond human capabilities. Machine learning algorithms, a subset of AI, excel in recognizing patterns and anomalies within data, allowing for the detection of potential threats with remarkable accuracy. This capability addresses a significant challenge in cybersecurity – the sheer volume and complexity of data generated by networks, systems, and user activities, making it increasingly difficult for traditional security measures to keep pace with the sophistication of modern cyber threats.

Machine learning algorithms leverage historical data to train models, enabling them to distinguish between normal and abnormal behavior within a given environment. This proactive approach to threat detection allows AI-powered systems to identify subtle deviations or anomalies that might indicate a security incident. Unlike rule-based systems that rely on predefined patterns, machine learning adapts and evolves over time, continuously improving its ability to discern between benign and malicious activities. This adaptability is particularly crucial in the face of polymorphic and zero-day threats, where attackers constantly modify their tactics to evade traditional signature-based detection methods.

One notable application of AI in threat detection is the use of anomaly detection algorithms. These algorithms establish a baseline of normal behavior within a network or system by analyzing historical data. Any deviation from this baseline is flagged as a potential anomaly, warranting further investigation. This approach is effective in identifying previously unknown threats, as it does not rely on predefined signatures but instead focuses on detecting unusual patterns of behavior that may indicate malicious activity. Anomaly detection is especially valuable in recognizing sophisticated threats that exhibit subtle and context-dependent behaviors, such as advanced persistent threats (APTs) that aim to remain undetected for extended periods.

AI-powered threat detection is also enhancing the identification of malicious files and malware. Traditional antivirus solutions rely on signature-based detection, matching known patterns of malicious code against a database of predefined signatures. However, this approach is limited when facing polymorphic malware that frequently changes its code to evade detection. AI-driven solutions, particularly those utilizing machine learning, can analyze the characteristics and behavior of files to identify potential threats without relying on fixed signatures. By understanding the underlying features that distinguish malicious files, AI models can recognize new variants of malware, providing a more adaptive and resilient defense against evolving cyber threats.

Behavioral analysis, another facet of AI-driven threat detection, focuses on understanding the behavior of users and entities within a network. By establishing baselines for normal behavior, AI models can identify deviations indicative of unauthorized or malicious activities. Behavioral analysis extends beyond traditional signature-based methods, allowing organizations to detect insider threats, compromised accounts, or unusual patterns of network traffic that may signal a security incident. This dynamic approach to threat detection is particularly effective in addressing the challenges posed by increasingly sophisticated and stealthy attacks.

In addition to anomaly detection and behavioral analysis, natural language processing (NLP) and sentiment analysis are emerging as powerful tools in AI-driven threat detection. Cybercriminals often exploit communication channels to coordinate attacks or distribute malicious content. NLP enables AI systems to analyze and understand human language, allowing for the identification of potential threats within textual data. Sentiment analysis further enhances this capability by assessing the tone and intent expressed in communication, helping to discern between normal and malicious content. These AI-driven linguistic capabilities contribute to a more comprehensive approach to threat detection, addressing the diverse range of cyber threats that involve social engineering, phishing, and other deceptive tactics.

Machine learning models, particularly those employing deep learning techniques, have demonstrated exceptional performance in image and pattern recognition. In the realm of cybersecurity, this capability is leveraged for the identification of visual indicators of compromise (IoCs), such as malicious code embedded within images or graphical elements. AI models can analyze images, screenshots, and visual data to uncover hidden threats that may go unnoticed by traditional signature-based methods. This visual analysis extends the scope of threat detection to encompass the diverse range of tactics employed by cybercriminals to obfuscate malicious activities.

The integration of threat intelligence feeds with AI-driven systems enhances the contextual understanding of potential threats. Threat intelligence provides up-to-date information about known threats, vulnerabilities, and attacker techniques. When combined with AI algorithms, organizations can correlate threat intelligence with real-time data from their own environments, allowing for more accurate and context-aware threat detection. This synergy enables AI-driven systems to prioritize and contextualize alerts, reducing the likelihood of false positives and empowering security teams to focus on the most critical security incidents.

Automation is a key enabler in the effectiveness of AI-driven threat detection. The speed and efficiency with which AI algorithms process and analyze data allow for real-time threat detection and response. Automated responses, triggered by AI-driven systems, can mitigate threats swiftly, reducing the potential impact of security incidents. This rapid response is particularly critical in scenarios where manual intervention might be delayed, allowing attackers to exploit vulnerabilities. The synergy between AI-driven threat detection and automated response mechanisms creates a dynamic and proactive cybersecurity posture, aligning with the evolving nature of cyber threats.

AI-driven threat detection is also playing a pivotal role in addressing the challenges posed by the sheer volume of security alerts generated within large-scale enterprise environments. Traditional security approaches often result in alert fatigue, overwhelming security teams with a high volume of alerts, many of which may be false positives. AI-powered solutions, equipped with the ability to analyze and prioritize alerts based on contextual information and historical data, significantly reduce the burden on security teams. By automating the initial stages of threat triage and analysis, AI allows security professionals to focus their expertise on more complex and nuanced aspects of threat response.

The concept of threat hunting is undergoing transformation with the integration of AI. Threat hunting traditionally involves skilled cybersecurity professionals actively seeking out signs of compromise within an organization's environment. AI-driven threat hunting, however, empowers security teams by automating the preliminary phases of investigation, identifying potential threats, and presenting relevant contextual information. This augmented intelligence approach enables human analysts to leverage their expertise in making informed decisions, enhancing the efficiency and efficacy of threat hunting initiatives.

As organizations embrace cloud computing and hybrid infrastructures, AI is proving instrumental in securing these dynamic environments. AI-driven threat detection adapts seamlessly to the distributed and scalable nature of cloud architectures, providing continuous monitoring and analysis of data across diverse platforms. The ability to detect threats in real time, regardless of the location or complexity of the infrastructure, aligns with the agility and flexibility demanded by modern digital ecosystems. AI-driven solutions are well-suited to address the unique challenges associated with cloud security, such as rapid scaling, diverse data sources, and the need for centralized threat visibility.

While AI has significantly advanced threat detection capabilities, it is not without its challenges. Adversarial attacks, where attackers intentionally manipulate data to deceive AI models, pose a notable concern. Cybercriminals may attempt to exploit vulnerabilities in AI algorithms by injecting subtle changes into data to evade detection. Continual research and development in adversarial machine learning are essential to fortify AI models against such attacks, ensuring the reliability and robustness of AI-driven threat detection mechanisms.

In conclusion, the integration of artificial intelligence into threat detection is transforming the cybersecurity landscape, empowering organizations to stay ahead of evolving cyber threats. From anomaly detection and behavioral analysis to natural language processing and automation, AI-driven approaches offer a holistic and adaptive defense against a diverse range of cyber threats. As cybercriminal tactics become more sophisticated, the proactive and dynamic nature of AI-driven threat detection positions organizations to effectively identify, mitigate, and respond to emerging security challenges. While challenges such as adversarial attacks persist, the ongoing development and refinement of AI technologies continue to reinforce their role as a cornerstone in the future of cybersecurity.

Discuss the use of machine learning algorithms to identify and respond to cyber threats.

Machine learning (ML) algorithms are playing a pivotal role in transforming the landscape of cybersecurity, offering advanced capabilities to identify and respond to an ever-evolving array of cyber threats. One fundamental aspect of machine learning lies in its ability to analyze vast datasets to discern patterns, anomalies, and trends, providing a proactive defense against a wide range of cyber threats. These algorithms leverage historical data to train models, enabling them to recognize normal patterns of behavior within networks, systems, and user activities. By understanding what is considered "normal," machine learning models can subsequently identify deviations or anomalies that may signify potential security incidents, a capability particularly crucial in the context of advanced persistent threats (APTs) and other sophisticated cyber attacks.

One of the key applications of machine learning in threat identification is anomaly detection. Traditional signature-based detection methods struggle to keep pace with the constant evolution of cyber threats, making them less effective against previously unseen attacks. Anomaly detection, on the other hand, does not rely on predefined patterns but rather focuses on identifying deviations from established baselines of normal behavior. Machine learning algorithms can dynamically adapt these baselines, learning from the evolving nature of data to identify subtle deviations indicative of potential threats. This adaptive approach enhances the capability to detect novel and sophisticated cyber threats that may not have recognizable signatures.

Behavioral analysis is another powerful application of machine learning algorithms in identifying and responding to cyber threats. By establishing baselines for normal user and entity behavior, machine learning models can recognize deviations that may indicate unauthorized access, compromised accounts, or other malicious activities. These models can analyze patterns of behavior within a network, identifying unusual activities or changes in user conduct. Behavioral analysis contributes to a more context-aware threat detection mechanism, allowing organizations to respond swiftly to potential security incidents and mitigate the impact of evolving threats.

Machine learning algorithms are also instrumental in the detection of malicious files and malware. Traditional antivirus solutions often rely on signature-based detection, matching known patterns of malicious code against a predefined database of signatures. However, this approach is limited when faced with polymorphic malware that frequently modifies its code to evade detection. Machine learning models, particularly those employing techniques like deep learning, can analyze the characteristics and behaviors of files to identify potential threats without relying on fixed signatures. By understanding the underlying features that distinguish malicious files, these algorithms can recognize new variants of malware, providing a more adaptive and resilient defense against rapidly evolving cyber threats.

Natural Language Processing (NLP) is emerging as a valuable tool in the identification and response to cyber threats, especially those involving social engineering, phishing, and deceptive tactics. Cybercriminals often exploit communication channels to coordinate attacks or distribute malicious content. NLP enables machine learning algorithms to analyze and understand human language, allowing for the identification of potential threats within textual data. Sentiment analysis, a component of NLP, further enhances this capability by assessing the tone and intent expressed in communication. Machine learning models can identify patterns associated with phishing attempts, fraudulent messages, or other malicious activities, contributing to a more comprehensive approach to threat detection.

Machine learning is proving particularly effective in image and pattern recognition, extending its application to the identification of visual indicators of compromise (IoCs). Cyber threats often involve the concealment of malicious code within images or graphical elements. Machine learning algorithms can analyze images, screenshots, and visual data to uncover hidden threats that may go unnoticed by traditional signature-based methods. This visual analysis broadens the scope of threat detection to encompass the diverse range of tactics employed by cybercriminals to obfuscate their activities, offering a more comprehensive defense against sophisticated attacks.

The integration of threat intelligence feeds with machine learning algorithms enhances the contextual understanding of potential threats. Threat intelligence provides up-to-date information about known threats, vulnerabilities, and attacker techniques. When combined with machine learning algorithms, organizations can correlate threat intelligence with real-time data from their own environments, allowing for more accurate and context-aware threat detection. This synergy enables machine learning systems to prioritize and contextualize alerts, reducing the likelihood of false positives and empowering security teams to focus on the most critical security incidents.

Automation is a key enabler in the effectiveness of machine learning-driven threat detection. The speed and efficiency with which machine learning algorithms process and analyze data allow for real-time threat detection and response. Automated responses, triggered by machine learning systems, can mitigate threats swiftly, reducing the potential impact of security incidents. This rapid response is particularly critical in scenarios where manual intervention might be delayed, allowing attackers to exploit vulnerabilities. The synergy between machine learning-driven threat detection and automated response mechanisms creates a dynamic and proactive cyber-security posture, aligning with the evolving nature of cyber threats.

Machine learning is also contributing to the evolution of traditional Intrusion Detection Systems (IDS) and Intrusion Prevention Systems (IPS). These systems traditionally relied on rule-based approaches, matching network traffic patterns against predefined signatures. However, this method struggles to adapt to the dynamic nature of cyber threats. Machine learning-based IDS and IPS solutions can analyze network traffic in real-time, identifying patterns indicative of potential attacks or anomalous behavior. By continuously learning from network data, these systems can enhance their accuracy over time, providing a more adaptive defense against a wide range of threats, including those that exhibit polymorphic characteristics.

The concept of threat hunting is undergoing transformation with the integration of machine learning. Threat hunting traditionally involves skilled cybersecurity professionals actively seeking out signs of compromise within an organization's environment. Machine learning-driven threat hunting, however, empowers security teams by automating the preliminary phases of investigation, identifying potential threats, and presenting relevant contextual information. This augmented intelligence approach enables human analysts to leverage their expertise in making informed decisions, enhancing the efficiency and efficacy of threat hunting initiatives.

As organizations increasingly adopt cloud computing and hybrid infrastructures, machine learning is proving instrumental in securing these dynamic environments. Machine learning-driven threat detection adapts seamlessly to the distributed and scalable nature of cloud architectures, providing continuous monitoring and analysis of data across diverse platforms. The ability to detect threats in real time, regardless of the location or complexity of the infrastructure, aligns with the agility and flexibility demanded by modern digital ecosystems. Machine learning solutions are well-suited to address the unique challenges associated with cloud security, such as rapid scaling, diverse data sources, and the need for centralized threat visibility. While machine learning has significantly advanced threat detection capabilities, it is not without its challenges. Adversarial attacks, where attackers intentionally manipulate data to deceive machine learning models, pose a notable concern. Cybercriminals may attempt to exploit vulnerabilities in machine learning algorithms by injecting subtle changes into data to evade detection. Continual research and development in adversarial machine learning are essential to fortify machine learning models against such attacks, ensuring the reliability and robustness of machine learning-driven threat detection mechanisms.

In conclusion, the use of machine learning algorithms has ushered in a new era of sophistication and adaptability in identifying and responding to cyber threats. From anomaly detection and behavioral analysis to natural language processing, automation, and integration with threat intelligence, machine learning offers a multifaceted and dynamic approach to cybersecurity. As the cyber threat landscape continues to evolve, machine learning's ability to continuously learn, adapt, and improve positions it as a cornerstone in the arsenal of tools employed by organizations to safeguard their digital assets. While challenges persist, the ongoing advancements in machine learning technologies promise to fortify the resilience of cybersecurity defenses and contribute to a more secure digital future.

Examine the role of AI in automating incident response processes.

Artificial Intelligence (AI) plays a transformative role in automating incident response processes within the realm of cybersecurity, revolutionizing how organizations detect, analyze, and mitigate security incidents in real-time. Incident response traditionally relied heavily on manual intervention, a process that often led to delays in identifying and mitigating threats, leaving organizations vulnerable to extended periods of compromise. AI-driven automation addresses these challenges by harnessing the power of machine learning, natural language processing, and other AI technologies to streamline incident response workflows, enabling organizations to respond rapidly to evolving cyber threats.

One of the primary contributions of AI in automating incident response lies in its ability to enhance the speed and efficiency of threat detection. Machine learning algorithms can continuously analyze vast datasets, including network traffic, logs, and system activities, to identify patterns indicative of potential security incidents. This proactive approach allows AI systems to detect anomalies, deviations from normal behavior, or known malicious patterns in real-time, reducing the time between the occurrence of a security event and its identification. By automating the initial stages of threat detection, AI-driven incident response processes significantly accelerate the overall incident response lifecycle.

Natural Language Processing (NLP) is a key component of AI that is instrumental in automating the analysis of textual data, such as security alerts, logs, and threat intelligence feeds. NLP enables AI systems to understand and interpret human language, facilitating the extraction of relevant information from unstructured data sources. In the context of incident response, this capability enables automated systems to process and contextualize textual information, making it easier to prioritize alerts, categorize incidents, and extract actionable insights. By automating the analysis of textual data, organizations can achieve greater efficiency in understanding the nature and context of security incidents.

AI-driven automation is particularly effective in automating the correlation of disparate security events and indicators of compromise (IoCs). Machine learning algorithms can dynamically correlate information from various sources, including network logs, endpoint data, and threat intelligence feeds, to create a comprehensive and contextualized view of an ongoing incident. This correlation capability is crucial in identifying complex attack patterns, recognizing coordinated campaigns, and attributing security events to specific threat actors. By automating the correlation process, organizations gain a holistic understanding of the threat landscape, enabling more informed and effective incident response decisions.

Automation extends to the enrichment of incident data with contextual information derived from external sources. AI-driven systems can automatically integrate threat intelligence feeds, vulnerability databases, and historical incident data to enhance the context surrounding a security incident. This enrichment process provides incident responders with a broader perspective on the threat landscape, including information about known threat actors, common attack techniques, and indicators of compromise. By automating the enrichment of incident data, organizations empower incident responders with the knowledge needed to make informed decisions and take appropriate actions during the incident response process.

Machine learning algorithms are instrumental in automating the categorization and prioritization of security incidents. By learning from historical data and incident patterns, AI systems can automatically assign risk levels or severity scores to incoming incidents, allowing incident responders to prioritize their efforts based on the potential impact and urgency of each incident. Automated categorization ensures that incidents are appropriately classified, streamlining the incident response workflow and enabling organizations to allocate resources effectively. This level of automation optimizes the use of human expertise, directing it toward addressing the most critical and high-priority security incidents.

The automation of decision-making processes is a significant aspect of AI-driven incident response. Machine learning models can be trained to make informed decisions based on predefined rules, historical data, and contextual information. Automated decision-making can include actions such as blocking malicious IP addresses, isolating compromised endpoints, or initiating containment measures. By automating these routine and predefined responses, organizations can achieve a more consistent and rapid response to security incidents, reducing the manual effort required to handle each incident individually. Automated decision-making is particularly valuable in scenarios where immediate action is crucial to prevent the escalation of a security incident.

Automation extends to the orchestration of incident response workflows, allowing organizations to define and execute predefined response playbooks. AI-driven orchestration enables the integration of diverse security tools, platforms, and technologies into a cohesive and automated incident response process. Automated playbooks can include tasks such as isolating affected systems, gathering forensic evidence, notifying stakeholders, and initiating remediation measures. The orchestration of incident response workflows ensures a coordinated and consistent approach to handling security incidents, regardless of the complexity or diversity of the organization's IT environment.

Machine learning models are increasingly employed in automating the identification and prioritization of vulnerabilities within an organization's infrastructure. By analyzing vulnerability data, historical attack patterns, and threat intelligence, AI-driven systems can prioritize vulnerabilities based on their potential risk and exploitability. Automated vulnerability prioritization allows organizations to focus their resources on addressing the most critical security weaknesses, reducing the attack surface and enhancing overall cybersecurity posture. This automation ensures that vulnerability management efforts align with the evolving threat landscape, optimizing the allocation of resources to address the most pressing security concerns.

AI-driven automation contributes to the acceleration of incident response through the optimization of communication and collaboration processes. Automated systems can facilitate the rapid exchange of information between security tools, incident responders, and relevant stakeholders. This includes automated notifications, alerts, and updates that keep all parties informed about the evolving status of a security incident. Automated communication processes enhance collaboration, reduce response times, and ensure that incident responders have real-time access to critical information needed for effective decision-making.

The integration of AI with Security Information and Event Management (SIEM) systems is a notable development in automating incident response. AI-powered SIEM solutions can analyze vast amounts of security event data, correlate information from multiple sources, and identify patterns indicative of potential security incidents. Automated alerting and notification mechanisms ensure that incident responders are promptly informed about suspicious activities. AI-driven SIEM systems also facilitate the automated collection and analysis of forensic data, aiding in the rapid investigation and response to security incidents.

AI-driven automation extends to the realm of threat hunting, enabling organizations to proactively seek out and identify potential threats within their environments. Machine learning algorithms can analyze historical data, patterns of behavior, and known threat indicators to identify areas of concern that may warrant further investigation. Automated threat hunting processes streamline the identification of potential threats, allowing security teams to focus their efforts on areas with the highest likelihood of containing hidden security risks. This level of automation enhances the organization's ability to detect and respond to emerging threats before they escalate.

Despite the many advantages of AI-driven automation in incident response, challenges persist. Adversarial attacks, where threat actors intentionally manipulate data to deceive AI models, pose a notable concern. Cybercriminals may attempt to exploit vulnerabilities in machine learning algorithms by injecting subtle changes into data to evade detection. Continuous research and development in adversarial machine learning are essential to fortify AI models against such attacks, ensuring the reliability and robustness of AI-driven incident response mechanisms.

In conclusion, AI plays a transformative role in automating incident response processes, offering organizations the ability to detect, analyze, and mitigate security incidents at unprecedented speeds. From the automation of threat detection, analysis, and decision-making to the orchestration of incident response workflows, AI-driven automation optimizes the efficiency and effectiveness of incident response teams. As cyber threats continue to evolve, the integration of AI technologies ensures that incident response processes adapt dynamically, providing organizations with a proactive and resilient defense against the ever-changing cybersecurity landscape. While challenges such as adversarial attacks persist, the ongoing advancements in AI-driven incident response promise to redefine the capabilities of cybersecurity teams and contribute to a more secure digital future.

Discuss the benefits and challenges associated with relying on AI for rapid response.

The reliance on Artificial Intelligence (AI) for rapid response in cybersecurity brings forth a multitude of benefits, transforming the way organizations detect, analyze, and respond to security incidents. However, alongside these advantages, there are notable challenges that organizations must navigate to maximize the efficacy of AI-driven rapid response.

One of the primary benefits of relying on AI for rapid response is the unprecedented speed and efficiency it brings to threat detection. Machine learning algorithms, a subset of AI, can analyze vast datasets at speeds and scales far beyond human capabilities. This enables organizations to detect security incidents in real-time, minimizing the time between a security event occurring and its identification. Rapid detection is crucial in the context of cybersecurity, as it allows organizations to respond swiftly and mitigate the impact of security incidents, reducing the window of vulnerability and preventing further compromise.

Automation, a key aspect of AI-driven rapid response, contributes significantly to the efficiency of incident response processes. AI systems can automate the initial stages of threat detection, analysis, and decision-making, streamlining workflows and allowing security teams to focus on more complex aspects of incident response. This automation not only accelerates the overall incident response lifecycle but also ensures a consistent and standardized approach to handling security incidents. Automated playbooks, for instance, can orchestrate predefined responses, allowing organizations to respond rapidly and consistently to known types of security incidents.

The speed of AI-driven rapid response extends to decision-making processes. Machine learning models can be trained to make informed decisions based on predefined rules, historical data, and contextual information. Automated decision-making can include actions such as blocking malicious IP addresses, isolating compromised endpoints, or initiating containment measures. This level of automation ensures a rapid and consistent response to security incidents, reducing the manual effort required to handle each incident individually and allowing organizations to respond swiftly to prevent further damage.

The ability of AI systems to continuously learn and adapt contributes to their effectiveness in rapid response. Machine learning algorithms, through ongoing training on new data, improve their accuracy and understanding of the evolving threat landscape. This adaptability is particularly crucial in the face of polymorphic threats and zero-day attacks, where attackers constantly modify their tactics to evade traditional security measures. AI-driven systems, by continuously learning from new data, can identify emerging threats and adjust their detection mechanisms accordingly, providing a dynamic defense against evolving cyber threats.

Natural Language Processing (NLP), a component of AI, enhances the efficiency of rapid response by automating the analysis of textual data. Security alerts, logs, and threat intelligence feeds often contain valuable information in unstructured text. NLP enables AI systems to understand and interpret human language, facilitating the extraction of relevant information from these data sources. This capability streamlines the analysis of textual data, enabling organizations to quickly derive insights, prioritize alerts, and make informed decisions during the incident response process.

The integration of AI with Security Information and Event Management (SIEM) systems is a notable advancement that benefits rapid response. AI-powered SIEM solutions can analyze vast amounts of security event data, correlate information from multiple sources, and identify patterns indicative of potential security incidents. Automated alerting and notification mechanisms ensure that incident responders are promptly informed about suspicious activities. AI-driven SIEM systems also facilitate the automated collection and analysis of forensic data, aiding in the rapid investigation and response to security incidents. This integration enhances the overall speed and effectiveness of incident response efforts.

Automated threat hunting is another advantage associated with relying on AI for rapid response. Machine learning algorithms can analyze historical data, patterns of behavior, and known threat indicators to proactively identify potential threats within an organization's environment. Automated threat hunting processes streamline the identification of areas of concern, allowing security teams to focus their efforts on areas with the highest likelihood of containing hidden security risks. This proactive approach to threat hunting contributes to rapid response by detecting and mitigating emerging threats before they escalate.

Despite these benefits, there are challenges organizations must consider when relying on AI for rapid response. One significant challenge is the potential for adversarial attacks, where threat actors intentionally manipulate data to deceive AI models. Cybercriminals may attempt to exploit vulnerabilities in machine learning algorithms by injecting subtle changes into data to evade detection. Continual research and development in adversarial machine learning are essential to fortify AI models against such attacks, ensuring the reliability and robustness of AI-driven rapid response mechanisms.

The interpretability of AI models poses another challenge. As machine learning models become more complex, understanding the reasoning behind their decisions becomes increasingly difficult. Interpretable AI is crucial in the context of cybersecurity, where the ability to explain why a particular decision was made is essential for building trust and ensuring accountability. Balancing the complexity of AI models with the need for interpretability is an ongoing challenge that organizations must address to foster confidence in AI-driven rapid response mechanisms.

The need for high-quality and diverse training data is a crucial consideration in the deployment of AI for rapid response. Machine learning models rely on historical data to train and improve their accuracy. If the training data is biased, incomplete, or not representative of the organization's specific threat landscape, the AI models may produce inaccurate or unreliable results. Ensuring the quality and diversity of training data is a continuous effort that requires ongoing monitoring and refinement to enhance the effectiveness of AI-driven rapid response.

AI-driven rapid response also raises concerns about the potential for false positives and false negatives. False positives occur when an AI system incorrectly identifies normal behavior as a security threat, leading to unnecessary alerts and potential disruption of legitimate activities. False negatives, on the other hand, occur when the system fails to detect an actual security threat. Striking the right balance between minimizing false positives and false negatives is a delicate challenge that requires continuous tuning and optimization of AI models to align with the organization's risk tolerance and operational requirements.

The ethical considerations surrounding AI-driven rapid response are paramount. The deployment of AI in cybersecurity raises questions about privacy, bias, and accountability. Organizations must carefully consider the ethical implications of using AI to make decisions that impact individuals, systems, and operations. Ensuring transparency, fairness, and adherence to ethical principles becomes essential in building and maintaining trust in AI-driven rapid response mechanisms.

The potential overreliance on AI without human oversight is a concern that organizations must address. While AI significantly enhances the speed and efficiency of rapid response, human expertise remains critical for complex decision-making, contextual understanding, and adapting to novel and evolving threats. Balancing the roles of AI and human analysts in incident response processes is essential to harness the strengths of both and create a resilient and adaptive cybersecurity posture.

In conclusion, relying on AI for rapid response in cybersecurity brings substantial benefits, including unprecedented speed, efficiency, and adaptability in threat detection and mitigation. Automation, machine learning, natural language processing, and integration with SIEM systems contribute to a dynamic and proactive incident response. However, organizations must navigate challenges related to adversarial attacks, interpretability, training data quality, false positives and negatives, ethical considerations, and the balance between AI and human expertise. Addressing these challenges is crucial to

harnessing the full potential of AI-driven rapid response while ensuring the reliability, transparency, and ethical use of these advanced
technologies in the ever-evolving landscape of cybersecurity.

**Introduce the concept of behavioral analytics in cybersecuri-
ty.**

Behavioral analytics is a transformative concept within the realm
of cybersecurity, offering a dynamic and proactive approach to threat
detection and risk management. At its core, behavioral analytics revolves around the analysis of patterns, trends, and anomalies in the
behavior of users, devices, and entities within an organization's digital environment. Unlike traditional security measures that rely on
static rules or predefined signatures, behavioral analytics leverages
the power of advanced analytics, machine learning, and statistical
modeling to discern deviations from established baselines of normal
behavior. This shift from rule-based detection to a more dynamic,
context-aware methodology enables organizations to identify subtle
and sophisticated threats that often evade conventional security measures.

The fundamental premise of behavioral analytics is grounded in
the understanding that every user and system within a network has
a unique digital fingerprint, characterized by their typical patterns of
activity. By establishing baselines for normal behavior, behavioral analytics systems can detect deviations that may indicate potential security incidents. This approach recognizes the inherent variability in
user behavior and adapts to the evolving nature of cyber threats, offering a more nuanced and accurate means of identifying anomalous
activities.

User behavior analytics (UBA) is a prominent application of behavioral analytics, focusing on the patterns and activities of individual users. UBA systems analyze user interactions with digital resources, such as login patterns, access to sensitive data, and the use of
applications. Deviations from established behavior baselines, such as

unusual login times, access to unfamiliar resources, or a sudden increase in data transfer, trigger alerts for further investigation. UBA is particularly valuable in detecting insider threats, where compromised or malicious users may exhibit behavior that deviates from their regular activities.

Device behavior analytics extends the scope of analysis to the activities and interactions of endpoints, IoT devices, and other connected entities within a network. By examining the behavior of devices, organizations can identify potential indicators of compromise, such as unusual network traffic, unexpected communication patterns, or suspicious access to critical systems. Device behavior analytics plays a crucial role in securing the increasingly complex and interconnected ecosystems of modern IT environments, where diverse devices contribute to the overall attack surface.

Entity behavior analytics broadens the focus to encompass the collective behavior of entities within a network, including users, devices, and applications. By correlating the behavior of multiple entities, organizations can detect sophisticated attack patterns, lateral movement, and coordinated campaigns that involve multiple elements working in concert. This holistic approach enhances the contextual understanding of potential security incidents, allowing organizations to respond more effectively to complex and orchestrated threats.

Behavioral analytics also extends to application behavior analysis, where the focus is on understanding the normal patterns and interactions of software applications. Anomalous behavior within applications, such as unexpected data access, privilege escalation attempts, or unusual system calls, can indicate potential security threats. Application behavior analytics aids in identifying and mitigating threats that target vulnerabilities within software, ensuring a comprehensive approach to securing the entire IT infrastructure.

Machine learning algorithms play a pivotal role in the success of behavioral analytics. These algorithms analyze historical data to establish baselines of normal behavior and learn from patterns associated with security incidents. As the system encounters new data, machine learning models adapt and refine their understanding of what constitutes normal or abnormal behavior. This adaptive learning process is essential for addressing the dynamic nature of cyber threats, including emerging attack techniques and evolving patterns of malicious behavior.

One notable strength of behavioral analytics is its ability to detect previously unknown or "zero-day" threats. Traditional security measures often rely on known signatures or patterns associated with known threats. Behavioral analytics, however, excels in identifying anomalies that may not have a predefined signature. By continuously learning and adapting to new data, behavioral analytics systems can uncover novel threats that exhibit subtle deviations from normal behavior, providing a proactive defense against emerging risks.

The contextual awareness inherent in behavioral analytics is a key differentiator. Rather than relying solely on isolated events or alerts, behavioral analytics systems consider the broader context of user and entity behavior. This contextual understanding enables organizations to distinguish between benign anomalies and potential security incidents, reducing false positives and allowing security teams to focus on the most critical threats. The ability to correlate diverse data points contributes to a more accurate and nuanced analysis of the overall security posture.

Behavioral analytics is particularly effective in addressing the challenges posed by advanced persistent threats (APTs). APTs are characterized by their stealthy and prolonged nature, often involving sophisticated tactics to remain undetected within a network. Behavioral analytics can identify subtle and persistent anomalies that may indicate the presence of an APT, such as unusual patterns of data exfiltration, lateral movement, or privilege escalation attempts. The continuous monitoring and analysis of behavior contribute to the early detection of APTs, minimizing the potential impact of these persistent and elusive threats.

The integration of behavioral analytics with threat intelligence feeds enhances its capabilities. Threat intelligence provides organizations with up-to-date information about known threats, vulnerabilities, and attacker techniques. By combining behavioral analytics with threat intelligence, organizations can contextualize their analysis, correlating observed behaviors with external knowledge about the current threat landscape. This synergy enables more informed decision-making, allowing organizations to prioritize and respond to potential security incidents based on the broader context of the threat landscape.

Despite its strengths, behavioral analytics is not without challenges. The need for high-quality and diverse training data is a critical consideration. Machine learning models rely on historical data to establish baselines and learn from patterns. If the training data is biased, incomplete, or not representative of the organization's specific environment, the behavioral analytics system may produce inaccurate or unreliable results. Ensuring the quality and diversity of training data is an ongoing effort that requires continuous monitoring and refinement to enhance the effectiveness of behavioral analytics.

Privacy concerns are another challenge associated with behavioral analytics. Analyzing the behavior of individual users or entities within a network raises questions about privacy, consent, and the ethical use of monitoring tools. Organizations must strike a balance between the need for enhanced security and the protection of individual privacy rights. Implementing transparent policies, obtaining informed consent, and anonymizing data where possible are crucial steps in addressing privacy concerns associated with behavioral analytics.

The interpretability of behavioral analytics findings poses a challenge, especially as machine learning models become more complex. Understanding the reasoning behind the identification of specific behaviors as anomalous or indicative of a security incident is essential for effective decision-making and incident response. Balancing the complexity of machine learning models with the need for interpretability is an ongoing challenge that organizations must address to build trust and confidence in the outputs of behavioral analytics systems.

In conclusion, behavioral analytics represents a paradigm shift in cybersecurity, offering a dynamic and context-aware approach to threat detection and risk management. By analyzing patterns, trends, and anomalies in the behavior of users, devices, and entities, behavioral analytics provides organizations with a proactive defense against a wide range of cyber threats. The integration of machine learning, contextual awareness, and correlation with threat intelligence enhances the effectiveness of behavioral analytics in addressing the complexities of modern cybersecurity landscapes. Despite challenges related to training data, privacy, and interpretability, behavioral analytics stands as a powerful tool in the arsenal of cybersecurity strategies, contributing to a resilient and adaptive security posture in the face of evolving threats.

Discuss how AI-driven anomaly detection enhances the identification of unusual patterns and potential threats.

Artificial Intelligence (AI)-driven anomaly detection stands as a cutting-edge technique in cybersecurity, revolutionizing the identification of unusual patterns and potential threats within complex and dynamic digital environments. At its core, anomaly detection leverages the power of advanced machine learning algorithms and statistical models to establish baselines of normal behavior, allowing for the dynamic identification of deviations that may indicate security incidents. This paradigm shift from rule-based approaches to a more adaptive and context-aware methodology addresses the limitations of traditional security measures and enhances organizations' ability to detect subtle, novel, and sophisticated threats that may elude conventional defenses.

Machine learning algorithms play a pivotal role in the success of AI-driven anomaly detection. These algorithms analyze vast amounts of historical data to learn and establish patterns associated with normal behavior. By understanding what is considered typical within a specific environment, these models can subsequently identify deviations or anomalies that fall outside established baselines. Unlike rule-based detection mechanisms that rely on predefined signatures, machine learning algorithms excel in recognizing patterns that may not have a fixed signature, making them particularly effective in detecting previously unknown or "zero-day" threats.

The dynamic adaptability of AI-driven anomaly detection is a significant advantage in the ever-evolving landscape of cyber threats. Traditional security measures often struggle to keep pace with rapidly changing tactics employed by cybercriminals. AI-driven anomaly detection systems continuously learn from new data, adapting and refining their understanding of normal and abnormal behavior over time. This adaptability ensures that organizations can proactively identify emerging threats, even those that exhibit novel characteristics or variations from known attack patterns.

One of the key applications of AI-driven anomaly detection is in the realm of network security. By analyzing patterns of network traffic, machine learning models can identify deviations indicative of potential security incidents. Unusual communication patterns, unexpected data transfers, or anomalies in user access to network resources can trigger alerts for further investigation. The contextual awareness provided by anomaly detection in network security allows organizations to distinguish between normal fluctuations in network activity and patterns that may signify malicious behavior, enhancing the accuracy and efficacy of threat detection.

Endpoint security is another domain where AI-driven anomaly detection proves invaluable. Endpoints, such as individual devices or systems within a network, are common targets for cyber attacks. Machine learning models can analyze the behavior of endpoints, identifying deviations such as unusual access patterns, unexpected system calls, or changes in file access that may indicate compromise. Anomaly detection at the endpoint level enables organizations to detect and respond to potential threats at an early stage, preventing the lateral movement of attackers within the network.

User behavior analytics (UBA) is a specialized application of AI-driven anomaly detection focused on understanding the patterns and activities of individual users. By analyzing user interactions with digital resources, UBA systems can identify deviations from established behavior baselines. Unusual login times, access to unfamiliar resources, or sudden increases in data transfer may trigger alerts for further investigation. UBA is particularly effective in detecting insider threats, where compromised or malicious users may exhibit behavior that deviates from their regular activities.

AI-driven anomaly detection contributes significantly to the identification of malicious activities related to application behavior. Anomalies in application behavior, such as unexpected data access, privilege escalation attempts, or abnormal system calls, can indicate potential security threats. By continuously analyzing application behavior, organizations can detect and respond to anomalies that may signify vulnerabilities or active attacks targeting software systems. This level of visibility into application behavior enhances the overall security posture by addressing threats at the software level.

Behavioral analysis within AI-driven anomaly detection extends beyond individual users and entities to encompass the collective behavior of users, devices, and applications within a network. By correlating the behavior of multiple entities, organizations can identify sophisticated attack patterns, lateral movement, and coordinated campaigns that involve multiple elements working in concert. This holistic approach enhances the contextual understanding of potential security incidents, allowing organizations to respond more effectively to complex and orchestrated threats.

The integration of AI-driven anomaly detection with threat intelligence feeds further enhances its capabilities. Threat intelligence provides organizations with up-to-date information about known threats, vulnerabilities, and attacker techniques. By combining anomaly detection with threat intelligence, organizations can correlate observed behaviors with external knowledge about the current threat landscape. This synergy enables more informed decision-making, allowing organizations to prioritize and respond to potential security incidents based on the broader context of the threat landscape.

AI-driven anomaly detection is particularly effective in addressing the challenges posed by advanced persistent threats (APTs). APTs are characterized by their stealthy and prolonged nature, often involving sophisticated tactics to remain undetected within a network. Anomaly detection can identify subtle and persistent anomalies that may indicate the presence of an APT, such as unusual patterns of data exfiltration, lateral movement, or privilege escalation attempts. The continuous monitoring and analysis of behavior contribute to the early detection of APTs, minimizing the potential impact of these persistent and elusive threats.

Contextual awareness is a key strength of AI-driven anomaly detection. Rather than relying solely on isolated events or alerts, anomaly detection systems consider the broader context of user and entity behavior. This contextual understanding enables organizations to distinguish between benign anomalies and potential security incidents, reducing false positives and allowing security teams to focus on the most critical threats. The ability to correlate diverse data points contributes to a more accurate and nuanced analysis of the overall security posture.

Despite its strengths, AI-driven anomaly detection is not without challenges. The need for high-quality and diverse training data is a critical consideration. Machine learning models rely on historical data to establish baselines and learn from patterns. If the training data is biased, incomplete, or not representative of the organization's specific environment, the anomaly detection system may produce inaccurate or unreliable results. Ensuring the quality and diversity of training data is an ongoing effort that requires continuous monitoring and refinement to enhance the effectiveness of anomaly detection.

Privacy concerns are another challenge associated with AI-driven anomaly detection. Analyzing the behavior of individual users or entities within a network raises questions about privacy, consent, and the ethical use of monitoring tools. Organizations must strike a balance between the need for enhanced security and the protection of individual privacy rights. Implementing transparent policies, obtaining informed consent, and anonymizing data where possible are crucial steps in addressing privacy concerns associated with anomaly detection.

Interpreting the findings of AI-driven anomaly detection poses a challenge, especially as machine learning models become more complex. Understanding the reasoning behind the identification of specific behaviors as anomalous or indicative of a security incident is essential for effective decision-making and incident response. Balancing the complexity of machine learning models with the need for interpretability is an ongoing challenge that organizations must address to build trust and confidence in the outputs of anomaly detection systems.

In conclusion, AI-driven anomaly detection represents a transformative approach to identifying unusual patterns and potential threats within cybersecurity.

By leveraging advanced machine learning algorithms and statistical models, organizations can establish dynamic baselines of normal behavior and detect deviations that may indicate security incidents. From network security and endpoint protection to user behavior analytics and application security, AI-driven anomaly detection offers a versatile and proactive defense against a wide range of cyber threats. Despite challenges related to training data, privacy, and interpretability, anomaly detection stands as a powerful tool in the arsenal of cybersecurity strategies, contributing to a resilient and adaptive security posture in the face of evolving threats.

Explore how artificial intelligence is applied to enhance identity and access management.

Artificial Intelligence (AI) has emerged as a transformative force in enhancing Identity and Access Management (IAM), revolutionizing the way organizations manage and secure user identities, permissions, and access to critical resources. At its core, IAM involves the processes, technologies, and policies that facilitate the management of digital identities and control access to systems and data. The integration of AI into IAM systems brings a range of capabilities that not only streamline administrative tasks but also significantly improve security by proactively identifying and mitigating risks associated with user access.

One of the key areas where AI enhances IAM is in the realm of user authentication. Traditional authentication methods, such as passwords or token-based systems, are increasingly vulnerable to sophisticated cyber attacks. AI-driven authentication introduces advanced methods like biometric recognition, facial recognition, voice authentication, and behavioral biometrics. These methods leverage machine learning algorithms to analyze and authenticate users based on unique physical or behavioral attributes. By continuously learning and adapting to users' changing behaviors, AI-driven authentication provides a more secure and user-friendly approach, reducing the reliance on easily compromised passwords.

Behavioral biometrics, a subset of AI-driven authentication, focuses on analyzing patterns of user behavior to establish a unique identity profile. Factors such as typing speed, mouse movements, and application usage patterns contribute to a user's behavioral biometric profile. AI algorithms continuously analyze these patterns, allowing the system to detect anomalies that may indicate unauthorized access. This dynamic and context-aware authentication method enhances security by recognizing users based on their behavior, even when traditional static credentials may be compromised.

AI plays a pivotal role in risk-based authentication within IAM systems. Risk-based authentication assesses the risk associated with a specific access request based on contextual factors such as the user's location, device used, time of access, and the sensitivity of the requested resource. AI algorithms analyze these contextual factors in real-time, assigning risk scores to access requests. High-risk requests may trigger additional authentication steps, while low-risk requests experience a smoother, frictionless authentication process. This adaptive approach enables organizations to balance security and user experience by applying stronger authentication only when necessary.

AI-driven anomaly detection is instrumental in identifying and mitigating insider threats within IAM systems. Insider threats, whether unintentional or malicious, pose a significant risk to organizations. AI algorithms continuously analyze user behavior, access patterns, and data usage to detect anomalies that may signify a potential insider threat. Unusual access attempts, changes in user behavior, or suspicious data transfers trigger alerts for further investigation. By proactively identifying anomalous activities, AI-driven anomaly detection enhances the ability to detect and respond to insider threats before they escalate.

The application of AI in IAM extends to privileged access management (PAM), where organizations manage and monitor privileged user accounts that have elevated access to critical systems and data. AI-driven PAM introduces capabilities such as just-in-time access, which dynamically grants elevated privileges for a specific time frame and purpose. AI algorithms assess the legitimacy of privileged access requests, considering contextual factors and historical behavior to ensure that privileged access is granted only when necessary. This approach minimizes the risk of unauthorized access and helps organizations adhere to the principle of least privilege.

User behavior analytics (UBA), powered by AI, enhances IAM by providing insights into patterns of user activity. UBA systems continuously analyze user interactions with digital resources, identifying deviations from established behavior baselines. AI algorithms can distinguish between normal and abnormal behavior, flagging activities that may indicate compromised accounts or malicious intent. UBA contributes to proactive threat detection within IAM systems, allowing organizations to respond swiftly to potential security incidents before they escalate.

AI-driven IAM systems excel in enhancing the accuracy and efficiency of identity verification processes. Facial recognition, voice authentication, and other biometric methods powered by AI offer more reliable and secure means of verifying a user's identity compared to traditional methods. AI algorithms can adapt to variations in biometric data, such as changes in appearance or voice over time, ensuring a robust and resilient identity verification process. This is particularly valuable in scenarios where a high level of confidence in user identity is crucial, such as financial transactions or access to sensitive information.

Automated provisioning and de-provisioning of user accounts is another area where AI streamlines IAM processes. AI-driven provisioning systems can analyze user roles, responsibilities, and historical access patterns to automatically assign or revoke access rights based on changing job roles or responsibilities. By automating these processes, organizations not only improve efficiency but also reduce the risk of human error in managing user access. AI-driven IAM systems can predict access needs based on historical data, ensuring that users have the appropriate permissions without unnecessary delays or security gaps.

In the context of AI-enhanced IAM, continuous monitoring is a key feature. AI algorithms continuously analyze user activities, access requests, and system events in real-time. This continuous monitoring enables organizations to detect and respond to security incidents promptly. Suspicious activities, deviations from normal behavior, or unauthorized access attempts trigger alerts, allowing security teams to investigate and mitigate potential threats in real-time. The proactive nature of continuous monitoring is crucial in preventing security incidents from escalating and minimizing the impact on the organization.

AI-driven IAM systems also contribute to adaptive access control, allowing organizations to dynamically adjust access permissions based on changing risk factors. AI algorithms assess contextual factors, such as the user's location, device health, and network conditions, in real-time. If the risk level associated with a specific access request changes, the system can dynamically adjust access permissions or trigger additional authentication measures. This adaptive access control approach ensures that security measures align with the evolving risk landscape, providing a more resilient defense against emerging threats.

AI-powered threat intelligence integration is a significant enhancement in IAM, enabling organizations to leverage external knowledge about known threats and vulnerabilities. AI algorithms correlate internal IAM data with threat intelligence feeds, providing context to user behavior and access patterns. This integration enhances the ability to detect and respond to threats by identifying access attempts associated with known malicious actors, compromised credentials, or emerging attack techniques. By staying informed about the broader threat landscape, organizations can proactively enhance their IAM defenses and preemptively address potential risks.

Despite the myriad benefits, the deployment of AI in IAM is not without challenges. Interpreting AI-driven decisions poses a challenge, especially as machine learning models become more complex. Understanding why specific access decisions or risk assessments are made is essential for building trust in AI-driven IAM systems. Striking the right balance between the complexity of machine learning models and the need for interpretability is an ongoing challenge that organizations must address to ensure effective decision-making and user trust.

Another challenge is the potential for adversarial attacks on AI-driven IAM systems. Adversarial attacks involve manipulating input data to deceive AI models and make incorrect decisions. In the context of IAM, attackers may attempt to exploit vulnerabilities in machine learning algorithms to gain unauthorized access or manipulate risk assessments. Ongoing research and development in adversarial machine learning are essential to fortify AI-driven IAM systems against such attacks and ensure the robustness of access control mechanisms.

Privacy considerations are paramount in AI-driven IAM, particularly when using biometric authentication methods. Collecting, storing, and processing biometric data raise concerns about user privacy and the potential for misuse. Organizations must implement stringent privacy measures, such as anonymizing biometric data where possible, obtaining informed consent, and adhering to relevant data protection regulations. Building transparent and ethical practices in AI-driven IAM is crucial for fostering user trust and ensuring the responsible use of biometric technologies.

In conclusion, the application of AI in enhancing Identity and Access Management represents a paradigm shift in cybersecurity, offering advanced capabilities that go beyond traditional IAM methods. From biometric authentication and risk-based access control to continuous monitoring and threat intelligence integration, AI-driven IAM systems provide a dynamic, adaptive, and context-aware defense against evolving cyber threats. While challenges related to interpretability, adversarial attacks, and privacy considerations persist, the benefits of improved security, efficiency, and user experience position AI as a driving force in the future of IAM. As organizations continue to evolve in the digital landscape, AI-enhanced IAM stands at the forefront of safeguarding identities and access to critical resources in an increasingly complex and dynamic cybersecurity landscape.

Discuss the role of AI in authentication and authorization processes.

The integration of Artificial Intelligence (AI) in authentication and authorization processes represents a significant advancement in the field of cybersecurity, redefining how organizations validate user identities and control access to sensitive resources. Authentication, the process of verifying the identity of users, and authorization, the process of granting or denying access based on authenticated identities, are foundational components of Identity and Access Management (IAM). By harnessing the capabilities of AI, organizations enhance the security, efficiency, and adaptability of these processes, addressing challenges posed by evolving cyber threats and the limitations of traditional authentication methods.

AI-driven authentication introduces a paradigm shift from traditional methods reliant on static credentials, such as passwords, to dynamic and adaptive approaches that leverage advanced biometric technologies. Biometric authentication, powered by AI algorithms, includes methods like facial recognition, fingerprint scanning, voice recognition, and behavioral biometrics. These technologies analyze unique physical or behavioral traits to establish and verify user identities. Unlike traditional passwords, biometric data is inherently tied to the individual, providing a more robust and user-friendly authentication experience. AI enhances the accuracy and reliability of biometric authentication by continuously learning and adapting to variations in biometric data over time.

Facial recognition, a prominent application of AI in authentication, analyzes facial features to uniquely identify individuals. AI algorithms can adapt to changes in appearance, lighting conditions, and facial expressions, improving the resilience of facial recognition systems. The widespread adoption of facial recognition in consumer devices, such as smartphones, demonstrates the efficacy and user acceptance of this AI-driven authentication method. Facial recognition not only enhances security but also streamlines user interactions by providing a seamless and non-intrusive authentication experience.

Voice recognition, another biometric authentication method empowered by AI, analyzes unique vocal characteristics to verify user identities. AI algorithms can distinguish between genuine and synthetic voices, enhancing the robustness of voice recognition systems. The natural and convenient nature of voice-based authentication contributes to its adoption in various applications, from customer service interactions to secure access to devices and systems. AI-driven voice recognition not only strengthens security but also aligns with user expectations for intuitive and frictionless authentication experiences.

Behavioral biometrics represent a sophisticated application of AI in authentication, focusing on analyzing patterns of user behavior to establish a unique identity profile. Factors such as typing speed, mouse movements, and application usage patterns contribute to a user's behavioral biometric profile. AI algorithms continuously analyze these patterns, allowing the system to detect anomalies that may indicate unauthorized access. Behavioral biometrics provide a dynamic and context-aware authentication method, recognizing users based on their behavior even when traditional static credentials may be compromised.

AI-driven anomaly detection plays a pivotal role in enhancing the security of authentication processes. Traditional authentication methods often struggle to detect sophisticated attacks, such as account takeover attempts or the use of stolen credentials. AI algorithms analyze patterns of user behavior, access requests, and contextual factors in real-time, identifying anomalies that may signify potential security threats. Unusual login times, atypical access patterns, or deviations from established behavior baselines trigger alerts for further investigation. AI-driven anomaly detection contributes to the proactive identification of security incidents during the authentication process, enabling organizations to respond swiftly to potential threats.

Risk-based authentication, powered by AI, introduces a dynamic and adaptive approach to access control. This method assesses the risk associated with a specific access request based on contextual factors such as the user's location, device used, time of access, and the sensitivity of the requested resource. AI algorithms analyze these contextual factors in real-time, assigning risk scores to access requests. High-risk requests may trigger additional authentication steps, such as multi-factor authentication, while low-risk requests experience a smoother, frictionless authentication process. Risk-based authentication optimizes security by tailoring the level of authentication to the perceived risk, balancing security requirements with user experience.

Multi-factor authentication (MFA), a widely adopted security practice, benefits from AI-driven advancements. MFA combines multiple authentication factors, such as passwords, biometrics, and one-time codes, to enhance security. AI algorithms contribute to the effectiveness of MFA by dynamically adjusting the combination of factors based on contextual factors and risk assessments. For example, a high-risk access request may trigger the use of additional authentication factors, while routine access from a familiar device may require fewer factors. AI-driven MFA enhances security by providing a flexible and adaptive approach to multi-layered authentication.

AI-driven fraud detection further strengthens authentication processes by identifying patterns indicative of fraudulent activities. Fraudulent activities, such as account takeover attempts or phishing attacks, often exhibit distinct patterns that AI algorithms can recognize. By continuously learning from historical data and adapting to emerging threats, AI-driven fraud detection contributes to the early identification of potential security incidents. This proactive approach enables organizations to prevent unauthorized access and mitigate the impact of fraudulent activities on user accounts and sensitive resources.

Authorization processes, determining the permissions and access levels granted to authenticated users, also benefit significantly from AI-driven advancements. Role-based access control (RBAC), a common authorization model, assigns access permissions based on user roles within an organization. AI enhances RBAC by dynamically adjusting user roles and permissions based on changing contextual factors and user behavior. For example, AI algorithms can identify changes in user responsibilities or access patterns, automatically updating roles to align with the principle of least privilege.

Privileged Access Management (PAM), which governs access to privileged accounts with elevated permissions, leverages AI to enhance security and accountability. AI-driven PAM introduces capabilities such as just-in-time access, which dynamically grants elevated privileges for a specific time frame and purpose. AI algorithms assess the legitimacy of privileged access requests, considering contextual factors and historical behavior to ensure that privileged access is granted only when necessary. This approach minimizes the risk of unauthorized access to critical systems and helps organizations adhere to stringent security controls.

User behavior analytics (UBA), powered by AI, provides insights into patterns of user activity that inform authorization decisions. UBA systems continuously analyze user interactions with digital resources, identifying deviations from established behavior baselines. AI algorithms can distinguish between normal and abnormal behavior, flagging activities that may indicate compromised accounts or malicious intent. UBA contributes to proactive threat detection within authorization processes, allowing organizations to respond swiftly to potential security incidents before they escalate.

The integration of AI with Zero Trust Security models further enhances authorization processes by continuously validating user identities and access permissions. Zero Trust Security assumes that no user or device can be inherently trusted, requiring continuous verification of user identities and authorization status. AI algorithms play a crucial role in real-time analysis of user behavior, device health, and contextual factors to determine access permissions. By dynamically adjusting access levels based on changing risk factors, AI-driven Zero Trust Security models provide a resilient defense against unauthorized access and lateral movement within networks.

Despite the numerous benefits, the deployment of AI in authentication and authorization processes is not without challenges. Privacy considerations, particularly in the context of biometric authentication, raise concerns about the collection, storage, and processing of sensitive user data. Organizations must implement robust privacy measures, such as anonymizing biometric data where possible, obtaining informed consent, and adhering to relevant data protection regulations. Transparency and ethical practices in the use of AI-driven authentication technologies are essential for building user trust and ensuring responsible data handling.

Interpreting AI-driven decisions poses another challenge, especially as machine learning models become more complex. Understanding why specific access decisions or risk assessments are made is essential for building trust in AI-driven authentication and authorization systems. Striking the right balance between the complexity of machine learning models and the need for interpretability is an ongoing challenge that organizations must address to ensure effective decision-making and user trust.

In conclusion, the role of AI in authentication and authorization processes represents a transformative shift in the landscape of cybersecurity. From biometric authentication and risk-based access control to anomaly detection and continuous monitoring, AI-driven advancements significantly improve the security, efficiency, and adaptability of IAM processes. While challenges related to privacy considerations, interpretability, and ethical use persist, the benefits of enhanced security, user experience, and proactive threat detection position AI as a driving force in shaping the future of authentication and authorization in an increasingly complex and dynamic cybersecurity landscape.

Address the ethical implications of using AI in cybersecurity.

The integration of Artificial Intelligence (AI) into the realm of cybersecurity brings forth a myriad of ethical considerations that span various dimensions, from privacy and accountability to bias and the potential misuse of advanced technologies. As AI algorithms become increasingly sophisticated and pervasive in defending against cyber threats, the ethical implications demand careful examination to ensure responsible and transparent practices in the use of these technologies.

One of the primary ethical concerns surrounding AI in cybersecurity revolves around the invasion of privacy. As AI-driven technologies analyze vast amounts of data to identify potential threats, there is an inherent tension between the need for robust security measures and the protection of individuals' private information. The collection, processing, and storage of sensitive data, especially when related to user behavior or biometric information for authentication, raise significant privacy concerns. Striking a balance between effective cybersecurity practices and respecting individuals' right to privacy becomes crucial in navigating this ethical dilemma.

The potential for bias in AI algorithms presents another ethical challenge. Machine learning models are trained on historical data, and if that data contains biases, the algorithms may perpetuate and even exacerbate those biases. In the context of cybersecurity, biased algorithms could lead to discriminatory outcomes, where certain groups or individuals are unfairly targeted or disproportionately affected. Addressing bias in AI requires ongoing efforts in diverse and representative data collection, transparent model development, and continuous monitoring to mitigate unintended consequences.

The transparency and interpretability of AI algorithms pose ethical concerns related to accountability and user trust. As AI systems become more complex, understanding the decision-making process behind these algorithms becomes increasingly challenging. Lack of transparency can lead to a "black box" problem, where users, administrators, and even the developers themselves may struggle to comprehend why a particular decision was made. This opacity raises questions about accountability in the event of errors, security reaches, or unintended consequences, emphasizing the need for ethical AI practices that prioritize transparency and explainability.

The deployment of AI in offensive cybersecurity measures, such as automated hacking or autonomous decision-making in cyber warfare, introduces significant ethical dilemmas. The use of AI in offensive operations raises concerns about the potential escalation of cyber conflicts and the development of autonomous cyber weapons. The lack of clear ethical guidelines and international norms in this domain heightens the risk of unintended consequences, including collateral damage, civilian impact, and the potential for cyber-attacks to spiral out of control. Establishing ethical frameworks for the responsible use of AI in offensive cybersecurity measures is imperative to prevent destabilization and ensure adherence to international laws and norms.

Another ethical consideration lies in the dual-use nature of AI technologies in cybersecurity. While AI is developed to defend against cyber threats, there is a risk that the same technologies can be repurposed for malicious activities. This dual-use dilemma raises questions about responsible research and development practices, export controls, and the potential unintended consequences of advancing AI capabilities. Striking a balance between fostering innovation and preventing the malicious use of AI in cybersecurity is a complex ethical challenge that requires international collaboration and regulatory frameworks.

The ethical implications of AI in cybersecurity extend to the human-machine collaboration aspect, particularly in the context of autonomous decision-making. As AI systems take on more responsibilities in threat detection, incident response, and decision-making, there is a need to delineate clear boundaries between automated processes and human oversight. The "human in the loop" approach becomes essential to ensure that critical decisions involving potential harm or escalation are subject to human judgment, ethical considerations, and a broader understanding of the context in which these decisions are made.

AI-powered threat intelligence, while essential for identifying and mitigating cyber threats, raises ethical concerns related to the sharing and dissemination of information. The collaborative nature of threat intelligence sharing among organizations and governments requires careful handling to avoid privacy violations, misuse of shared information, or the potential for threat intelligence to be weaponized. Establishing ethical guidelines for responsible threat intelligence sharing is critical to fostering a collective defense against cyber threats without compromising individual privacy or enabling offensive actions.

The ethical considerations surrounding AI in cybersecurity extend to the accountability of AI developers and organizations. In the event of a cybersecurity incident or breach involving AI technologies, questions arise about responsibility, liability, and the role of human oversight. Ensuring that AI developers adhere to ethical standards, conduct thorough risk assessments, and prioritize security in AI system design becomes paramount. Establishing clear lines of responsibility and accountability in the development, deployment, and maintenance of AI-driven cybersecurity solutions is essential for addressing potential ethical lapses and ensuring the protection of users and organizations.

The ethical implications of AI in cybersecurity also intersect with broader societal concerns related to job displacement and economic inequality. The automation of routine cybersecurity tasks through AI may lead to changes in the job market, potentially rendering some traditional roles obsolete. Addressing the ethical dimensions of job displacement requires proactive efforts, including retraining and upskilling initiatives, to ensure a smooth transition for workers affected by the integration of AI in cybersecurity. Additionally, ethical considerations include efforts to minimize the impact of AI-driven advancements on economic inequality and disparities in access to opportunities.

The ethical use of AI in cybersecurity requires ongoing scrutiny of the potential for unintended consequences, including the creation of new vulnerabilities and attack vectors. As AI technologies evolve, there is a need for ethical considerations that prioritize the security and resilience of AI systems themselves. Ensuring that AI algorithms are robust against adversarial attacks, transparent in their decision-making processes, and continuously monitored for emerging risks becomes essential for maintaining the integrity of cybersecurity defenses.

AI in cybersecurity also raises ethical considerations related to its impact on democratic processes and individual freedoms. The use of AI in influence campaigns, misinformation, or social engineering attacks can have profound consequences on public discourse, political stability, and societal trust. The ethical responsibility of AI developers, organizations, and governments involves safeguarding against the misuse of AI technologies to manipulate public opinion, disrupt democratic processes, or infringe on individual freedoms. Striking a balance between leveraging AI for cybersecurity and safeguarding democratic principles is a complex ethical challenge that requires ongoing vigilance.

The ethical considerations of using AI in cybersecurity extend to issues of international cooperation and governance. As cyber threats transcend national borders, establishing ethical norms, frameworks, and agreements for the responsible use of AI in cybersecurity becomes crucial. International collaboration is essential to address common challenges, harmonize ethical standards, and prevent the proliferation of AI-driven cyber threats. The absence of globally accepted ethical guidelines poses a risk of fragmented approaches and potential conflicts, emphasizing the need for concerted efforts in shaping international norms for the ethical use of AI in cybersecurity.

In conclusion, the ethical implications of using AI in cybersecurity encompass a wide range of concerns that require careful attention, deliberation, and responsible practices. From privacy and bias to accountability, dual-use challenges, and societal impacts, navigating the ethical dimensions of AI in cybersecurity demands a multifaceted approach. Establishing clear ethical frameworks, fostering transparency, ensuring human oversight, and promoting international collaboration are essential steps in harnessing the benefits of AI while mitigating potential risks and upholding ethical standards in the evolving landscape of cybersecurity.

Discuss the importance of responsible AI practices and avoiding biases.

The importance of responsible Artificial Intelligence (AI) practices, particularly in the context of avoiding biases, cannot be overstated as AI systems play an increasingly pervasive role in shaping various aspects of our lives. Responsible AI practices encompass a set of principles and guidelines aimed at ensuring that AI technologies are developed, deployed, and used ethically and equitably. The ethical imperative is grounded in the recognition that AI systems, driven by machine learning algorithms, can inadvertently perpetuate and even exacerbate biases present in the data on which they are trained. Addressing biases in AI is crucial not only for promoting fairness and inclusivity but also for preventing unintended consequences that may have profound societal impacts.

At the heart of responsible AI practices is the acknowledgment that the data used to train machine learning models may reflect historical biases present in society. These biases can manifest in various forms, including gender, race, ethnicity, socioeconomic status, and other demographic factors. When AI systems are trained on biased data, they can learn and reproduce these biases, leading to discriminatory outcomes in decision-making processes. For instance, biased AI algorithms in hiring or lending processes may perpetuate historical disparities, reinforcing existing inequalities rather than mitigating them.

One key aspect of responsible AI practices involves meticulous data curation and preprocessing to identify and mitigate biases in training datasets. Data scientists and AI developers must critically evaluate the datasets used for training, testing, and validation to identify potential biases and ensure that they do not disproportionately represent certain groups or perspectives. This proactive approach to bias detection and mitigation is foundational for fostering fairness in AI systems and aligns with the ethical commitment to avoid perpetuating societal inequities.

Algorithmic transparency is another critical component of responsible AI practices. Transparency ensures that the decision-making processes of AI models are understandable and interpretable by humans. This transparency facilitates accountability and allows stakeholders, including developers, regulators, and end-users, to comprehend how decisions are reached. When AI systems operate as "black boxes" with opaque decision-making processes, it becomes challenging to identify and rectify biases, leading to potential ethical lapses and diminished trust in AI technologies.

Ensuring diversity and inclusivity in AI development teams is a pivotal element of responsible AI practices. The composition of development teams influences the perspectives, values, and considerations embedded in AI systems. Diverse teams are more likely to identify and address biases effectively, bringing a range of viewpoints and experiences to the design, development, and testing phases. Inclusivity in AI development extends beyond demographic diversity to encompass interdisciplinary collaboration, including input from ethicists, social scientists, and experts in relevant domains, contributing to a more comprehensive and responsible approach to AI development.

Continuous monitoring and auditing of AI systems post-deployment are imperative for identifying and rectifying biases that may emerge in real-world scenarios. Responsible AI practices involve establishing mechanisms for ongoing evaluation, feedback, and refinement of AI models to ensure that they adapt to changing contexts and evolving societal norms. Regular audits can uncover biases introduced by shifts in user behavior, emerging patterns, or changes in the underlying data distribution. This iterative and adaptive approach to monitoring aligns with the ethical commitment to address biases as they emerge and enhance the overall reliability of AI systems.

Educating and raising awareness among stakeholders about the ethical implications of AI and biases is a fundamental aspect of responsible AI practices. Developers, data scientists, decision-makers, and end-users should be well-informed about the potential biases in AI systems, their societal impact, and the ethical considerations involved. This awareness fosters a culture of responsibility and encourages proactive efforts to mitigate biases at every stage of the AI development lifecycle. Moreover, educating end-users about the limitations and potential biases of AI systems promotes transparency and empowers individuals to critically assess the outputs and decisions made by these systems.

An essential principle of responsible AI practices is the commitment to fairness in algorithmic decision-making. Fairness, in this context, implies treating all individuals and groups equitably, without favoring or discriminating against any particular demographic. Various fairness metrics and techniques, such as demographic parity, equalized odds, and disparate impact analysis, can be employed to assess and promote fairness in AI models. Integrating fairness considerations into the design and evaluation of AI algorithms is crucial for avoiding discriminatory outcomes and fostering an ethical and inclusive deployment of AI technologies.

Responsible AI practices extend beyond avoiding biases to encompass broader ethical considerations, including accountability and the responsible use of AI in decision-making. Establishing clear lines of responsibility for AI systems, including defining roles and accountability mechanisms for developers, organizations, and decision-makers, is essential. The ethical use of AI involves considering the potential impact on individuals and society, adhering to legal and regulatory frameworks, and prioritizing the well-being and rights of individuals affected by AI decisions. Mitigating biases in AI also involves exploring techniques and approaches that explicitly address fairness considerations. Fairness-aware machine learning algorithms aim to incorporate fairness constraints during the training process, minimizing disparate impacts on different demographic groups. Additionally, adversarial training, counterfactual fairness, and other advanced methods are emerging as tools to enhance fairness in AI models. Responsible AI practices involve staying abreast of these advancements and integrating them into the development pipeline to continually improve the fairness and ethical soundness of AI systems.

The deployment of AI in sensitive domains, such as criminal justice, healthcare, and finance, amplifies the ethical considerations surrounding biases. Responsible AI practices demand heightened scrutiny and accountability in these contexts, where the potential impact on individuals' lives is significant. Special attention must be given to avoiding biases that could result in unfair treatment, discrimination, or other adverse consequences. Ethical considerations in these domains include ensuring transparency, accountability, and the involvement of domain experts and affected communities in the development and deployment of AI systems.

Global collaboration and the establishment of international standards for responsible AI practices are essential for addressing biases on a broader scale. As AI technologies transcend national boundaries, creating a shared understanding of ethical principles and guidelines is imperative. Collaborative efforts among governments, industry stakeholders, and academia can contribute to the development of ethical frameworks, best practices, and regulatory standards that promote responsible AI use globally. This collaborative approach is instrumental in fostering a collective commitment to addressing biases and ensuring the ethical development and deployment of AI technologies.

In conclusion, the importance of responsible AI practices, particularly in avoiding biases, is paramount for fostering ethical, equitable, and trustworthy AI systems. From meticulous data curation and transparency to diversity in development teams, continuous monitoring, and global collaboration, responsible AI practices encompass a comprehensive set of principles and actions. By prioritizing fairness, accountability, and the responsible use of AI, society can harness the benefits of AI technologies while mitigating potential harms and advancing a future where AI systems contribute positively to the well-being of individuals and the broader global community.

Chapter 7: Incident Response: Strategies for a Cyber Crisis

Discuss the importance of having a dedicated incident response team.

The importance of having a dedicated incident response team within an organization cannot be overstated in today's complex and dynamic cybersecurity landscape. An incident response team plays a pivotal role in safeguarding the organization's digital assets, mitigating the impact of security incidents, and ensuring a swift and effective response to cyber threats. In the face of an increasingly sophisticated and persistent threat landscape, having a dedicated team with the expertise, tools, and protocols to handle security incidents is essential for minimizing the potential damage, protecting sensitive information, and maintaining the overall resilience of the organization's cybersecurity posture.

One of the primary functions of a dedicated incident response team is to provide a proactive and organized approach to cybersecurity incidents. This proactive stance involves anticipating and preparing for potential threats rather than reacting only when incidents occur. The team is responsible for developing and implementing incident response plans, conducting risk assessments, and identifying vulnerabilities within the organization's infrastructure. By having a dedicated team focused on incident response, organizations can establish a robust framework that aligns with industry best practices, regulatory requirements, and the unique risk profile of the organization.

In the event of a cybersecurity incident, the timeliness of the response is critical to minimizing the impact and preventing further damage. A dedicated incident response team is equipped to respond swiftly and decisively, employing predefined processes and procedures to contain, eradicate, and recover from security incidents. The team's expertise enables them to navigate the complexities of various types of incidents, including malware infections, data breaches, denial-of-service attacks, and other cyber threats. Their ability to act quickly and efficiently is instrumental in preventing the escalation of incidents, limiting the scope of compromise, and restoring normal operations promptly.

A dedicated incident response team also contributes to the organization's overall resilience by fostering a culture of continuous improvement and learning. Through regular training, simulations, and knowledge sharing, the team stays abreast of the latest cybersecurity trends, emerging threats, and evolving attack vectors. This ongoing education ensures that the incident response team remains well-equipped to address new challenges and adapt their strategies to the ever-changing threat landscape. The learning culture cultivated within the team enhances the organization's overall cybersecurity posture and contributes to its ability to stay ahead of potential threats.

The forensic capabilities of a dedicated incident response team are instrumental in understanding the root causes of security incidents and gathering evidence for subsequent investigations. When a security incident occurs, the team conducts thorough forensic analyses to determine how the incident occurred, what systems and data were affected, and whether there are indicators of compromise that may indicate broader vulnerabilities. This forensic insight not only aids in the immediate response efforts but also informs long-term security improvements, helping the organization implement measures to prevent similar incidents in the future.

Another critical aspect of the incident response team's role is communication and coordination. Effective communication is essential during a security incident to ensure that all relevant stakeholders are informed, from internal staff and executives to external partners, customers, and regulatory authorities. A dedicated incident response team is well-versed in crafting clear and timely communications that convey the severity of the incident, the steps being taken to address it, and any actions that affected individuals or entities need to take. This transparent and coordinated communication approach helps build trust, manage reputational damage, and comply with regulatory reporting requirements.

Compliance with regulatory frameworks and legal requirements is a significant consideration for organizations across various industries. A dedicated incident response team is well-versed in the regulatory landscape, ensuring that the organization's response efforts align with legal obligations and industry standards. The team assists in preparing for regulatory audits, maintaining documentation of incident response activities, and liaising with legal and compliance teams to address any legal implications arising from security incidents. Compliance is not just a legal obligation but also a crucial element in building trust with stakeholders and demonstrating a commitment to cybersecurity best practices.

The proactive threat intelligence capabilities of an incident response team contribute to the organization's ability to anticipate and defend against emerging threats. By continuously monitoring and analyzing threat intelligence sources, the team gains insights into the tactics, techniques, and procedures (TTPs) employed by threat actors. This intelligence allows the organization to bolster its defenses, adjust security controls, and implement preventive measures to thwart potential attacks before they can manifest. The ability to stay ahead of adversaries is a testament to the strategic value of a dedicated incident response team in maintaining a proactive cybersecurity stance.

Collaboration with other internal and external entities is a hallmark of an effective incident response team. Internally, the team collaborates with IT, security operations, legal, human resources, and other relevant departments to ensure a holistic and coordinated response. Externally, the team engages with law enforcement, regulatory bodies, cybersecurity information sharing communities, and industry peers to share threat intelligence, collaborate on investigations, and contribute to collective defense efforts. This collaborative approach strengthens the organization's overall cybersecurity ecosystem and fosters a sense of community resilience against cyber threats.

The integration of technology and automation is a key enabler for the incident response team to streamline processes and enhance efficiency. Automation tools can assist in rapidly detecting and responding to security incidents, correlating disparate sources of data, and orchestrating response actions. By leveraging technology, the incident response team can focus on higher-level decision-making, analysis, and strategic planning, while routine and repetitive tasks are handled by automated systems. This combination of human expertise and technological efficiency enhances the overall effectiveness of incident response efforts.

A dedicated incident response team is instrumental in conducting post-incident reviews and learning from each security incident. These reviews, also known as post-mortems or after-action reports, analyze the organization's response to the incident, identify areas for improvement, and propose enhancements to incident response plans and processes. This iterative learning cycle ensures that the incident response team evolves and adapts based on real-world experiences, continuously enhancing the organization's ability to respond effectively to new and evolving threats.

In conclusion, the importance of having a dedicated incident response team within an organization cannot be overstated. The team serves as a cornerstone of the organization's cybersecurity strategy, providing proactive, swift, and effective responses to security incidents. From preparing for potential threats to conducting forensic analyses, ensuring compliance, fostering a learning culture, and collaborating with internal and external stakeholders, the incident response team plays a multifaceted role in enhancing the organization's overall cybersecurity resilience. In an era where cyber threats are persistent and evolving, the presence of a dedicated incident response team is a strategic imperative for organizations seeking to protect their digital assets, maintain stakeholder trust, and navigate the complexities of the modern cybersecurity landscape.

Outline the key roles and responsibilities within the team.

Within a dedicated incident response team, various key roles and responsibilities are assigned to ensure the team's effectiveness in responding to cybersecurity incidents. One of the pivotal roles is that of the Incident Response Manager, who is responsible for overseeing the entire incident response process. The Incident Response Manager plays a crucial role in coordinating the team's efforts, making strategic decisions, and liaising with other stakeholders within the organization. This role requires a deep understanding of the organization's cybersecurity posture, the ability to prioritize and allocate resources effectively, and strong communication skills to convey incident details to executive leadership and other relevant parties.

Another essential role within the incident response team is that of the Incident Responder. These individuals are at the forefront of incident detection, analysis, and containment. Incident Responders possess a deep technical understanding of various cyber threats, attack vectors, and malicious techniques. They are adept at using specialized tools for analyzing logs, network traffic, and system artifacts to identify indicators of compromise (IOCs). Incident Responders play a critical role in the initial assessment of incidents, determining the scope and severity, and executing containment measures to prevent further damage. Their quick and accurate decision-making is instrumental in the early stages of incident response.

Forensic Analysts form another integral part of the incident response team, specializing in digital forensics and the investigation of security incidents. These professionals possess expertise in collecting and analyzing digital evidence, reconstructing cyber incidents, and providing insights into the methods used by attackers. Forensic Analysts work closely with Incident Responders to conduct in-depth examinations of compromised systems, networks, and applications. Their findings contribute to understanding the root causes of incidents, aiding in the development of effective response strategies, and providing valuable input for legal and regulatory requirements.

The role of Threat Intelligence Analysts is crucial in ensuring that the incident response team remains proactive and well-informed about emerging cyber threats. Threat Intelligence Analysts monitor and analyze threat intelligence feeds, open-source intelligence, and industry reports to identify potential threats and vulnerabilities. They provide the team with timely and relevant information on the tactics, techniques, and procedures (TTPs) employed by threat actors. This threat intelligence is instrumental in enhancing the organization's overall cybersecurity defenses, preparing for potential threats, and informing incident response strategies.

Network Security Analysts play a pivotal role in monitoring and securing the organization's network infrastructure. They are responsible for analyzing network traffic, detecting anomalous patterns, and identifying potential security incidents. Network Security Analysts collaborate closely with Incident Responders to investigate incidents affecting the network, analyze communication between systems, and assess the impact on critical assets. Their expertise in network protocols, traffic analysis, and intrusion detection systems contributes to the early detection and response to cyber threats targeting the organization's network.

The role of Malware Analysts is dedicated to understanding and combating malicious software. Malware Analysts specialize in analyzing malware samples to identify their functionality, origins, and potential impact on systems. They dissect malware code, reverse engineer binaries, and analyze the behavior of malicious programs. Malware Analysts collaborate with Incident Responders to identify and mitigate malware infections, develop signatures for detection, and contribute to threat intelligence by providing insights into emerging malware trends. Their expertise is essential in countering one of the most prevalent threats in the cybersecurity landscape.

The Legal and Compliance Advisor within the incident response team ensures that all response actions align with legal requirements and regulatory frameworks. This role is responsible for guiding the team in understanding the legal implications of security incidents, providing advice on regulatory reporting obligations, and liaising with legal teams to address any legal consequences. The Legal and Compliance Advisor plays a critical role in maintaining the organization's adherence to privacy laws, data protection regulations, and other legal considerations that may arise during incident response efforts.

Public Relations and Communication Specialists contribute to the incident response team by managing external and internal communications during a security incident. This role involves crafting clear and accurate messages to communicate with stakeholders, customers, the media, and regulatory authorities. Public Relations and Communication Specialists play a crucial role in managing the organization's reputation, building trust, and ensuring transparency during and after a security incident. Their ability to convey complex technical information in a comprehensible manner is essential in maintaining open communication channels and managing the public perception of the incident.

A critical function within the incident response team is that of the Business Continuity and Recovery Specialist. This role is focused on ensuring the continuity of essential business operations during and after a security incident. Business Continuity and Recovery Specialists develop and implement strategies for maintaining critical functions, restoring services, and minimizing downtime. They work closely with other team members to assess the impact of incidents on business processes, identify dependencies, and develop recovery plans. Their expertise is vital in ensuring that the organization can recover swiftly and resume normal operations following a security incident.

Project Managers play a key role in coordinating the various tasks and activities within the incident response team. They are responsible for managing timelines, allocating resources, and ensuring that response efforts are executed efficiently. Project Managers work closely with the Incident Response Manager to develop project plans, track progress, and communicate with team members and stakeholders. Their organizational skills and ability to manage complex projects contribute to the overall effectiveness of the incident response team, ensuring that response efforts are well-coordinated and meet established objectives.

The Education and Training Coordinator focuses on building a culture of awareness, preparedness, and continuous learning within the organization. This role is responsible for developing and delivering training programs for employees, raising awareness about cybersecurity best practices, and conducting simulations and drills to test the organization's incident response capabilities. The Education and Training Coordinator ensures that all team members are well-prepared for their roles, stay abreast of emerging threats, and contribute to the overall resilience of the organization through a commitment to ongoing education and skill development.

Lastly, the Quality Assurance and Improvement Analyst is responsible for evaluating the effectiveness of incident response processes and identifying areas for improvement. This role involves conducting post-incident reviews, analyzing response actions, and providing recommendations for refining incident response plans and procedures. The Quality Assurance and Improvement Analyst contribute to the team's continuous improvement by identifying lessons learned from each incident, assessing the efficiency of response efforts, and proposing enhancements to strengthen the organization's overall incident response capabilities.

In conclusion, the various roles within a dedicated incident response team collectively contribute to building a resilient and effective response capability. From strategic decision-making and technical analysis to legal considerations, communication, and training, each role is integral to the overall success of the team in mitigating the impact of cybersecurity incidents. The collaborative efforts of these diverse roles ensure that organizations are well-prepared, well-coordinated, and well-equipped to navigate the challenges posed by the evolving cybersecurity landscape.

Provide guidance on identifying and classifying cybersecurity incidents.

Identifying and classifying cybersecurity incidents is a fundamental aspect of an effective incident response strategy, essential for organizations seeking to proactively manage and mitigate the impact of security threats. Incident identification involves recognizing abnormal activities, suspicious patterns, or potential security breaches within an organization's IT infrastructure. These incidents can range from relatively minor anomalies to serious security breaches with significant consequences. To aid in the identification process, organizations deploy a variety of monitoring tools, intrusion detection systems, security information and event management (SIEM) solutions, and user behavior analytics, which collectively contribute to the early detection of potential threats.

The first step in identifying cybersecurity incidents is establishing a baseline of normal behavior within the organization's network, systems, and applications. This baseline serves as a reference point against which anomalies and deviations can be identified. Deviations from the norm may include unusual network traffic, atypical user behavior, unexpected system access, or irregular patterns in system logs. Continuous monitoring and analysis of network traffic and system logs enable organizations to detect indicators of compromise (IOCs) that may suggest the presence of malicious activity. Automated tools, such as anomaly detection systems, contribute to the identification process by flagging deviations that may indicate a potential security incident.

User awareness and reporting mechanisms are crucial components in identifying cybersecurity incidents. Employees, being the first line of defense, are often the ones who observe unusual activities or receive suspicious emails. Establishing clear reporting channels and encouraging a culture of cybersecurity awareness empower users to promptly report any perceived anomalies or security concerns. Incident identification benefits significantly from a collaborative approach, where employees actively participate in the organization's cybersecurity efforts by reporting incidents, phishing attempts, or other suspicious activities they encounter.

Organizations often employ threat intelligence feeds to enhance incident identification capabilities. Threat intelligence provides context about known cyber threats, their tactics, techniques, and procedures (TTPs), and indicators of compromise. By integrating threat intelligence into their security operations, organizations can proactively identify and respond to potential threats based on the latest information about emerging risks. Regularly updating threat intelli-

gence sources and correlating this information with internal teleme-
try aids in identifying incidents aligned with known threat profiles.

Once an incident is identified, the next crucial step is classifying
its severity and impact. The classification process involves assessing
the nature and scope of the incident to determine its potential consequences for the organization. Security incidents can be classified
based on various factors, including the type of attack, the assets affected, the level of compromise, and the potential business impact.
Common incident classifications include malware infections, phishing attacks, data breaches, denial-of-service (DoS) attacks, and insider threats. Each classification provides insights into the nature of
the incident, guiding the incident response team in tailoring their response strategies to the specific characteristics of the threat.

The Common Vulnerability Scoring System (CVSS) is a widely
used framework for classifying and prioritizing security vulnerabilities and incidents. CVSS assigns a severity score to vulnerabilities
and incidents based on various factors, including the ease of exploitation, the impact on confidentiality, integrity, and availability, and the
level of user interaction required. This scoring system aids in objec-
tively assessing the severity of incidents, allowing organizations to
prioritize their response efforts based on the potential risk and impact associated with each incident.

The impact of a cybersecurity incident extends beyond technical
considerations and often includes legal, regulatory, and reputational
consequences. The incident response team must assess the potential
impact on sensitive data, compliance with data protection regulations, and any legal obligations for reporting the incident to authorities. Classifying incidents based on their legal and regulatory implications enables organizations to navigate the complex landscape of
compliance requirements and take appropriate actions to meet reporting obligations, thereby mitigating potential legal repercussions.

Understanding the motives and goals of threat actors is a crucial aspect of incident classification. Incidents may be categorized based on the threat actor's objectives, such as financial gain, industrial espionage, hacktivism, or state-sponsored cyber-espionage. Recognizing the motives behind an incident aids in determining the level of sophistication, persistence, and resources employed by the threat actor, influencing the organization's response strategy. For instance, incidents associated with nation-state actors may require a different level of response than those stemming from financially motivated cybercriminals.

The speed and agility with which incidents are classified impact the effectiveness of incident response efforts. Automated incident classification tools, leveraging machine learning and artificial intelligence, can enhance the efficiency of this process by analyzing large datasets, identifying patterns, and categorizing incidents based on predefined criteria. Automation in incident classification is particularly valuable in handling high volumes of security alerts, allowing the incident response team to focus on the most critical and impactful incidents that require immediate attention.

Collaboration and information-sharing within the cybersecurity community contribute to incident identification and classification. Participation in Information Sharing and Analysis Centers (ISACs), industry forums, and collaborative threat intelligence platforms facilitates the exchange of insights and experiences related to cybersecurity incidents. By staying informed about the tactics employed by threat actors across various sectors, organizations can improve their incident identification and classification capabilities, benefiting from collective knowledge and shared best practices.

The contextualization of incidents plays a pivotal role in accurate classification. Contextual factors include the organization's industry, geographic location, the value of compromised assets, and the potential impact on critical business processes. By considering these contextual elements, organizations can tailor their incident response strategies to address the unique challenges and priorities specific to their environment. Context-aware incident classification ensures that response efforts align with the organization's business objectives and risk tolerance.

In conclusion, identifying and classifying cybersecurity incidents are foundational steps in an organization's incident response strategy. From baseline establishment and continuous monitoring to user awareness, threat intelligence integration, and collaboration within the cybersecurity community, multiple factors contribute to the identification of security incidents. Automated tools, frameworks like CVSS, and contextual considerations aid in the efficient classification of incidents, guiding organizations in prioritizing and tailoring their response efforts. A proactive and collaborative approach to incident identification and classification empowers organizations to effectively manage and mitigate the impact of cybersecurity threats in an ever-evolving threat landscape.

Discuss the significance of rapid detection for effective response.

The significance of rapid detection in the realm of cybersecurity cannot be overstated, as it serves as the linchpin for effective incident response strategies. In the dynamic landscape of cyber threats, where adversaries constantly evolve their tactics and exploit vulnerabilities, the ability to detect and identify security incidents swiftly is paramount to minimizing the impact and thwarting potential damage. Rapid detection enables organizations to detect malicious activities, intrusions, and abnormal behaviors at an early stage, allowing for a timely and targeted response that can disrupt ongoing attacks, prevent further compromise, and mitigate the potential consequences of a security incident.

Time is of the essence in cybersecurity, and the "detection deficit" – the time it takes to discover a security incident – significantly influences the overall effectiveness of incident response efforts. The faster an organization can detect a security incident, the greater the likelihood of limiting the damage and preventing the lateral movement of attackers within the network. Rapid detection shortens the "dwell time," representing the duration a threat actor remains undetected within an environment, and consequently reduces the window of opportunity for malicious activities.

One of the critical aspects of rapid detection is the ability to identify indicators of compromise (IOCs) promptly. IOCs are artifacts or patterns that indicate potential security incidents, such as unusual network traffic, suspicious file modifications, or anomalous user behavior. Automated threat detection systems, including intrusion detection systems (IDS), endpoint detection and response (EDR) solutions, and advanced threat intelligence feeds, play a pivotal role in identifying IOCs and alerting security teams to potential threats. By leveraging these technologies, organizations can achieve real-time or near-real-time detection, enhancing their capacity to respond swiftly to emerging threats.

The significance of rapid detection becomes even more pronounced in the context of advanced and persistent threats. Advanced adversaries often employ sophisticated techniques, such as zero-day exploits and polymorphic malware, to evade traditional security measures. Rapid detection mechanisms that incorporate behavioral analysis, anomaly detection, and heuristic approaches can effectively identify novel and evolving threats that may not have known signatures. Machine learning and artificial intelligence-driven detection systems contribute to the agility required to recognize patterns indicative of sophisticated attacks, enabling organizations to respond proactively to emerging threats.

In the face of a constantly evolving threat landscape, where new vulnerabilities and attack vectors emerge regularly, the importance of timely detection becomes a strategic imperative. The rise of ransomware, supply chain attacks, and targeted threats against critical infrastructure underscores the need for organizations to fortify their defenses and enhance their detection capabilities. Rapid detection mechanisms serve as a proactive defense layer, enabling organizations to stay ahead of cyber adversaries, identify emerging threats quickly, and deploy countermeasures to mitigate potential risks.

The significance of rapid detection is heightened when considering the potential consequences of delayed or inadequate response. A delayed response can allow threat actors to escalate their activities, exfiltrate sensitive data, and achieve their objectives with greater impunity. In cases of data breaches, for example, the longer it takes to detect and respond, the more time adversaries have to exploit the compromised environment and exfiltrate valuable information. Rapid detection is, therefore, instrumental in preventing the exfiltration of sensitive data, protecting intellectual property, and preserving the confidentiality and integrity of critical information assets.

Rapid detection is not only about identifying external threats but also about detecting insider threats and inadvertent security incidents caused by employees or trusted entities. Insider threats, whether malicious or unintentional, pose a significant risk to organizations. Swift detection of anomalous user behavior, unauthorized access, or unusual data transfer patterns can help organizations identify and address insider threats promptly, mitigating the potential impact on data security and safeguarding against insider-driven attacks.

The significance of rapid detection extends beyond merely identifying security incidents; it also plays a pivotal role in reducing the mean time to respond (MTTR). MTTR represents the time taken to respond to and mitigate the impact of a security incident once detected. Rapid detection expedites the initiation of incident response activities, allowing security teams to investigate, contain, eradicate, and recover from incidents swiftly. The correlation between rapid detection and a shortened MTTR is critical for minimizing downtime, preserving business continuity, and reducing the overall financial and operational impact of security incidents. Effective incident response is contingent on the ability to prioritize and respond to the most critical threats promptly. Rapid detection facilitates the categorization and prioritization of incidents based on their severity, potential impact, and relevance to the organization's critical assets. Security teams can allocate resources judiciously, focusing on addressing high-priority incidents that pose the greatest risk to the organization. This strategic approach to incident response is particularly crucial in environments where security teams face resource constraints and must optimize their efforts to address the most pressing threats first.

The significance of rapid detection is intertwined with the concept of threat hunting – the proactive and systematic search for indicators of compromise within an organization's environment. Threat hunting involves leveraging human expertise, advanced analytics, and threat intelligence to identify hidden threats that may evade automated detection systems. Rapid detection, coupled with threat hunting capabilities, empowers organizations to proactively seek out potential threats, identify novel attack vectors, and continually refine their detection mechanisms based on evolving threat landscapes.

Timely detection is a fundamental requirement for complying with regulatory mandates and legal obligations. Many data protection regulations and cybersecurity standards, such as the General Data Protection Regulation (GDPR) and the Health Insurance Portability and Accountability Act (HIPAA), mandate organizations to implement measures for the timely detection and reporting of security incidents. Failure to detect and report incidents within stipulated timeframes may result in legal consequences, financial penalties, and reputational damage. Rapid detection, therefore, aligns with regulatory compliance requirements, ensuring that organizations fulfill their obligations and responsibilities in the event of a security incident.

The evolution of security operations toward a more proactive and intelligence-driven model underscores the strategic importance of rapid detection. Security Operations Centers (SOCs) are increasingly adopting Threat Intelligence Platforms (TIPs), Security Orchestration, Automation, and Response (SOAR) solutions, and advanced analytics to enhance their capabilities for rapid incident detection and response. Automation, in particular, enables organizations to automate routine tasks, orchestrate incident response processes, and respond at machine speed, complementing human expertise and accelerating the overall incident response lifecycle.

In conclusion, the significance of rapid detection in cybersecurity is integral to the overall efficacy of incident response strategies. Rapid detection empowers organizations to identify security incidents swiftly, reduce dwell time, and respond effectively to emerging threats. Whether combating advanced adversaries, mitigating the impact of insider threats, or adhering to regulatory requirements, organizations that prioritize rapid detection enhance their resilience in the face of an ever-evolving and dynamic cyber threat landscape. In an era where time is a critical factor in cybersecurity, the ability to detect and respond rapidly is a strategic imperative for organizations seeking to safeguard their digital assets, maintain business continuity, and fortify their defenses against cyber adversaries.

Detail strategies for containing and eradicating cybersecurity threats.

Containment and eradication of cybersecurity threats are pivotal phases in the incident response lifecycle, aiming to prevent further damage, mitigate the impact of incidents, and restore the integrity of compromised systems. These strategies are crucial components of a comprehensive incident response plan, allowing organizations to efficiently address security breaches and minimize the potential consequences of cyber threats. Containment involves isolating the affected systems and preventing the lateral movement of threat actors within the network, while eradication focuses on permanently removing the presence of malicious entities, artifacts, or vulnerabilities from the environment.

One effective strategy for containment involves leveraging network segmentation to isolate compromised systems and limit the potential spread of threats. Network segmentation divides the network into distinct segments, with restricted communication pathways between them. In the event of a security incident, isolating the affected segment containing compromised systems helps prevent the lateral movement of attackers to other parts of the network. Implementing micro-segmentation, where even individual systems are isolated from each other, enhances the precision and effectiveness of containment efforts. This strategy serves as a proactive measure to restrict the impact of incidents and safeguard critical assets.

The rapid deployment of firewalls, intrusion prevention systems (IPS), and network access controls is a critical containment strategy. By configuring these security controls to block or restrict traffic associated with the incident, organizations can prevent malicious communication, unauthorized access, and data exfiltration. Firewalls, in particular, play a crucial role in enforcing access policies and controlling the flow of network traffic. IPS systems can detect and block known attack signatures, while network access controls help manage user permissions and restrict access to critical resources. The coordinated use of these technologies fortifies containment efforts and impedes the progression of cyber threats.

Endpoint security plays a pivotal role in containment by isolating compromised devices and preventing them from interacting with other systems. Endpoint detection and response (EDR) solutions enable security teams to identify and respond to suspicious activities on individual endpoints. When a compromised endpoint is detected, it can be isolated from the network, limiting the impact of the incident. Automated response capabilities in EDR solutions facilitate the swift containment of threats by quarantining affected endpoints, terminating malicious processes, and preventing further compromise. Endpoint security measures are essential in containing threats that target specific devices within an organization's infrastructure.

Another containment strategy involves leveraging deception technologies to mislead and confuse attackers attempting to move laterally within the network. Deception technologies create decoy assets, such as fake servers, credentials, or files, designed to attract and divert the attention of attackers. When threat actors interact with these decoys, security teams receive alerts, allowing them to identify and contain the attackers. Deception technologies not only serve as early-warning systems but also disrupt the attacker's tactics by leading them into controlled environments, minimizing the risk of lateral movement and providing valuable time for containment efforts.

Isolation of compromised systems from critical network resources is a crucial containment measure, especially in the context of ransomware attacks. When a system is identified as compromised, isolating it from the network prevents the rapid spread of ransomware and limits the encryption of files on other connected devices. Network isolation can be achieved by disconnecting affected systems from the network, suspending network shares, or employing virtual local area networks (VLANs) to restrict communication. This containment strategy is essential in preventing the escalation of ransomware incidents and minimizing the impact on organizational data.

Cloud environments require specific containment strategies due to their dynamic nature. Implementing identity and access management (IAM) controls in cloud platforms allows organizations to restrict access to compromised accounts and prevent unauthorized activities. Cloud security posture management (CSPM) tools can be utilized to monitor and enforce security policies across cloud resources, facilitating the rapid detection and containment of misconfigurations or unauthorized access. Additionally, leveraging cloud-native security controls, such as virtual firewalls and network security groups, enhances the ability to isolate and contain threats within cloud environments.

Incident response playbooks, predefined sets of procedures for responding to specific types of incidents, are invaluable tools for swift and effective containment. Developing incident response playbooks enables organizations to outline containment actions based on the characteristics of different threats. Playbooks provide a structured and standardized approach to containment efforts, reducing response times and ensuring that security teams follow established best practices. Well-designed playbooks consider various scenarios, including malware infections, data breaches, and denial-of-service attacks, and provide step-by-step guidance for containing and mitigating each type of incident.

Eradication strategies focus on permanently removing the elements of a security incident, including malware, vulnerabilities, and unauthorized access points, to prevent the possibility of reinfection. One fundamental eradication measure involves patching and updating systems to address vulnerabilities exploited by the threat. Regularly applying security patches and updates to operating systems, applications, and software components helps eliminate the entry points used by attackers. Automated patch management systems streamline the process, ensuring that all systems are promptly updated and protected against known vulnerabilities.

The thorough scanning and cleaning of systems for malware and malicious artifacts are essential eradication strategies. Leveraging antivirus and antimalware solutions aids in the identification and removal of malicious software. Advanced threat hunting techniques, including file integrity monitoring and memory analysis, assist security teams in detecting and eradicating lingering malware that may attempt to evade traditional security measures. In the case of persistent threats, organizations may need to employ specialized malware removal tools and engage in manual analysis to ensure complete eradication.

Credential hygiene is a critical eradication strategy, focusing on resetting compromised credentials and implementing stronger authentication measures. In the aftermath of a security incident, especially those involving unauthorized access or credential theft, organizations must revoke compromised credentials, force password resets, and implement multi-factor authentication (MFA) to enhance account security. This eradication measure prevents threat actors from using stolen or compromised credentials to maintain unauthorized access and ensures the integrity of user accounts within the organization.

Security teams can employ threat intelligence to inform eradication efforts by understanding the tactics, techniques, and procedures (TTPs) employed by threat actors. Threat intelligence feeds provide insights into the indicators of compromise (IOCs) associated with specific threats, guiding security teams in the identification and removal of malicious entities. Integrating threat intelligence into security tools and platforms automates the process of matching IOCs with network and endpoint data, expediting the eradication of threats based on the latest threat intelligence.

Regular and comprehensive system audits contribute to the eradication of security threats by identifying and remediating unauthorized changes, configurations, or access rights. Audits help ensure that systems are configured securely, adhere to organizational policies, and do not contain lingering artifacts from previous incidents. Automated configuration management tools assist in maintaining the desired state of systems, rolling back unauthorized changes, and preventing the persistence of malicious configurations. A robust incident response team with expertise in digital forensics plays a crucial role in the eradication phase. Digital forensics involves the systematic examination of digital evidence to reconstruct events, identify the root causes of incidents, and trace the actions of threat actors. Forensic analysts use specialized tools and techniques to analyze logs, memory dumps, and file systems, uncovering the extent of the compromise and identifying residual artifacts. The insights gained from digital forensics inform eradication strategies, ensuring a thorough and meticulous removal of all traces of a security incident.

Collaboration with external partners, including incident response service providers, law enforcement agencies, and industry peers, enhances the efficacy of eradication efforts. External partners bring specialized expertise, threat intelligence, and additional resources to bear on the eradication process. Law enforcement collaboration may be particularly relevant in cases of cybercrime, facilitating the legal pursuit of threat actors and contributing to the broader cybersecurity ecosystem's collective defense against sophisticated adversaries.

Post-incident reviews and lessons learned sessions are critical components of the eradication phase. Analyzing the effectiveness of containment and eradication measures used during an incident provides valuable insights for improving incident response processes. Organizations can identify areas for enhancement, refine their incident response playbooks, and implement proactive measures to prevent similar incidents in the future. The continuous improvement cycle ensures that the organization's incident response capabilities evolve to match the evolving threat landscape.

In conclusion, containment and eradication strategies form the cornerstone of effective incident response, enabling organizations to respond swiftly and decisively to cybersecurity threats. By isolating compromised systems, preventing lateral movement, and permanently removing malicious entities, organizations can minimize the impact of incidents, protect critical assets, and restore the integrity of their digital environment. The holistic approach to incident response, encompassing technical controls, human expertise, threat intelligence, and collaborative efforts, ensures a resilient defense against the dynamic and evolving nature of cyber threats.

Discuss the importance of isolating affected systems to prevent further damage.

The importance of isolating affected systems in cybersecurity cannot be overstated, as it stands as a foundational and proactive measure to prevent further damage, contain the spread of threats, and ultimately safeguard the overall security and functionality of an organization's digital infrastructure. In the dynamic landscape of cyber threats, where adversaries constantly refine their tactics and exploit vulnerabilities, the swift and strategic isolation of affected systems serves as a crucial linchpin in the broader incident response strategy.

One of the primary reasons for the emphasis on isolating affected systems lies in the rapid pace at which cyber threats evolve and propagate. Cybersecurity incidents, ranging from malware infections to advanced persistent threats, often leverage vulnerabilities to move laterally within a network. By isolating affected systems promptly, security teams can disrupt the potential spread of threats, preventing the lateral movement that could lead to the compromise of additional assets. This containment strategy is particularly critical in environments where interconnected systems create pathways for threat actors to navigate and escalate their activities.

Isolation plays a pivotal role in breaking the chain of attack progression, especially in scenarios where malware or malicious actors attempt to move laterally to compromise more resources. Whether it's a ransomware attack attempting to encrypt files on shared network drives or an advanced threat seeking to compromise privileged accounts, isolating affected systems creates a barrier, limiting the impact on critical assets and preventing the broader compromise of an organization's digital ecosystem. This containment strategy aligns with the principle of minimizing the attack surface, reducing the potential avenues for exploitation.

Moreover, the importance of isolating affected systems extends beyond merely disrupting the lateral movement of threats; it is integral to preserving the integrity of data and critical assets. In instances of a data breach or unauthorized access, isolating the compromised system prevents further exfiltration of sensitive information. By creating a controlled environment around the affected system, security teams can limit the potential exposure of sensitive data, protecting intellectual property, customer information, and other valuable assets from unauthorized access or theft.

The swift isolation of affected systems is particularly crucial in scenarios involving advanced persistent threats (APTs) or targeted attacks. These sophisticated adversaries often employ stealthy techniques to maintain a foothold within a network for extended periods. Isolation disrupts their ability to persist and move stealthily, forcing them to reevaluate their tactics. This containment measure not only mitigates the immediate impact but also introduces uncertainty and complexity into the attacker's operational plan, potentially revealing their presence and thwarting their objectives.

The importance of isolating affected systems becomes even more pronounced in the context of emerging threats, such as zero-day exploits or polymorphic malware. These threats may not have known signatures, making them challenging to detect using traditional security measures. Isolation provides a proactive defense mechanism by limiting the potential damage while security teams investigate and develop effective countermeasures. It buys valuable time for analysis, allowing organizations to understand the nature of the threat and deploy targeted responses without waiting for signature updates or predefined detection methods.

Beyond the technical aspects, the isolation of affected systems aligns with broader risk management and compliance objectives. In the face of regulatory requirements and data protection laws, organizations must demonstrate due diligence in safeguarding sensitive information. Isolation, as part of an incident response strategy, showcases a commitment to containing incidents promptly, reducing the likelihood of regulatory penalties, legal consequences, and reputational damage associated with the compromise of sensitive data.

Furthermore, the importance of isolating affected systems is underscored by the need for a methodical and well-coordinated response to security incidents. Isolation is not a standalone action but an integral component of a broader incident response plan. Coordinated efforts in isolating affected systems help ensure that security teams act in a synchronized manner, minimizing disruptions to normal business operations while containing the impact of the incident. This collaborative approach enhances the organization's resilience and ability to respond effectively to the evolving threat landscape.

In situations where immediate isolation is not possible, organizations may opt for containment measures such as network segmentation. Network segmentation involves dividing the network into distinct segments with restricted communication pathways. While not equivalent to isolating a specific system, this strategy limits the lateral movement of threats and contains their impact within defined segments. It exemplifies the adaptability of containment strategies to suit the unique characteristics of different environments, considering factors such as business continuity requirements, operational dependencies, and the specific nature of the incident.

The proactive nature of isolating affected systems aligns with the principles of risk mitigation and incident prevention. Rather than relying solely on reactive measures, such as signature-based detection or post-incident remediation, isolating affected systems empowers organizations to take preemptive action, disrupting the progression of cyber threats before they can inflict substantial damage. This proactive stance is particularly essential in an era where the volume and sophistication of cyber threats demand a holistic and anticipatory approach to cybersecurity.

In conclusion, the importance of isolating affected systems in cybersecurity is multifaceted, addressing the dynamic and evolving nature of cyber threats. It is a strategic and proactive measure that not only prevents further damage but also preserves the integrity of critical assets, minimizes the risk of data breaches, and demonstrates compliance with regulatory requirements. As an integral component of incident response, isolating affected systems reflects a commitment to resilience, risk management, and the ongoing effort to stay ahead of adversaries in an ever-changing digital landscape.

Outline effective communication protocols for internal and external stakeholders.

Establishing effective communication protocols for both internal and external stakeholders is a cornerstone of successful organizational management and crisis response. These protocols serve as a framework for conveying information in a clear, timely, and transparent manner, fostering collaboration, maintaining trust, and enabling informed decision-making. Whether addressing routine business matters, navigating organizational changes, or responding to crises, well-defined communication protocols contribute to the overall efficiency and resilience of an organization.

Internally, fostering open and transparent communication is essential for maintaining a cohesive and informed workforce. Establishing regular channels of communication, such as company-wide emails, intranet updates, and town hall meetings, creates a sense of transparency and inclusivity. Providing employees with a clear understanding of organizational goals, changes, and developments enhances their engagement and alignment with the company's mission. In times of change or uncertainty, organizations can leverage targeted communication strategies, such as interactive Q&A sessions or dedicated forums, to address employee concerns, gather feedback, and ensure that accurate information is disseminated promptly.

Moreover, effective internal communication protocols involve tailoring messages to different stakeholders within the organization. Executives may require concise, high-level updates, while frontline employees may benefit from more detailed and context-rich information. Utilizing a multi-channel approach, including email, team meetings, and collaboration platforms, ensures that information is disseminated comprehensively and reaches all levels of the organization. Additionally, providing avenues for two-way communication, such as employee surveys or suggestion boxes, fosters a culture of feedback and continuous improvement.

In times of crisis or change, internal communication protocols take on added significance. Establishing a crisis communication plan with predefined roles, responsibilities, and communication channels helps organizations respond swiftly and effectively. This plan should include a designated crisis communication team, a centralized communication hub, and predefined templates for various communication scenarios. Clear and consistent messaging, aligned with the organization's values and priorities, is paramount during crises, helping to manage uncertainties and reassure employees. Training key personnel in crisis communication, conducting regular drills, and maintaining updated contact lists contribute to the readiness of the organization to handle unforeseen challenges.

External communication protocols are equally crucial, as they determine how an organization engages with clients, partners, regulators, and the wider community. Maintaining transparency and consistency in external messaging builds credibility and trust, essential elements for sustaining positive relationships. Establishing a centralized point of contact for external communication ensures a unified voice and reduces the risk of conflicting messages. Regular updates through official channels, such as press releases, website announcements, and social media platforms, keep external stakeholders informed and mitigate the potential spread of misinformation.

For public-facing communications, organizations must align their messaging with the broader organizational narrative and values. This ensures that external stakeholders perceive a consistent brand image and understand the organization's stance on relevant issues. Clear communication of corporate social responsibility initiatives, ethical business practices, and environmental sustainability efforts contributes to a positive public image and fosters goodwill among external stakeholders. Social media, in particular, offers a dynamic platform for engaging with the public, responding to inquiries, and showcasing the organization's commitment to transparency and accountability.

Navigating external communications during a crisis demands a well-coordinated and agile approach. Establishing a crisis communication team with representatives from key departments, including public relations, legal, and executive leadership, ensures a comprehensive and unified response. The team should be equipped with pre-approved crisis communication templates, guidelines for media interactions, and protocols for addressing the public. A designated spokesperson, trained in crisis communication, serves as the primary conduit for official information, reducing the risk of conflicting messages and ensuring that the organization's narrative remains controlled.

In the realm of external communication, managing stakeholder expectations is vital. Clearly articulating organizational goals, timelines, and potential challenges contributes to realistic expectations, minimizing the risk of disappointment or dissatisfaction among stakeholders. In the case of project updates, product releases, or service changes, organizations benefit from establishing proactive communication schedules and providing stakeholders with opportunities for feedback. This collaborative approach fosters a sense of partnership and inclusivity, reinforcing the organization's commitment to transparency and customer-centricity.

External communication protocols also extend to regulatory compliance and reporting. Organizations must ensure that they adhere to legal requirements regarding the disclosure of information, data protection, and industry-specific regulations. Establishing a clear process for regulatory reporting, including the identification of responsible parties, timelines, and documentation requirements, helps organizations fulfill their obligations and mitigate the risk of legal repercussions. Timely and accurate reporting to regulatory bodies and stakeholders contributes to the organization's reputation for compliance and ethical business practices.

Crisis communication with external stakeholders requires a nuanced and empathetic approach. Acknowledging the impact of a crisis, expressing empathy, and outlining concrete steps being taken to address the situation contribute to a sense of accountability and trust. Organizations should leverage multiple communication channels, including press releases, media briefings, and social media, to reach diverse audiences. Transparency about the organization's response, mitigation efforts, and plans for recovery helps manage external perceptions and reinforces the commitment to resolving challenges responsibly.

In summary, effective communication protocols, both internal and external, are integral to the overall success, resilience, and reputation of an organization. Internally, clear and transparent communication fosters employee engagement, alignment with organizational goals, and a culture of continuous improvement. Externally, well-defined communication strategies contribute to positive relationships with clients, partners, and the wider community, building trust and credibility. During crises or periods of change, these protocols become even more critical, serving as a guide for navigating challenges, managing perceptions, and ensuring that the organization's narrative remains consistent and controlled.

Discuss transparency and accountability in communicating cybersecurity incidents.

Transparency and accountability play pivotal roles in effectively communicating cybersecurity incidents, reflecting the principles of openness, honesty, and responsibility. In an era where cyber threats are pervasive, and organizations face an ever-increasing risk of security breaches, how an organization communicates about cybersecurity incidents profoundly influences its reputation, customer trust, and overall resilience. Transparent communication involves openly sharing information about the incident, its impact, and the steps taken for mitigation. Accountability, on the other hand, entails taking responsibility for the incident, acknowledging any shortcomings, and demonstrating a commitment to addressing vulnerabilities. These two principles are interconnected, forming the foundation of a robust and ethical approach to managing cybersecurity incidents.

When a cybersecurity incident occurs, transparency is paramount in building trust with internal and external stakeholders. This begins with a timely and clear acknowledgment of the incident. Organizations must communicate promptly, avoiding delays that could lead to speculation or the spread of misinformation. Transparency extends to providing a comprehensive understanding of the nature of the incident, the potential impact on affected parties, and the steps being taken to investigate and address the issue. By sharing this information openly, organizations demonstrate a commitment to accountability and provide stakeholders with the clarity needed to navigate the situation.

Disclosing the scope and impact of a cybersecurity incident is a delicate but necessary aspect of transparency. Organizations may be tempted to downplay the severity of an incident to protect their reputation, but such an approach is counterproductive. Stakeholders, including customers, employees, and partners, value honesty and openness. A transparent communication strategy involves providing a realistic assessment of the incident's impact on sensitive data, systems, and services. This enables affected parties to understand the potential risks and take appropriate actions to protect themselves, such as changing passwords or monitoring accounts for suspicious activities.

Transparency also extends to the organization's communication about the root causes of the incident. While investigations may take time, providing insights into how the incident occurred helps build credibility. Sharing technical details without compromising security, such as the attack vector, exploited vulnerabilities, or the type of malware involved, enhances transparency and demonstrates a commitment to addressing systemic weaknesses. This level of disclosure not only informs stakeholders but also contributes to the broader cybersecurity community's collective knowledge, fostering a collaborative and learning-oriented approach to incident response.

Acknowledging the challenges and uncertainties surrounding incident response is another facet of transparency. Cybersecurity incidents are dynamic, and investigations may uncover new information over time. Organizations should communicate transparently about the evolving nature of the incident, updating stakeholders as new details emerge. This openness helps manage expectations, demonstrating that the organization is actively engaged in understanding the incident and adapting its response accordingly. In cases where the full extent of the incident is not immediately apparent, regular updates contribute to maintaining trust and credibility.

While transparency focuses on sharing information openly, accountability addresses the organization's responsibility for the incident and its aftermath. Accountability begins with accepting that a cybersecurity incident has occurred, regardless of its scale or complexity. Organizations must resist the temptation to conceal incidents out of fear of reputational damage. Instead, embracing accountability involves acknowledging that no system is entirely invulnerable and that incidents are an unfortunate reality in the digital age. By doing so, organizations position themselves as responsible stewards of data and technology, committed to addressing challenges head-on.

One of the key elements of accountability is taking ownership of any mistakes or shortcomings that may have contributed to the incident. This involves conducting a thorough post-incident analysis to identify gaps in cybersecurity controls, lapses in security hygiene, or failures in incident detection and response. Publicly acknowledging these shortcomings, along with a commitment to remediation, demonstrates a genuine commitment to learning from the incident and improving the organization's security posture. This level of transparency instills confidence among stakeholders that the organization is serious about preventing similar incidents in the future.

Organizations must also be accountable for their response to a cybersecurity incident. This includes the effectiveness and timeliness of incident detection, containment, and recovery efforts. Communication about these response activities should be transparent, providing stakeholders with insights into the measures being taken to mitigate the impact of the incident. Organizations should be prepared to answer questions about their incident response plan, the involvement of external experts, and any third-party collaborations to resolve the incident. This proactive communication underscores the organization's commitment to accountability and its dedication to resolving the situation promptly and thoroughly.

Legal and regulatory compliance is a critical aspect of accountability in cybersecurity incident communication. Organizations must navigate a complex landscape of data protection laws, industry regulations, and reporting requirements. Adhering to these compliance obligations ensures that the organization is accountable to regulatory bodies and legal frameworks. Transparent communication about compliance efforts, investigations, and any legal consequences arising from the incident is essential. Organizations should be clear about their commitment to fulfilling reporting requirements, cooperating with authorities, and maintaining the highest standards of ethical conduct throughout the incident response process.

Public relations and external communications are integral to the accountability component of incident communication. Organizations must craft clear, consistent, and coordinated messages to external stakeholders, such as customers, partners, and the public. Public statements should align with the facts of the incident, avoiding misleading or overly optimistic language. Demonstrating accountability involves being forthcoming about the steps being taken to address the incident, prevent future occurrences, and support affected individuals. A well-managed public relations strategy reinforces the organization's commitment to transparency and accountability.

Moreover, accountability extends to the ongoing efforts to improve cybersecurity practices and resilience. Post-incident, organizations should conduct a comprehensive review of their security policies, procedures, and technical controls. This self-assessment should be communicated transparently, outlining the identified areas for improvement and the strategic initiatives planned to enhance the organization's cybersecurity posture. Sharing lessons learned from the incident fosters a culture of continuous improvement and positions the organization as a proactive advocate for cybersecurity best practices.

In conclusion, transparency and accountability are inseparable components of effective communication in the aftermath of a cybersecurity incident. Transparency involves openly sharing information about the incident, its impact, and the steps taken for mitigation, while accountability entails taking responsibility for the incident, acknowledging any shortcomings, and demonstrating a commitment to addressing vulnerabilities. Together, these principles form the bedrock of ethical and responsible incident communication, fostering trust, credibility, and a resilient cybersecurity posture for organizations in the face of evolving cyber threats.

Discuss the importance of post-incident analysis for continuous improvement.

The importance of post-incident analysis in the realm of cybersecurity cannot be overstated, as it serves as a linchpin for continuous improvement, resilience, and the evolution of organizational defenses in the face of dynamic and persistent cyber threats. Post-incident analysis, often referred to as incident debriefing, involves a systematic examination of the events, actions, and outcomes surrounding a cybersecurity incident. This comprehensive review aims not only to understand the specific circumstances of the incident but, more importantly, to extract valuable insights that inform strategic enhancements to an organization's security posture. The significance of post-incident analysis lies in its ability to transform a cybersecurity incident from a disruptive event into a catalyst for learning, adaptability, and proactive defense measures.

One primary importance of post-incident analysis is its role in identifying the root causes and contributing factors of a cybersecurity incident. Understanding how and why an incident occurred is fundamental to preventing similar occurrences in the future. This analysis delves into the technical aspects of the incident, including the vulnerabilities exploited, the tactics employed by threat actors, and the weaknesses in existing security controls. By unraveling the intricacies of the incident, organizations gain a nuanced understanding of the specific areas where their defenses were breached, paving the way for targeted and strategic improvements.

The knowledge gained from post-incident analysis extends beyond the technical details to encompass the human and process-related aspects of incident response. It provides insights into how well the incident response plan was executed, the effectiveness of communication protocols, and the collaboration between different teams and stakeholders. Evaluating the human factors involved in incident response helps organizations identify areas for training, skill development, or the refinement of internal processes. This holistic understanding contributes to a more resilient and adaptive cybersecurity posture that acknowledges the interconnected nature of technology, people, and processes.

Moreover, post-incident analysis plays a crucial role in refining and optimizing an organization's incident response plan. Incident response plans are dynamic documents that should evolve based on the lessons learned from real-world incidents. By scrutinizing the organization's response to a cybersecurity incident, the analysis can identify gaps, bottlenecks, or inefficiencies in the established procedures. This, in turn, enables organizations to update their incident response plans to better align with the evolving threat landscape, emerging attack vectors, and the unique characteristics of their own IT environment.

The continuous improvement facilitated by post-incident analysis extends to the enhancement of detection and monitoring capabilities. By examining how the incident was initially detected, organizations can refine their detection mechanisms to identify similar threats more rapidly in the future. This may involve updating or deploying new intrusion detection systems, fine-tuning security information and event management (SIEM) rules, or incorporating threat intelligence feeds to bolster the organization's ability to proactively identify and respond to emerging threats.

Post-incident analysis is instrumental in addressing the concept of "dwell time," referring to the duration between the initial compromise and the detection and containment of a cybersecurity incident. By scrutinizing the timeline of events during an incident, organizations can pinpoint where delays occurred and what contributed to prolonged dwell times. Reducing dwell time is crucial in minimizing the potential impact of incidents, preventing further lateral movement by threat actors, and mitigating the risk of data exfiltration. The insights gained from this analysis inform strategies for accelerating incident detection, response, and containment efforts.

Organizations can leverage post-incident analysis to assess the effectiveness of their incident containment measures. Understanding how well the organization prevented the lateral movement of attackers, isolated affected systems, and mitigated the impact on critical assets provides crucial feedback for refining containment strategies. This analysis helps organizations evaluate the effectiveness of security controls, such as firewalls, intrusion prevention systems, and endpoint protection, and fine-tune these measures to thwart similar tactics employed by threat actors in the future.

Another vital aspect of post-incident analysis is its contribution to risk management and vulnerability management processes. By identifying the specific vulnerabilities exploited during an incident, organizations can prioritize patching and remediation efforts. This strategic approach ensures that resources are allocated to address the most critical vulnerabilities first, reducing the overall risk exposure. Additionally, organizations can use the insights gained from the analysis to enhance their vulnerability scanning programs, ensuring a proactive and continuous assessment of the security landscape.

Furthermore, post-incident analysis plays a pivotal role in fostering a culture of organizational learning and resilience. Rather than viewing incidents solely as disruptive events, organizations that embrace post-incident analysis as a cornerstone of their cybersecurity strategy see incidents as opportunities to learn, adapt, and fortify their defenses. This cultural shift promotes a proactive mindset among cybersecurity teams, encouraging them to seek continuous improvement, stay informed about emerging threats, and anticipate potential weaknesses in the organization's security posture.

Post-incident analysis contributes significantly to the development of threat intelligence within an organization. The analysis provides a wealth of information about the tactics, techniques, and procedures (TTPs) employed by threat actors. This intelligence is invaluable for creating or refining threat models specific to the organization's industry, sector, or geographic location. Armed with this contextual understanding, organizations can bolster their threat intelligence feeds, ensuring that their defenses are informed by real-world incidents and the evolving tactics of cyber adversaries.

The insights derived from post-incident analysis are instrumental in communicating effectively with internal and external stakeholders. Internally, the analysis findings can be used to educate employees about the evolving threat landscape, the importance of cybersecurity best practices, and the role each individual plays in maintaining a secure environment. Externally, organizations can leverage the lessons learned to communicate transparently with customers, partners, and regulatory bodies. Open and honest communication about incident response efforts, improvements made, and steps taken to prevent future incidents enhances an organization's credibility and builds trust.

In conclusion, the importance of post-incident analysis for continuous improvement in cybersecurity cannot be overstated. This process goes beyond a retrospective examination of incidents; it serves as a catalyst for learning, adaptation, and strategic refinement of an organization's cybersecurity posture. By dissecting the technical, human, and procedural aspects of incidents, organizations gain valuable insights that inform targeted improvements to their defenses, incident response capabilities, and overall resilience. Post-incident analysis is not just a reactive measure; it is a proactive strategy that transforms cybersecurity incidents into opportunities for growth, strengthening an organization's ability to navigate the ever-changing landscape of cyber threats.

Provide a framework for remediating vulnerabilities and strengthening future incident response efforts.

Establishing a robust framework for remediating vulnerabilities and fortifying future incident response efforts is critical for organizations seeking to enhance their cybersecurity resilience in the face of evolving threats. This comprehensive framework encompasses a continuum of proactive measures, reactive responses, and continuous improvement cycles, aligning with industry best practices and standards. The process begins with a thorough vulnerability management program that includes vulnerability identification, prioritization, remediation, and ongoing monitoring. Simultaneously, incident response efforts are refined through continuous training, scenario-based exercises, and the integration of lessons learned from past incidents. This dynamic framework, driven by a commitment to proactive defense and continuous improvement, serves as a strategic blueprint for organizations aiming to strengthen their cybersecurity posture.

The foundation of the framework lies in establishing a robust vulnerability management program. This program begins with the systematic identification of vulnerabilities within the organization's IT infrastructure. This entails regular vulnerability scanning of systems, networks, and applications to identify potential weaknesses. Automated scanning tools, combined with manual assessments, contribute to a comprehensive understanding of the organization's attack surface. This initial step sets the stage for informed decision-making by providing a baseline of vulnerabilities that need to be addressed.

Once vulnerabilities are identified, prioritization becomes a crucial component of the framework. Not all vulnerabilities pose the same level of risk, and organizations must prioritize remediation efforts based on factors such as the severity of the vulnerability, the criticality of the affected systems, and the potential impact on business operations. A risk-based approach ensures that resources are allocated efficiently, addressing the most critical vulnerabilities that pose the greatest threat to the organization's security.

Remediating vulnerabilities involves deploying patches, updates, or configuration changes to eliminate or mitigate the identified weaknesses. This process requires a well-defined and agile patch management system that can promptly address critical vulnerabilities as soon as patches become available. Automated patch deployment tools, coupled with testing procedures to ensure minimal disruption to operations, contribute to a streamlined and effective remediation process. Additionally, organizations should consider employing compensating controls or temporary mitigations to reduce the risk associated with unpatched vulnerabilities while maintaining business continuity.

Simultaneously, the framework recognizes the importance of ongoing monitoring and assessment to ensure the sustained effectiveness of vulnerability remediation efforts. Continuous vulnerability scanning, penetration testing, and red teaming contribute to the identification of new vulnerabilities introduced by system changes, updates, or evolving threat landscapes. Regular assessments provide organizations with the agility to adapt their remediation strategies based on the dynamic nature of cybersecurity threats, technologies, and organizational changes.

In conjunction with the vulnerability management program, organizations should integrate incident response into the framework to create a holistic approach to cybersecurity. This involves developing and maintaining a well-documented incident response plan that outlines roles, responsibilities, and procedures for responding to security incidents. The incident response plan should be regularly updated to reflect changes in the organizational environment, emerging threat vectors, and the lessons learned from past incidents. Additionally, the plan should be accessible to all relevant stakeholders and should undergo regular testing through tabletop exercises and simulated incident scenarios.

Training and awareness play a crucial role in strengthening incident response capabilities within the framework. Employees, ranging from IT staff to executives, should receive regular training on recognizing and reporting security incidents. This training not only empowers individuals to contribute to incident detection but also ensures a coordinated and informed response when incidents occur. Furthermore, organizations should conduct realistic and scenario-based training exercises that simulate various cyber threats, allowing incident response teams to practice their skills, test the effectiveness of the response plan, and identify areas for improvement.

The framework emphasizes the importance of real-time incident detection and response capabilities to minimize the impact of security incidents. Organizations should invest in advanced threat detection tools, security information and event management (SIEM) systems, and threat intelligence feeds that enable the proactive identification of anomalous activities or potential security breaches. Automated incident detection, combined with manual analysis by skilled cybersecurity professionals, enhances the organization's ability to detect and respond to incidents swiftly.

Post-incident analysis is a crucial component of the framework, serving as a feedback loop for continuous improvement. After an incident is resolved, organizations should conduct a comprehensive analysis to understand the root causes, the effectiveness of the incident response plan, and the overall lessons learned. This analysis contributes valuable insights to both the incident response and vulnerability management components of the framework, informing strategies to prevent similar incidents in the future and improve the organization's overall cybersecurity posture.

The framework places a strong emphasis on collaboration and communication throughout the incident response lifecycle. Effective communication ensures that all relevant stakeholders are informed promptly and accurately during an incident. This includes internal teams, external partners, regulatory bodies, and, when necessary, the public. Transparent and timely communication builds trust, manages expectations, and demonstrates the organization's commitment to addressing security incidents responsibly.

Integration with threat intelligence is a key aspect of the framework, enhancing the organization's ability to anticipate and respond to emerging threats. By leveraging threat intelligence feeds, organizations can proactively update their incident response plans, fine-tune detection capabilities, and prioritize remediation efforts based on the latest threat landscape. This integration ensures that incident response efforts are informed by real-time and relevant threat data, contributing to a more adaptive and resilient cybersecurity posture.

Continuous improvement is woven into the fabric of the framework, creating a cyclical process that drives ongoing enhancement of cybersecurity capabilities. The insights gained from post-incident analyses, vulnerability assessments, and threat intelligence integration feed into a continuous improvement loop. Organizations use this information to refine incident response plans, update vulnerability management strategies, and invest in technologies that address emerging threats. This iterative approach ensures that the organization's cybersecurity posture evolves in tandem with the ever-changing threat landscape.

The framework also recognizes the importance of regular audits and assessments to validate the effectiveness of vulnerability management and incident response efforts. External audits, internal assessments, and penetration testing provide an objective evaluation of the organization's security controls, policies, and procedures. These assessments contribute to the refinement of the framework by identifying areas of strength, uncovering weaknesses, and validating the organization's overall cybersecurity resilience.

Moreover, the framework acknowledges the necessity of legal and regulatory compliance in the realm of cybersecurity. Organizations must align their vulnerability management and incident response efforts with relevant laws, regulations, and industry standards. This includes data protection regulations, breach notification requirements, and sector-specific compliance mandates. By ensuring adherence to legal and regulatory frameworks, organizations demonstrate a commitment to ethical conduct, transparency, and accountability in their cybersecurity practices.

In conclusion, the framework for remediating vulnerabilities and strengthening incident response efforts is a dynamic and multifaceted approach that integrates vulnerability management, incident response, continuous improvement, collaboration, and compliance. By establishing a well-defined and adaptive framework, organizations can systematically address vulnerabilities, enhance incident detection and response capabilities, and fortify their overall cybersecurity posture. This strategic blueprint ensures that cybersecurity efforts align with industry best practices, legal requirements, and the evolving nature of cyber threats, contributing to a resilient and proactive defense against the challenges of the digital landscape.

Chapter 8: Emerging Technologies and Future Trends in Cybersecurity

Explore the potential impact of quantum computing on cybersecurity.

Quantum computing, a paradigm-shifting approach to computation, has the potential to revolutionize various fields, and its impact on cybersecurity is a topic of intense scrutiny and speculation. Classical computers process information using bits that exist in one of two states, 0 or 1, whereas quantum computers leverage quantum bits or qubits, which can exist in multiple states simultaneously due to the principles of superposition and entanglement. This unique property enables quantum computers to perform certain calculations exponentially faster than classical computers, posing both opportunities and challenges for the realm of cybersecurity.

One of the most significant impacts of quantum computing on cybersecurity lies in its ability to break widely used encryption algorithms. Many contemporary encryption protocols, such as RSA and ECC, rely on the difficulty of certain mathematical problems—such as factoring large numbers or solving discrete logarithms—for their security. Shor's algorithm, a quantum algorithm developed by mathematician Peter Shor, has demonstrated the potential to solve these problems exponentially faster than the best-known classical algorithms. As a result, once large-scale, fault-tolerant quantum computers become a reality, they could compromise the security of widely deployed cryptographic systems, undermining the confidentiality and integrity of sensitive data transmitted over the internet.

To mitigate the impending threat posed by quantum computing to classical cryptographic systems, the field of post-quantum cryptography has emerged. Researchers are actively developing cryptographic algorithms that are believed to be secure against quantum attacks. These algorithms, often based on mathematical problems considered hard even for quantum computers, aim to provide a secure transition for digital communication in the quantum era. The National Institute of Standards and Technology (NIST) is spearheading standardization efforts to select quantum-resistant cryptographic algorithms through a public competition, acknowledging the need for a seamless transition to quantum-safe encryption.

However, the impact of quantum computing on cybersecurity extends beyond encryption. Quantum computers could also enhance certain aspects of cybersecurity, particularly in the realm of secure communication. Quantum key distribution (QKD), a quantum cryptographic protocol, leverages the principles of quantum mechanics to enable the secure exchange of cryptographic keys between parties. Unlike classical key exchange methods, QKD is theoretically immune to attacks by quantum computers, providing a foundation for the development of quantum-safe communication channels. While practical implementation challenges remain, QKD holds promise as a secure method for key distribution in the post-quantum era.

In addition to its implications for encryption and secure communication, quantum computing introduces challenges to the field of digital signatures. Digital signatures, a fundamental component of cybersecurity, are used to verify the authenticity and integrity of digital messages or documents. Similar to encryption, many digital signature schemes rely on mathematical problems that are vulnerable to quantum attacks. The development of quantum-resistant digital signature algorithms is, therefore, a critical aspect of preparing for the quantum era, ensuring the continued integrity of digital signatures in a world where classical digital signatures could be compromised by quantum computers.

Furthermore, the advent of quantum computing raises concerns about the potential impact on hash functions, which are essential cryptographic tools used for data integrity and authentication. Quantum computers could potentially break widely used hash functions, compromising the security of systems that rely on them. The development and adoption of quantum-resistant hash functions become imperative to address these vulnerabilities. The NIST post-quantum cryptography competition also includes categories for quantum-resistant hash functions, emphasizing the need for robust solutions in this critical area.

As quantum computing progresses, the security landscape is expected to witness a paradigm shift, prompting organizations to reevaluate and adapt their cybersecurity strategies. The timeline for the practical realization of large-scale, fault-tolerant quantum computers is uncertain, with estimates ranging from a decade to several decades. However, the long lifespan of certain sensitive data, such as classified information or long-term strategic plans, necessitates proactive measures to ensure their security against future quantum threats.

Quantum-safe migration strategies are essential for organizations to future-proof their cybersecurity infrastructure. This involves identifying cryptographic systems that will be vulnerable to quantum attacks and transitioning to quantum-resistant alternatives. The migration process is intricate, involving careful planning, investment, and coordination. Organizations must assess the cryptographic algorithms used in their systems, prioritize their migration based on sensitivity and longevity of data, and collaborate with industry partners and standards bodies to stay informed about emerging quantum-resistant cryptographic standards.

Moreover, the impact of quantum computing on cybersecurity extends to the realm of cybersecurity awareness and education. As quantum computing becomes more prevalent in discussions about the future of technology, there is a growing need for cybersecurity professionals to understand the implications of quantum advancements. This includes staying informed about the progress of quantum computing research, the development of quantum-resistant cryptographic solutions, and the evolving threat landscape. Educational programs and training initiatives must incorporate quantum cybersecurity concepts to equip professionals with the knowledge and skills necessary to navigate the quantum era.

The rise of quantum computing also introduces geopolitical considerations in the realm of cybersecurity. Countries and organizations investing heavily in quantum research and development gain a strategic advantage, not only in terms of technological prowess but also in shaping the global cybersecurity landscape. Quantum technologies have implications for national security, economic competitiveness, and the balance of power in cyberspace. Policymakers and international bodies must grapple with the geopolitical dimensions of quantum computing, considering the potential for both collaboration and competition in this emerging frontier.

In conclusion, the potential impact of quantum computing on cybersecurity is multifaceted, introducing both challenges and opportunities. While the advent of large-scale, fault-tolerant quantum computers poses a threat to widely used encryption algorithms, efforts in post-quantum cryptography aim to develop secure alternatives. Quantum-resistant cryptographic solutions, including those for secure communication, digital signatures, and hash functions, are crucial for ensuring the long-term security of digital systems. Organizations need to proactively embrace quantum-safe migration strategies and educate cybersecurity professionals to navigate the complexities of the quantum era. Geopolitical considerations further underscore the importance of strategic investments and collaborations in quantum research and development. As the quantum revolution unfolds, the cybersecurity community faces a transformative period, requiring adaptive strategies to navigate the evolving landscape of quantum threats and opportunities.

Discuss strategies for adapting current security measures to quantum-resistant standards.

Adapting current security measures to quantum-resistant standards is a complex and crucial undertaking, given the impending threat quantum computing poses to traditional cryptographic systems. This process requires a strategic and proactive approach, involving a careful evaluation of existing cryptographic infrastructure, the identification of vulnerabilities, and the implementation of quantum-resistant alternatives. As organizations embark on this journey, they must navigate challenges related to migration costs, interoperability, and the evolving landscape of quantum-resistant cryptography. This comprehensive strategy involves a phased transition, collaboration with industry partners, and ongoing awareness and education initiatives.

A fundamental aspect of adapting to quantum-resistant standards involves assessing the current cryptographic algorithms used for encryption, key exchange, digital signatures, and hash functions. Organizations need to identify algorithms that are susceptible to quantum attacks and prioritize their replacement with quantum-resistant alternatives. This evaluation should consider the sensitivity and longevity of data, as well as the potential timeline for the practical realization of large-scale, fault-tolerant quantum computers. In many cases, this may involve a mix of classical and quantum-resistant cryptographic algorithms during the transitional period.

One key area for adaptation is in the realm of encryption. Quantum computers pose a significant threat to widely used encryption algorithms, such as RSA and ECC, which rely on the difficulty of factoring large numbers or solving discrete logarithms. Quantum-resistant encryption algorithms, based on mathematical problems believed to be hard even for quantum computers, are under development. Organizations must plan for the integration of these quantum-safe encryption methods, ensuring a seamless transition to algorithms that withstand quantum attacks. The National Institute of Standards and Technology (NIST) is leading standardization efforts in post-quantum cryptography, providing a framework for organizations to select and implement quantum-resistant encryption standards.

In addition to encryption, organizations must adapt their key exchange mechanisms to quantum-resistant standards. Quantum Key Distribution (QKD) emerges as a promising quantum-resistant key exchange solution. QKD leverages the principles of quantum mechanics to enable the secure exchange of cryptographic keys, offering a level of security believed to be immune to attacks by quantum computers. Integrating QKD into communication channels requires careful consideration of practical challenges, such as distance limitations and the development of reliable quantum key distribution infrastructure. This adaptation enhances the resilience of key exchange processes against quantum threats.

Digital signatures, a critical component of cybersecurity, also require adaptation to quantum-resistant standards. Classical digital signature algorithms, including those based on RSA and ECDSA, are vulnerable to Shor's algorithm and other quantum attacks. The transition to quantum-resistant digital signature algorithms is essential to ensure the continued integrity and authenticity of digital messages. The NIST post-quantum cryptography competition includes categories for quantum-resistant digital signature algorithms, providing organizations with a roadmap for selecting robust alternatives.

Hash functions, employed for data integrity and authentication, constitute another area where adaptation is necessary. Widely used hash functions, such as SHA-2, are vulnerable to quantum attacks. Quantum-resistant hash functions, designed to withstand quantum computing capabilities, are essential for maintaining the security of data integrity mechanisms. Organizations must plan for the integration of quantum-resistant hash functions into their systems, preventing potential vulnerabilities associated with quantum attacks on classical hash functions.

As organizations transition to quantum-resistant standards, they must also consider the interoperability of cryptographic solutions. Ensuring seamless communication between systems using classical and quantum-resistant algorithms is crucial. Hybrid cryptographic protocols, capable of supporting both classical and quantum-resistant algorithms, may be necessary during the transition period. Organizations should collaborate with industry partners, standardization bodies, and vendors to establish interoperable solutions that facilitate a smooth migration to quantum-resistant cryptographic standards.

The phased transition to quantum-resistant standards involves a delicate balance between security, cost, and practical considerations. Organizations must prioritize the protection of sensitive and long-term data while managing the costs associated with implementing quantum-resistant cryptography. A risk-based approach, considering the potential timeline for quantum computing advancements and the sensitivity of data, guides the prioritization of cryptographic upgrades. Collaboration with industry partners, research institutions, and vendors helps organizations stay informed about emerging quantum-resistant cryptographic solutions and navigate the complexities of migration.

Quantum-safe migration strategies should include a comprehensive awareness and education component. Cybersecurity professionals must be equipped with the knowledge and skills required to understand the implications of quantum computing on cryptographic systems and implement quantum-resistant alternatives. Training programs, workshops, and educational initiatives ensure that organizations have a skilled workforce capable of navigating the intricacies of quantum-resistant cryptography. Additionally, ongoing awareness efforts help organizations stay abreast of developments in quantum computing research, emerging quantum-resistant standards, and evolving cybersecurity best practices.

The development of a quantum-resistant cryptographic infrastructure requires collaboration and standardization across the cybersecurity landscape. Organizations should actively participate in industry forums, consortia, and standardization bodies working on quantum-resistant cryptographic standards. Engaging with these entities allows organizations to contribute to the development of robust standards, share insights and experiences with other stakeholders, and stay informed about the latest advancements in quantum-resistant cryptography. The NIST post-quantum cryptography competition serves as a pivotal platform for such collaboration, guiding the selection of standardized quantum-resistant cryptographic algorithms.

Furthermore, organizations must consider the geopolitical and regulatory landscape as they adapt to quantum-resistant standards. The global nature of the cybersecurity landscape requires a harmonized approach to quantum-safe migration strategies. Policymakers and regulatory bodies play a crucial role in shaping the legal and regulatory frameworks surrounding quantum-resistant cryptography. International cooperation, the development of common standards, and adherence to established cybersecurity best practices contribute to a cohesive and effective response to the quantum threat.

In conclusion, the adaptation of current security measures to quantum-resistant standards is a multifaceted and strategic process that involves evaluating existing cryptographic infrastructure, identifying vulnerabilities, and implementing quantum-resistant alternatives. Organizations must navigate challenges related to migration costs, interoperability, and the evolving landscape of quantum-resistant cryptography. A phased transition, collaboration with industry partners, ongoing awareness and education initiatives, and active participation in standardization efforts are crucial components of a comprehensive strategy. As organizations proactively embrace quantum-resistant standards, they enhance their cybersecurity resilience, ensuring the security and integrity of data in the era of quantum computing.

EXAMINE THE ROLE OF blockchain in enhancing decentralized security.

Blockchain, originally devised as the underlying technology for the digital currency Bitcoin, has evolved into a powerful and versatile tool with far-reaching implications for decentralized security across various industries. At its core, blockchain is a distributed and decentralized ledger that records transactions in a secure, transparent, and tamper-resistant manner. The decentralized nature of blockchain, achieved through a consensus mechanism among network participants, is key to its role in enhancing security in a variety of contexts.

One of the primary contributions of blockchain to decentralized security lies in its ability to establish trust in a trustless environment. Traditional centralized systems often rely on a central authority to validate and record transactions, introducing a single point of failure and vulnerability. In contrast, blockchain operates on a decentralized network of nodes, where each participant holds a copy of the entire ledger. Transactions are grouped into blocks, cryptographically linked to form a chain, and distributed across the network. This decentralized architecture eliminates the need for a central authority, reducing the risk of manipulation, fraud, or unauthorized access.

Smart contracts, self-executing code stored on the blockchain, further enhance decentralized security by automating and enforcing contractual agreements. Smart contracts operate within predefined rules and conditions, executing actions automatically when trigger conditions are met. This eliminates the need for intermediaries and reduces the potential for disputes or breaches of contract. Decentralized applications (DApps) leverage smart contracts to enable trustless interactions, providing a secure and transparent environment for various services, from finance to supply chain management.

In the realm of identity management, blockchain offers a decentralized solution to the challenges of securing and verifying personal information. Traditional identity systems often involve the collection and storage of sensitive data by centralized entities, making them attractive targets for hackers. Blockchain-based identity systems, on the other hand, enable users to control and manage their own identity information. Individuals can grant or revoke access to specific attributes, enhancing privacy and reducing the risk of identity theft. Decentralized identity solutions also eliminate the need for users to create multiple accounts across various platforms, streamlining the authentication process.

Blockchain's impact on decentralized security extends to the domain of supply chain management. In traditional supply chains, the lack of transparency and traceability can lead to issues such as counterfeiting, fraud, and inefficiencies. By utilizing blockchain, supply chain participants can record every transaction and movement of goods on an immutable ledger. This transparency ensures that all stakeholders have real-time visibility into the provenance and authenticity of products. Smart contracts can automate aspects of supply chain operations, such as triggering payments upon the successful delivery of goods, reducing the risk of disputes and fraud.

Decentralized finance (DeFi) represents a prominent and transformative application of blockchain in the financial sector. DeFi platforms leverage smart contracts to recreate traditional financial services, such as lending, borrowing, and trading, without the need for intermediaries like banks. Blockchain's decentralized architecture ensures that users retain control of their assets, mitigating the risk of funds being frozen or mismanaged by a central authority. While the DeFi space has introduced novel financial opportunities, it has also faced challenges, including smart contract vulnerabilities and regulatory considerations that underscore the importance of ongoing security measures and governance.

Blockchain's role in enhancing decentralized security is particularly evident in the context of voting and governance systems. By utilizing blockchain, voting processes can be made more transparent, secure, and resistant to manipulation. Each vote is recorded as a transaction on the blockchain, ensuring an immutable and auditable trail. This not only enhances the integrity of elections but also enables secure and decentralized decision-making in various organizational and governance structures. However, challenges such as ensuring voter privacy and addressing potential attacks on the network require careful consideration in the design and implementation of blockchain-based voting systems.

The decentralized nature of blockchain contributes to the resilience of the network against attacks and disruptions. Traditional centralized systems are vulnerable to single points of failure, where a targeted attack on a central server can compromise the entire system. In contrast, a blockchain network consists of multiple nodes distributed across the globe. Each node maintains a copy of the ledger, and the consensus mechanism ensures agreement on the state of the blockchain. This redundancy and decentralization make blockchain networks inherently resistant to censorship, tampering, and denial-of-service attacks.

Furthermore, blockchain's role in decentralized security is exemplified in its application to combat data breaches and secure the Internet of Things (IoT). In a blockchain-based IoT ecosystem, devices can communicate and transact autonomously with a high level of security and integrity. The decentralized ledger records all device interactions, providing an immutable history of events. This ensures that data generated by IoT devices is trustworthy and has not been tampered with. Additionally, blockchain's cryptographic features contribute to the secure and private exchange of data between devices, addressing concerns related to data ownership and unauthorized access.

In the realm of intellectual property and content distribution, blockchain provides a decentralized solution to issues of piracy, copyright infringement, and royalty distribution. Content creators can register their work on a blockchain, creating an immutable record of ownership. Smart contracts embedded in the blockchain can automate royalty payments to creators based on predefined rules, ensuring fair compensation and reducing the reliance on intermediaries. This decentralized approach empowers creators and promotes a more transparent and efficient content distribution ecosystem.

Blockchain also plays a pivotal role in securing digital assets and enabling tokenization. Through the tokenization of real-world assets, such as real estate or art, blockchain facilitates fractional ownership and transparent transactions. The ownership of digital tokens is recorded on the blockchain, providing a secure and decentralized representation of ownership rights. This not only enhances liquidity but also mitigates the risk of fraud and disputes associated with traditional asset ownership.

While blockchain introduces innovative solutions for decentralized security, it is not without challenges. Scalability, energy consumption, regulatory considerations, and interoperability between different blockchain networks are among the complex issues that require ongoing research and development. The choice of consensus mechanisms, such as proof-of-work or proof-of-stake, also influences the security and sustainability of blockchain networks.

In conclusion, the role of blockchain in enhancing decentralized security is multifaceted and transformative. From redefining trust in transactions to enabling decentralized finance and securing the Internet of Things, blockchain's decentralized architecture provides a foundation for innovative and secure solutions across various industries. As organizations continue to explore and implement blockchain applications, addressing challenges, fostering interoperability, and ensuring responsible governance are essential for unlocking the full potential of blockchain in decentralized security. The journey towards a more secure, transparent, and decentralized future is underway, driven by the foundational principles of blockchain technology.

Discuss its applications in securing transactions and data.

Blockchain technology, originally conceptualized as the underlying architecture for the digital currency Bitcoin, has evolved into a versatile tool with profound applications in securing transactions and data across various industries. At its core, blockchain is a decentralized and distributed ledger that records transactions in a secure, transparent, and tamper-resistant manner. This decentralized architecture, combined with cryptographic principles and consensus mechanisms, introduces a paradigm shift in how transactions and data are secured, eliminating the need for central authorities and enhancing trust in a trustless environment.

One of the primary applications of blockchain in securing transactions is evident in the realm of finance. Cryptocurrencies, which operate on blockchain technology, provide a decentralized alternative to traditional financial systems. Bitcoin, the first and most well-known cryptocurrency, enables secure and pseudonymous transactions without the need for intermediaries such as banks. The decentralized nature of blockchain ensures that transactions are recorded on a public ledger, providing transparency and immutability. Beyond Bitcoin, a myriad of cryptocurrencies and blockchain-based tokens have emerged, each with its unique features and use cases, contributing to a more decentralized and inclusive financial ecosystem.

Smart contracts, self-executing code stored on a blockchain, represent a revolutionary application in securing and automating transactions. Smart contracts operate within predefined rules and conditions, executing actions automatically when trigger conditions are met. These contracts, often written in languages like Solidity, are deployed on blockchain platforms such as Ethereum. Their execution is tamper-resistant and transparent, reducing the risk of fraud or disputes. Smart contracts find applications in various sectors, including finance, supply chain management, and decentralized applications (DApps), providing a secure and programmable layer for automated agreements and transactions.

The decentralized finance (DeFi) movement showcases the transformative potential of blockchain in securing financial transactions. DeFi platforms leverage blockchain and smart contracts to recreate traditional financial services, such as lending, borrowing, and trading, without the need for traditional intermediaries. Decentralized exchanges (DEXs), decentralized lending platforms, and liquidity pools operate on blockchain networks, enabling users to retain control of their assets while participating in a variety of financial activities. However, the nascent nature of DeFi also introduces challenges, including smart contract vulnerabilities, regulatory considerations, and the need for robust governance mechanisms to ensure the security and stability of these decentralized financial systems.

Blockchain's role in securing transactions extends to cross-border payments and remittances. Traditional international transactions often involve multiple intermediaries, leading to delays, high fees, and a lack of transparency. Blockchain-based solutions, such as Ripple's XRP or Stellar, aim to streamline cross-border payments by leveraging blockchain's speed, transparency, and cost-effectiveness. These solutions enable near-instantaneous transactions, traceable and auditable through the blockchain, reducing the friction and inefficiencies associated with traditional cross-border payment systems.

In the domain of identity management, blockchain introduces decentralized and secure solutions for securing personal information. Traditional identity systems often involve the collection and storage of sensitive data by central authorities, making them lucrative targets for hackers. Blockchain-based identity systems enable users to control and manage their own identity information. Individuals can grant or revoke access to specific attributes, enhancing privacy and reducing the risk of identity theft. Decentralized identity solutions, built on blockchain principles, also eliminate the need for users to create multiple accounts across various platforms, simplifying and securing the authentication process.

Supply chain management represents another application where blockchain secures transactions and data. The lack of transparency and traceability in traditional supply chains can lead to issues such as counterfeiting, fraud, and inefficiencies. Blockchain's decentralized and transparent ledger provides a solution by recording every transaction and movement of goods. Each participant in the supply chain, from manufacturers to retailers, has real-time visibility into the provenance and authenticity of products. This transparency ensures that stakeholders can trace the journey of products, reducing the risk of counterfeit goods entering the market and enhancing overall supply chain security.

Blockchain's impact on securing transactions is particularly pronounced in the field of intellectual property and content distribution. Content creators face challenges related to piracy, copyright infringement, and fair compensation. Blockchain provides a decentralized solution by allowing content creators to register their work on a blockchain, creating an immutable record of ownership. Smart contracts embedded in the blockchain can automate royalty payments to creators based on predefined rules, ensuring fair compensation and reducing the reliance on intermediaries. This decentralized approach empowers creators and promotes a more transparent and efficient content distribution ecosystem.

The secure and transparent nature of blockchain also finds applications in the voting and governance systems. Traditional voting processes are susceptible to various issues, including fraud, manipulation, and lack of transparency. By utilizing blockchain, voting processes can be made more secure and tamper-resistant. Each vote is recorded as a transaction on the blockchain, ensuring an immutable and auditable trail. This not only enhances the integrity of elections but also enables secure and decentralized decision-making in various organizational and governance structures. However, challenges such as ensuring voter privacy and addressing potential attacks on the network require careful consideration in the design and implementation of blockchain-based voting systems.

The use of blockchain in securing transactions and data is pivotal in combatting data breaches and ensuring the integrity of information. Traditional databases, often centralized and vulnerable to single points of failure, are lucrative targets for hackers seeking unauthorized access or tampering. Blockchain's decentralized architecture distributes the ledger across multiple nodes in a network, reducing the risk of a single point of failure. Each transaction is cryptographically linked to the previous one, creating an immutable chain of blocks. This ensures that once a block is added to the blockchain, altering or tampering with the data within it becomes computationally infeasible, providing a high level of security against unauthorized changes.

In the context of the Internet of Things (IoT), where billions of interconnected devices generate and exchange vast amounts of data, blockchain introduces a secure and decentralized solution.

Blockchain's cryptographic features contribute to the secure and private exchange of data between devices. Each device's interaction is recorded on the blockchain, providing an immutable history of events. This ensures that data generated by IoT devices is trustworthy and has not been tampered with. Additionally, blockchain's decentralized nature reduces the risk of a single point of failure in the IoT ecosystem, enhancing overall security and reliability.

Securing healthcare data and ensuring patient privacy are critical concerns in the healthcare industry. Blockchain's decentralized and cryptographic features can be applied to create secure and interoperable electronic health records (EHRs). Patients can control access to their health data, granting permission to healthcare providers or researchers as needed. Blockchain ensures the integrity of health records, reducing the risk of data manipulation or unauthorized access. This application not only enhances data security but also facilitates seamless and secure sharing of health information among different stakeholders in the healthcare ecosystem.

In conclusion, blockchain technology has emerged as a transformative force in securing transactions and data across diverse industries. From revolutionizing financial systems through decentralized currencies and smart contracts to enhancing identity management, supply chain security, and content distribution, blockchain's impact is profound. Its decentralized architecture, cryptographic principles, and transparent ledger provide a foundation for secure and tamper-resistant transactions. As organizations continue to explore and implement blockchain applications, addressing scalability, energy consumption, regulatory considerations, and interoperability challenges remains imperative. The journey towards a more secure, transparent, and decentralized future is propelled by the foundational principles of blockchain technology.

Investigate the cybersecurity challenges posed by the Internet of Things (IoT).

The proliferation of Internet of Things (IoT) devices has brought unprecedented connectivity to various aspects of our daily lives, ranging from smart homes and wearable devices to industrial systems and critical infrastructure. However, this rapid expansion of IoT also introduces a myriad of cybersecurity challenges, creating vulnerabilities that can be exploited by malicious actors. One significant challenge is the sheer scale and heterogeneity of IoT ecosystems, encompassing a vast array of devices with varying levels of security measures. Many IoT devices are resource-constrained, lacking the computational power and memory to implement robust security features, making them susceptible to exploitation. The diverse nature of IoT devices, ranging from sensors and actuators to embedded systems, complicates the establishment of standardized security protocols, leading to a fragmented and often inconsistent security landscape.

Inadequate security measures in IoT devices create a fertile ground for various attack vectors. Device-level vulnerabilities, such as weak authentication mechanisms, easily guessable passwords, and unencrypted communication channels, make it possible for attackers to compromise individual devices. The absence of standardized security practices across the IoT ecosystem exacerbates the situation, allowing attackers to exploit common vulnerabilities across a multitude of devices. Moreover, the lack of regular software updates and patch management mechanisms in many IoT devices makes them susceptible to known vulnerabilities, as manufacturers may not prioritize or provide ongoing support for their products. This challenge is further amplified in scenarios where devices are deployed in critical infrastructure or industrial settings, where outdated and unpatched devices pose significant risks to operational continuity and overall security.

Interoperability issues among IoT devices and platforms contribute to cybersecurity challenges. The diverse range of communication protocols and standards utilized by different manufacturers often hinders seamless integration and communication between devices. This diversity not only complicates the implementation of standardized security measures but also introduces the potential for misconfigurations and insecure data exchanges. Interconnected IoT devices form complex networks where a compromise in one device could lead to a domino effect, allowing attackers to move laterally within the network and potentially gain access to more critical systems. Additionally, the lack of robust identity management and authentication mechanisms in IoT ecosystems can result in unauthorized access, data breaches, and the compromise of sensitive information.

The pervasive nature of IoT devices, spanning both personal and industrial domains, raises privacy concerns. Many IoT devices collect vast amounts of data, often including personal information and behavioral patterns. The insecure handling and transmission of this data could expose individuals to privacy violations, identity theft, and unauthorized surveillance. Furthermore, the aggregation of data from multiple sources within an IoT ecosystem creates a rich target for cybercriminals seeking to exploit sensitive information for financial gain or to orchestrate more sophisticated attacks. As IoT devices become integral to smart homes, healthcare systems, and smart cities, the potential impact of privacy breaches extends beyond individual users to encompass broader societal implications.

The concept of 'security by obscurity,' a practice where the reliance on the secrecy of design or implementation is considered a primary security measure, is prevalent in many IoT devices. Manufacturers often prioritize functionality and time-to-market over rigorous security practices, leading to the use of proprietary protocols and closed systems that obscure the inner workings of IoT devices. However, relying solely on security through obscurity is a flawed approach, as it assumes that attackers will not discover or reverse engineer the underlying systems. Once vulnerabilities are exposed, the lack of transparency and open standards hinders the ability of the security community to collaborate on effective mitigation strategies, leaving users and organizations at the mercy of potential exploits.

The lifecycle management of IoT devices presents a significant challenge to cybersecurity. Many IoT devices are deployed with extended operational lifetimes, sometimes spanning decades, particularly in industrial and critical infrastructure settings. The long lifespan poses difficulties in ensuring that devices remain secure and up-to-date with evolving cybersecurity threats. Manufacturers may discontinue support or fail to provide updates for older devices, leaving them susceptible to known vulnerabilities. Additionally, the integration of legacy IoT devices with newer technologies may introduce compatibility issues, making it challenging to implement consistent security measures across the entire IoT ecosystem.

The dynamic and evolving nature of IoT environments complicates the task of monitoring and detecting security incidents. Traditional security solutions are often ill-equipped to handle the diverse range of devices, communication patterns, and data flows inherent in IoT ecosystems. Anomalies and malicious activities may go unnoticed amidst the sheer volume of data generated by interconnected devices. Furthermore, the distributed nature of IoT networks, where devices operate at the edge of the network, creates challenges in centralized monitoring and response. As a result, timely detection of security breaches and the mitigation of threats become complex tasks, requiring specialized tools and strategies tailored to the unique characteristics of IoT environments.

The susceptibility of IoT devices to physical attacks introduces an additional layer of cybersecurity challenges. Many IoT devices, especially those deployed in industrial settings, may be physically accessible to potential attackers. This physical proximity allows adversaries to tamper with devices, extract sensitive information, or manipulate the functionality of the devices to cause disruptions. The integration of IoT devices into critical infrastructure, such as energy grids and transportation systems, amplifies the potential impact of physical attacks. Securing IoT devices against physical tampering requires the implementation of robust physical security measures, including tamper-evident designs, secure enclosures, and environmental monitoring to detect unauthorized access.

The lack of a comprehensive regulatory framework for IoT security contributes to the challenges in addressing cybersecurity issues. Unlike other technology domains, such as telecommunications or aviation, where regulatory standards and certifications are well-established, the IoT landscape lacks a universally accepted set of security standards. This absence of regulatory cohesion allows manufacturers to prioritize cost and functionality over robust security measures. Regulatory bodies and industry alliances are working towards the development of security frameworks and standards for IoT devices, but achieving widespread adoption and enforcement remains a complex task.

The emerging threat landscape in the context of IoT includes the potential for large-scale, orchestrated attacks leveraging compromised devices to form botnets. These botnets, comprised of a multitude of IoT devices, can be harnessed to launch distributed denial-of-service (DDoS) attacks, overwhelm network infrastructure, or engage in other malicious activities. The Mirai botnet, which targeted insecure IoT devices to launch massive DDoS attacks, served as a wake-up call to the cybersecurity community regarding the potential scale and impact of IoT-based attacks. The evolving landscape of IoT threats underscores the need for proactive cybersecurity measures, collaboration among stakeholders, and the development of effective incident response strategies.

In conclusion, the cybersecurity challenges posed by the Internet of Things (IoT) are multifaceted and demand a comprehensive, collaborative, and proactive approach from manufacturers, policymakers, and cybersecurity practitioners. The scale, diversity, and inherent vulnerabilities of IoT ecosystems require the development and adoption of standardized security measures, including robust authentication mechanisms, encryption protocols, and regular software updates. Addressing interoperability issues, improving device lifecycle management, and establishing a regulatory framework are essential components of mitigating the cybersecurity risks associated with IoT. As IoT continues to shape the digital landscape, a collective effort to prioritize security will be crucial to harnessing the benefits of interconnected devices while safeguarding against the potential threats they pose.

Provide solutions and best practices for securing IoT devices and networks.

Securing Internet of Things (IoT) devices and networks is paramount in mitigating the cybersecurity challenges inherent in the expanding landscape of interconnected devices. A comprehensive approach to IoT security involves a combination of technical solutions, best practices, and ongoing collaboration among stakeholders. One fundamental aspect is the implementation of robust authentication mechanisms. Strong, unique credentials for each IoT device, coupled with secure methods of key exchange, help prevent unauthorized access. The use of multi-factor authentication adds an extra layer of security, requiring users or devices to provide multiple forms of identification before gaining access to sensitive data or systems. Furthermore, the adoption of certificate-based authentication enhances the overall security posture, ensuring the integrity and authenticity of device identities within the IoT ecosystem.

Encryption plays a pivotal role in safeguarding data transmitted between IoT devices and networks. Employing end-to-end encryption ensures that data remains confidential and secure throughout its journey, protecting it from interception or tampering. This is especially crucial for IoT devices that collect and transmit sensitive information, such as personal data in smart homes or critical data in industrial settings. Advanced encryption protocols, including Transport Layer Security (TLS) for communication between devices and networks, contribute to the overall resilience of IoT security. Regularly updating encryption protocols to adhere to the latest standards helps address evolving cybersecurity threats and vulnerabilities.

Device manufacturers play a crucial role in enhancing IoT security by prioritizing security in the design and development phases. Implementing the principle of "security by design" involves integrating security measures into the core architecture of IoT devices from the outset. Manufacturers should conduct thorough security assessments, identify potential vulnerabilities, and implement robust security controls, such as secure boot processes and hardware-based security features. Additionally, ongoing security audits and regular firmware updates enable manufacturers to address emerging threats and vulnerabilities, ensuring that devices remain resilient throughout their operational lifecycle.

Fostering a culture of continuous monitoring is essential for identifying and responding to potential security incidents in IoT networks. Implementing intrusion detection systems (IDS) and intrusion prevention systems (IPS) enables real-time monitoring of network traffic, helping to detect anomalous activities or potential security breaches. By leveraging machine learning and artificial intelligence, these systems can analyze patterns of behavior and identify deviations that may indicate malicious activity. Continuous monitoring provides organizations with the visibility needed to respond swiftly to security incidents, reducing the dwell time of potential threats and minimizing the impact on IoT networks.

The principle of least privilege should be applied rigorously in IoT environments to limit the potential damage that can occur in the event of a security breach. Devices and users should only be granted the minimum level of access necessary for their intended functionality. This involves implementing proper access controls and segmenting IoT networks to contain potential threats. Network segmentation ensures that even if one segment is compromised, the impact is limited to that specific area, preventing lateral movement within the network. Additionally, regularly reviewing and updating access permissions based on the principle of least privilege helps organizations adapt to evolving security requirements and maintain a robust security posture.

Implementing secure over-the-air (OTA) update mechanisms is critical for ensuring that IoT devices remain resilient against evolving threats. Manufacturers should design devices with the capability to receive and install firmware updates securely. This involves the use of code signing to verify the authenticity of updates and prevent the installation of malicious or tampered firmware. Organizations should establish clear processes for distributing and managing updates, ensuring that patches for known vulnerabilities are deployed promptly. Encouraging users to enable automatic updates whenever possible reduces the risk of devices running outdated and vulnerable firmware, enhancing the overall security of IoT ecosystems.

The integration of network-based firewalls and intrusion detection and prevention systems is essential for safeguarding IoT devices from external threats. Firewalls help filter incoming and outgoing network traffic, blocking malicious actors and unauthorized access attempts. Intrusion detection and prevention systems provide an additional layer of defense by monitoring network and system activities for signs of suspicious behavior and taking preventive measures when potential threats are identified. The combination of these security measures contributes to the establishment of a robust perimeter defense, protecting IoT networks from a wide range of cyber threats.

Device lifecycle management is a critical component of securing IoT devices from the point of deployment to decommissioning. Establishing a clear and well-defined process for managing the entire lifecycle ensures that devices are monitored, updated, and retired in a secure manner. This involves maintaining an inventory of all deployed devices, tracking their operational status, and identifying those that may be nearing the end of their lifecycle. Secure decommissioning procedures, including the removal of sensitive data and the disposal of devices in accordance with industry standards, prevent the potential for security breaches arising from retired IoT devices.

Incorporating blockchain technology into IoT security frameworks can enhance the integrity and transparency of transactions within interconnected devices. Blockchain's decentralized and tamper-resistant ledger ensures that data recorded on the blockchain remains immutable, providing a reliable record of transactions. This is particularly valuable in scenarios such as supply chain management, where the transparency and traceability offered by blockchain contribute to the prevention of counterfeiting and fraud. Additionally, blockchain-based identity management systems enhance the security and privacy of user information, as individuals retain control over their identity data, reducing the risk of unauthorized access.

Implementing comprehensive threat modeling and risk assessment practices is instrumental in identifying potential vulnerabilities and weaknesses within IoT ecosystems. Organizations should conduct thorough assessments of the entire IoT architecture, considering both technical and non-technical aspects of security. This involves evaluating the potential impact of security breaches, understanding the attack surface of IoT devices, and identifying potential points of compromise. Threat modeling enables organizations to prioritize security measures based on the level of risk associated with different components of the IoT ecosystem, ensuring that resources are allocated effectively to address the most critical security challenges.

Collaboration among industry stakeholders is vital for establishing standards and best practices that promote a consistent and effective approach to IoT security. Industry alliances, regulatory bodies, and standardization organizations play a key role in developing and disseminating guidelines for secure IoT deployment. Collaborative initiatives foster information sharing, enabling organizations to stay abreast of emerging threats and vulnerabilities. Moreover, the exchange of best practices and lessons learned contributes to the collective improvement of IoT security across diverse industries. Engaging in collaborative efforts allows stakeholders to address the multifaceted nature of IoT security challenges and build a more resilient and secure IoT ecosystem.

In conclusion, securing IoT devices and networks requires a holistic and collaborative approach that encompasses technical solutions, best practices, and ongoing efforts to adapt to the evolving threat landscape. Robust authentication mechanisms, encryption protocols, and secure OTA updates form the foundation of technical solutions, while a proactive security culture, continuous monitoring, and collaboration among stakeholders contribute to a resilient security posture. As IoT continues to shape the digital landscape, organizations must prioritize cybersecurity measures to harness the benefits of interconnected devices while safeguarding against potential threats and vulnerabilities.

Explore emerging innovations in cloud security.

The landscape of cloud security is continually evolving, driven by the dynamic nature of cyber threats and the rapid adoption of cloud technologies across industries. One of the emerging innovations in cloud security is the integration of artificial intelligence (AI) and machine learning (ML) into security frameworks. AI and ML enable cloud security solutions to analyze vast amounts of data, detect patterns, and identify anomalies that may indicate potential security threats. These technologies enhance threat detection capabilities, allowing for real-time monitoring of cloud environments and swift response to security incidents. By leveraging AI and ML algorithms, cloud security platforms can adapt to evolving threats, offering a proactive defense against sophisticated cyber attacks.

Another key innovation in cloud security is the development of cloud-native security solutions. As organizations increasingly migrate their operations to the cloud, traditional security tools may become less effective in addressing the unique challenges posed by cloud environments. Cloud-native security solutions are designed to seamlessly integrate with cloud infrastructure and services, providing enhanced visibility, control, and protection. These solutions leverage the native capabilities of cloud platforms to offer dynamic and scalable security measures. Whether it's container security, serverless security, or security for cloud-based applications, these cloud-native approaches are tailored to the specific requirements of modern cloud architectures.

The concept of "zero trust" has gained prominence as a paradigm shift in cloud security. Zero trust security models operate on the principle of not trusting any entity, whether internal or external, by default. This approach challenges the traditional perimeter-based security model and assumes that threats can exist both inside and outside the traditional network. Zero trust architectures verify and authenticate every user, device, or application trying to access resources, regardless of their location. This model is particularly relevant in the context of cloud environments, where users and data may traverse different networks and locations. Zero trust security minimizes the risk of unauthorized access and lateral movement within cloud networks.

The advent of Secure Access Service Edge (SASE) represents a transformative innovation in cloud security architecture. SASE converges network security functions with WAN (Wide Area Network) capabilities to support the dynamic, secure access needs of organizations. By integrating functions like secure web gateways, firewall-as-a-service, and zero trust network access, SASE enables organizations to adopt a more flexible and scalable approach to network security. This innovation is particularly beneficial for businesses embracing cloud-centric and mobile-friendly operations, providing a unified and cloud-native security framework that adapts to the evolving digital landscape.

Containerization and orchestration technologies, such as Docker and Kubernetes, have become integral to modern cloud architectures. As organizations increasingly deploy applications in containers, the need for robust container security solutions has grown. Innovations in container security focus on securing the entire container lifecycle, from development and deployment to runtime and eventual decommissioning. Container security platforms offer features such as vulnerability scanning, image signing, and runtime protection to ensure the integrity and security of containerized applications. Additionally, the integration of security into the DevOps pipeline facilitates the seamless and secure deployment of containerized applications in cloud environments.

The rise of serverless computing introduces new challenges and opportunities in cloud security. Serverless architectures, where applications run in stateless compute containers known as functions, eliminate the need for traditional server management. However, securing serverless environments requires a shift in mindset, focusing on securing code and functions rather than infrastructure. Innovations in serverless security include runtime protection, vulnerability scanning, and security monitoring tailored for serverless applications. By embracing a serverless security model, organizations can leverage the benefits of reduced operational overhead while ensuring the resilience and integrity of serverless workloads in the cloud.

Identity and access management (IAM) have become crucial components of cloud security, and innovations in this space aim to enhance authentication and authorization mechanisms. Multi-factor authentication (MFA) is increasingly becoming a standard practice to add an extra layer of security beyond traditional password-based authentication. Adaptive authentication is another innovation that evaluates contextual factors, such as user behavior and device characteristics, to dynamically adjust the level of authentication required. Additionally, innovations in continuous authentication enable real-time verification of a user's identity throughout their session, reducing the risk of unauthorized access, especially in cloud environments where user access may span different devices and locations.

In response to the growing sophistication of cyber threats, threat intelligence platforms have emerged as a critical innovation in cloud security. These platforms aggregate and analyze threat data from various sources, providing organizations with insights into current and emerging cyber threats. By leveraging threat intelligence, organizations can enhance their proactive threat detection capabilities, prioritize security measures based on the relevance of threats, and fortify their defenses against known and unknown adversaries. Threat intelligence platforms contribute to a more informed and resilient security posture in the dynamic landscape of cloud computing.

Compliance and regulatory requirements are driving innovations in cloud security to ensure that organizations can meet industry-specific standards. Cloud security posture management (CSPM) solutions offer continuous monitoring and assessment of cloud configurations to ensure compliance with industry regulations and best practices. These tools provide real-time insights into potential misconfigurations or vulnerabilities that may impact compliance. Automated remediation features enable organizations to address issues promptly, reducing the risk of non-compliance and associated penalties. As regulations evolve, innovations in CSPM aim to provide adaptive and comprehensive solutions for maintaining a secure and compliant cloud environment.

Quantum-resistant cryptography is emerging as a proactive response to the potential threat posed by quantum computers to current cryptographic algorithms. Quantum computers have the theoretical capability to break widely used encryption methods, posing a significant risk to the security of data transmitted and stored in the cloud. Quantum-resistant cryptography aims to develop algorithms that can withstand attacks from quantum computers. Innovations in this field focus on creating cryptographic solutions that ensure the confidentiality and integrity of data in a post-quantum computing era, reinforcing the long-term security of cloud-based systems.

Cloud security orchestration and automation represent a significant innovation in streamlining security operations and response. Security orchestration platforms enable the integration of security tools, workflows, and processes to automate repetitive tasks and response actions. Automation in cloud security helps organizations respond swiftly to security incidents, reducing the time to detect and mitigate threats. Innovations in security orchestration include the development of playbooks and workflows that can adapt to dynamic cloud environments. By automating routine security tasks, organizations can free up resources, improve response times, and enhance overall security efficacy in the cloud.

In conclusion, the landscape of cloud security is evolving with innovations that address the unique challenges posed by the dynamic and interconnected nature of cloud environments. The integration of artificial intelligence and machine learning, cloud-native security solutions, zero trust architectures, Secure Access Service Edge (SASE), and advancements in container, serverless, and identity security are shaping the future of cloud security. Additionally, innovations in threat intelligence, compliance management, quantum-resistant cryptography, and security orchestration contribute to building resilient and adaptive security frameworks. As organizations continue to embrace the cloud, these innovations play a pivotal role in safeguarding sensitive data, ensuring compliance, and maintaining the integrity of cloud-based operations in the face of evolving cyber threats.

Discuss the evolving landscape of cloud-based cybersecurity solutions.

The landscape of cloud-based cybersecurity solutions has undergone significant evolution, fueled by the growing complexity of cyber threats and the widespread adoption of cloud technologies across industries. One prominent aspect of this evolution is the shift towards integrated and comprehensive security platforms that provide a unified approach to securing diverse cloud environments. These platforms typically offer a range of security services, including threat detection, identity and access management, encryption, and compliance management. The integration of these services within a single platform allows organizations to streamline their security operations, gain holistic visibility into their cloud infrastructure, and respond more effectively to emerging threats.

As organizations increasingly migrate their operations to the cloud, the need for cloud-native security solutions has become paramount. Cloud-native security is designed to seamlessly integrate with cloud environments, leveraging the native features and APIs (Application Programming Interfaces) provided by cloud platforms. This approach enables security solutions to adapt to the dynamic nature of cloud architectures, providing scalable and agile protection. Whether it's securing containers, serverless applications, or cloud-based databases, cloud-native security solutions are tailored to the specific requirements of modern cloud deployments, ensuring that organizations can harness the benefits of the cloud without compromising on security.

Identity and Access Management (IAM) have become foundational components of cloud security, reflecting the recognition that user identities and access controls are critical aspects of securing cloud environments. The evolving landscape of IAM in the cloud emphasizes the adoption of Zero Trust principles, which assume that trust should not be automatically granted based on a user's location or network. Zero Trust IAM models require continuous verification of user identities and their access privileges, irrespective of their location or network context. This approach is particularly relevant in cloud environments where users may access resources from various locations and devices, necessitating a more dynamic and risk-aware IAM framework.

The advent of Secure Access Service Edge (SASE) represents a paradigm shift in cloud-based cybersecurity. SASE converges network security functions with WAN (Wide Area Network) capabilities to provide a comprehensive and cloud-native security framework. By integrating services such as secure web gateways, firewall-as-a-service, and zero-trust network access, SASE accommodates the evolving needs of organizations embracing cloud-centric and mobile-friendly operations. This innovation not only simplifies the security architecture but also enhances the overall flexibility and scalability of security measures, aligning them with the distributed and dynamic nature of modern cloud networks.

The rise of DevSecOps, an integration of development, security, and operations practices, is reshaping how organizations approach security in the cloud. DevSecOps emphasizes the incorporation of security measures throughout the entire software development lifecycle, from code development to deployment and beyond. Integrating security into the DevOps pipeline allows for the continuous assessment and remediation of vulnerabilities, fostering a culture of proactive security measures rather than reactive responses. Cloud-based cybersecurity solutions that support DevSecOps practices enable organizations to automate security checks, implement policy as code, and ensure that security is an integral part of the software development process.

Containerization technologies, such as Docker and Kubernetes, have become instrumental in cloud-based application deployment. With the rise of containerized applications, the need for dedicated container security solutions has become apparent. Cloud-native container security platforms offer capabilities such as vulnerability scanning, runtime protection, and compliance checks specific to containerized environments. These solutions ensure the integrity and security of containerized applications throughout their lifecycle, addressing the unique challenges posed by the dynamic and ephemeral nature of containers in the cloud.

The emergence of serverless computing introduces a new dimension to cloud security considerations. Serverless architectures, where applications run in stateless compute containers known as functions, require a shift in security practices. Cloud-based security solutions for serverless computing focus on securing the code and functions themselves, as opposed to traditional infrastructure-based security. Innovations in serverless security include runtime protection, serverless-specific vulnerability scanning, and security monitoring tailored for serverless applications. By adopting a serverless security model, organizations can leverage the benefits of reduced operational overhead while ensuring the resilience and integrity of serverless workloads in the cloud.

Quantum computing poses a potential threat to traditional cryptographic algorithms, prompting the development of quantum-resistant cryptography. Cloud-based cybersecurity solutions are actively exploring and implementing quantum-resistant cryptographic techniques to safeguard sensitive data against the future threat of quantum-enabled attacks. These cryptographic innovations aim to ensure the long-term security of data stored and transmitted in the cloud, even in the face of advancements in quantum computing that may render current encryption methods vulnerable.

The integration of Artificial Intelligence (AI) and Machine Learning (ML) into cloud-based cybersecurity solutions is becoming increasingly prevalent. AI and ML technologies enhance threat detection capabilities by analyzing vast amounts of data, identifying patterns, and predicting potential security incidents. Cloud security platforms leverage these technologies to detect anomalies, correlate events, and automate responses to known and emerging threats. The adaptive nature of AI and ML allows cloud-based cybersecurity solutions to continuously learn and evolve, providing a proactive defense against sophisticated cyber attacks in the dynamic cloud environment.

Compliance management in the cloud has become a critical aspect of cybersecurity, driven by the need to adhere to industry-specific regulations and standards. Cloud Security Posture Management (CSPM) solutions play a crucial role in automating the continuous monitoring and assessment of cloud configurations to ensure compliance. These solutions provide real-time insights into potential misconfigurations or vulnerabilities that may impact compliance. Automated remediation features enable organizations to address issues promptly, reducing the risk of non-compliance and associated penalties. As regulations evolve, cloud-based cybersecurity solutions in compliance management aim to provide adaptive and comprehensive solutions for maintaining a secure and compliant cloud environment.

Threat intelligence platforms have gained prominence in the evolving landscape of cloud-based cybersecurity. These platforms aggregate and analyze threat data from various sources, providing organizations with insights into current and emerging cyber threats. By leveraging threat intelligence, organizations can enhance their proactive threat detection capabilities, prioritize security measures based on the relevance of threats, and fortify their defenses against known and unknown adversaries. Threat intelligence platforms contribute to a more informed and resilient security posture in the dynamic landscape of cloud computing.

Automation and orchestration are pivotal aspects of cloud-based cybersecurity solutions, streamlining security operations and response efforts. Security Orchestration, Automation, and Response (SOAR) platforms integrate security tools, workflows, and processes to automate repetitive tasks and response actions. Automation in cloud security helps organizations respond swiftly to security incidents, reducing the time to detect and mitigate threats. Cloud-based SOAR solutions enhance overall security efficacy by automating routine security tasks, freeing up resources, and improving response times in the face of evolving cyber threats.

The integration of blockchain technology into cloud-based cybersecurity solutions is gaining attention as a means to enhance data integrity, transparency, and trust in the cloud. Blockchain's decentralized and tamper-resistant ledger ensures the immutability of data recorded on the blockchain, providing a reliable record of transactions and changes. In cloud environments, blockchain can be utilized to secure data transactions, establish transparent audit trails, and enhance the overall integrity of data stored in the cloud. While still in the early stages of exploration, the potential applications of blockchain in cloud-based cybersecurity signify a growing area of innovation.

In conclusion, the evolving landscape of cloud-based cybersecurity solutions reflects the dynamic nature of cyber threats and the transformative impact of cloud technologies. From integrated security platforms and cloud-native security solutions to quantum-resistant cryptography and innovations in DevSecOps, the cloud security ecosystem continues to adapt to the ever-changing digital landscape. The integration of AI, ML, and blockchain, along with the emphasis on identity and access management, compliance, and threat intelligence, underscores the comprehensive and multi-faceted approach required to secure cloud environments effectively. As organizations navigate the complexities of the cloud, the continuous evolution of cloud-based cybersecurity solutions remains essential for maintaining a resilient defense against emerging threats and ensuring the security of digital assets in the cloud.

Discuss the evolving role of individuals in shaping the future of cybersecurity.

The evolving role of individuals in shaping the future of cybersecurity is a critical aspect of the rapidly changing digital landscape. As technology becomes more ingrained in our daily lives, individuals find themselves at the forefront of efforts to safeguard personal and organizational digital assets. One of the notable shifts is the increasing awareness among individuals regarding the importance of cybersecurity. As cyber threats become more sophisticated, the general populace is becoming more informed about the potential risks and the need for proactive measures. This awareness extends beyond the realm of IT professionals and cybersecurity experts, emphasizing that everyone, from the average user to business executives, plays a vital role in the collective defense against cyber threats.

Individuals are becoming more accountable for their online actions and are recognizing the impact of their behaviors on overall cybersecurity. This includes practicing good cyber hygiene, such as regularly updating passwords, being cautious about clicking on suspicious links, and keeping software up to date. The understanding that simple actions, like using strong and unique passwords or enabling multi-factor authentication, can significantly contribute to the overall resilience against cyber threats is gaining traction. The evolving role of individuals involves not only being aware of potential risks but actively taking steps to mitigate those risks in their personal and professional digital environments.

The integration of cybersecurity education into mainstream learning and professional development is another aspect of the evolving role of individuals. As digital literacy becomes a fundamental skill, there is a growing emphasis on including cybersecurity education in school curricula and professional training programs. This proactive approach aims to equip individuals with the knowledge and skills needed to navigate the digital landscape securely. By fostering a cybersecurity-aware culture from an early age, individuals are better prepared to make informed decisions and understand the implications of their actions in the online realm.

The rise of remote work and the increasing reliance on digital communication tools have further highlighted the importance of individuals in the cybersecurity equation. With the boundary between personal and professional digital environments becoming more blurred, individuals are tasked with ensuring the security of their work-related data and communications. This includes being vigilant about phishing attempts, securing home networks, and adhering to organizational cybersecurity policies. The evolving role of individuals in remote work scenarios underscores the need for a proactive and collaborative approach, where employees actively engage in securing their digital workspaces.

The concept of "cybersecurity citizenship" is emerging as a way to frame the evolving role of individuals in the digital age. Cybersecurity citizenship goes beyond individual actions and encompasses a sense of responsibility towards the broader online community. It involves understanding the interconnected nature of the digital ecosystem and recognizing that secure online behavior benefits not only the individual but also the collective security of the digital community. Individuals, as cybersecurity citizens, are encouraged to report suspicious activities, share threat intelligence, and contribute to the overall resilience of the digital environment.

The evolution of individuals' roles in cybersecurity extends to the concept of "user empowerment." Traditionally seen as potential weak links in the security chain, individuals are now being empowered to actively participate in their own defense. This empowerment involves providing individuals with the tools and knowledge needed to make informed security decisions. For example, organizations are implementing user-friendly security interfaces, conducting regular cybersecurity training sessions, and fostering a culture where individuals feel comfortable reporting security incidents. By empowering individuals, organizations leverage the human element as an asset in the cybersecurity strategy rather than viewing it solely as a potential vulnerability.

The advent of privacy-focused regulations, such as the General Data Protection Regulation (GDPR), has further emphasized the role of individuals in shaping the future of cybersecurity. These regulations grant individuals greater control over their personal data and require organizations to implement robust security measures to protect this data. Individuals are now more aware of their rights regarding the privacy and security of their personal information, and organizations are compelled to prioritize cybersecurity practices that align with these regulatory requirements. The evolving role of individuals in this context involves actively exercising their privacy rights and holding organizations accountable for ensuring the security of their data.

The rapid evolution of technology, including the Internet of Things (IoT) and the proliferation of smart devices, introduces new dimensions to the role of individuals in cybersecurity. As homes and workplaces become more interconnected, individuals are tasked with securing a broader range of devices, from smart thermostats to wearable fitness trackers. The responsibility extends to understanding the security implications of these devices, configuring them securely, and being aware of potential privacy risks. The evolving role of individuals in the era of IoT emphasizes the need for a holistic understanding of cybersecurity that goes beyond traditional computing devices.

Social engineering, encompassing tactics such as phishing and pretexting, remains a prevalent threat in the cybersecurity landscape. The evolving role of individuals involves developing a heightened awareness of social engineering tactics and exercising critical judgment in online interactions. Cybersecurity education programs often emphasize the importance of skepticism and verifying the authenticity of communications, especially when receiving unsolicited emails or messages. Individuals are becoming more adept at recognizing social engineering attempts and taking proactive steps to protect themselves and their organizations from falling victim to these deceptive tactics.

The concept of "digital resilience" captures the essence of the evolving role of individuals in cybersecurity. Digital resilience goes beyond mere awareness and education, emphasizing the ability of individuals to adapt and respond effectively to evolving cyber threats. This involves cultivating a mindset that embraces continuous learning, staying informed about emerging threats, and being prepared to implement security measures in response to changing circumstances. The evolving role of individuals as digitally resilient actors recognizes that cybersecurity is not a static state but a dynamic and ongoing process that requires active engagement.

Collaboration and information-sharing within the cybersecurity community exemplify the interconnected nature of the evolving role of individuals. Platforms for sharing threat intelligence, participating in online forums, and engaging in collaborative initiatives contribute to a collective defense against cyber threats. Individuals, whether they are cybersecurity professionals, researchers, or enthusiasts, play a crucial role in this ecosystem by actively contributing their expertise, insights, and experiences. The evolving role of individuals as contributors to the broader cybersecurity community emphasizes the importance of a united front against the constantly evolving landscape of cyber threats.

In conclusion, the evolving role of individuals in shaping the future of cybersecurity encompasses a multifaceted and dynamic set of responsibilities. From fostering awareness and education to actively participating in the defense of personal and organizational digital environments, individuals are central to the resilience of the digital ecosystem. The concepts of cybersecurity citizenship, user empowerment, and digital resilience underscore the transformative potential of individuals in the face of evolving cyber threats. As technology continues to advance, the role of individuals will remain pivotal in determining the overall success of cybersecurity strategies and shaping a secure digital future.

Explore the integration of human-centric approaches in technological advancements.

The integration of human-centric approaches in technological advancements signifies a paradigm shift in the design, development, and deployment of technology, placing human needs, experiences, and values at the core of innovation. This approach acknowledges that technology should not merely be a tool or solution but should enhance and complement human capabilities while addressing societal challenges. Human-centric design, often synonymous with user-centered design, emphasizes the importance of understanding and incorporating user perspectives throughout the entire technology development lifecycle.

One notable aspect of integrating human-centric approaches is the emphasis on empathy in design thinking. Design thinking, a problem-solving methodology that prioritizes understanding user needs, involves immersing designers in the user's environment, observing their behaviors, and empathizing with their challenges. By fostering a deep understanding of the user's experience, design thinking enables the creation of solutions that resonate with the user's context, preferences, and aspirations. This empathetic approach not only leads to more user-friendly products but also cultivates a deeper connection between technology and the end-users it serves.

Accessibility is a crucial dimension of human-centric technology integration, ensuring that advancements are inclusive and cater to diverse user needs. The principles of universal design advocate for creating products and systems that are accessible to people with varying abilities and disabilities. Technologies that incorporate accessibility features, such as screen readers, voice commands, and tactile interfaces, empower individuals with disabilities to participate more fully in the digital world. The integration of accessibility into technological advancements aligns with the broader goal of fostering inclusivity and breaking down barriers to digital participation.

The field of human-computer interaction (HCI) plays a pivotal role in driving human-centric approaches in technological advancements. HCI focuses on understanding the interactions between humans and computers, aiming to design systems that are intuitive, efficient, and satisfying for users. Usability studies, user testing, and iterative design processes are integral to HCI, ensuring that technology aligns with user expectations and preferences. As technologies become more complex, HCI principles guide the development of interfaces that facilitate seamless and enjoyable interactions, ultimately enhancing user engagement and satisfaction.

The rise of artificial intelligence (AI) and machine learning (ML) has brought forth new opportunities and challenges in integrating human-centric approaches. Ethical considerations in AI development emphasize transparency, fairness, and accountability to prevent biases and ensure that AI systems align with societal values. Human-in-the-loop approaches, where human input is integrated into AI systems, enable better decision-making and allow humans to intervene when necessary. By incorporating human oversight, AI technologies can strike a balance between automation and human judgment, fostering trust and ethical use of these powerful tools.

The concept of human augmentation envisions using technology to enhance human capabilities, both physically and cognitively. From wearable devices that monitor health metrics to brain-machine interfaces that enable communication for individuals with paralysis, human augmentation technologies aim to improve the quality of life and overcome limitations. The integration of human-centric approaches in this context involves not only technological innovation but also ethical considerations, privacy safeguards, and user consent. Balancing the potential benefits of human augmentation with ethical considerations ensures that these advancements prioritize the well-being and autonomy of individuals.

In the realm of healthcare, the integration of human-centric approaches is evident in the development of patient-centric technologies. Personalized medicine leverages advancements in genomics and data analytics to tailor medical treatments to individual patients based on their genetic makeup, lifestyle, and environmental factors. Telehealth and remote patient monitoring technologies enhance accessibility to healthcare services, particularly in remote or underserved areas. The convergence of technology and healthcare prioritizes patient empowerment, engagement, and personalized care, reflecting a shift towards more human-centered and holistic healthcare solutions.

The Internet of Things (IoT) represents another domain where human-centric approaches play a crucial role. The integration of IoT devices into daily life, ranging from smart home appliances to wearable fitness trackers, revolves around enhancing user experiences and addressing specific needs. Designing IoT devices with user privacy and security in mind is a fundamental aspect of human-centric approaches, ensuring that individuals can trust and control the connected devices in their lives. The success of IoT technologies hinges on their ability to seamlessly integrate into human routines and offer tangible benefits without compromising user trust.

The intersection of human-centric design and cybersecurity is gaining prominence as technology becomes more ingrained in everyday life. Recognizing that users are often the weakest link in cybersecurity, human-centric cybersecurity approaches focus on creating security solutions that are not only effective but also user-friendly. This involves designing interfaces that communicate security information clearly, educating users about potential risks, and implementing authentication mechanisms that balance security and usability. By understanding the psychology of user behavior, human-centric cybersecurity aims to empower individuals to make secure choices in their digital interactions.

In the educational domain, technology is increasingly being designed with human-centric principles to enhance learning experiences. EdTech platforms leverage personalized learning algorithms, interactive interfaces, and gamification to cater to individual student needs and preferences. The integration of human-centric approaches in educational technology recognizes the diverse learning styles and abilities of students, fostering a more inclusive and engaging learning environment. As technology continues to shape the future of education, human-centric design ensures that technological advancements align with the goals of effective learning and knowledge acquisition.

The integration of human-centric approaches is reshaping the way organizations approach innovation and product development. Design thinking methodologies, user feedback loops, and participatory design processes involve end-users throughout the development lifecycle, ensuring that products resonate with their intended audience. This collaborative approach not only leads to more successful and user-friendly products but also cultivates a sense of co-creation and shared ownership between developers and users. The result is technology that is not imposed on users but rather emerges from a collaborative and iterative process that values user input and experiences.

The ethical considerations inherent in human-centric technology development are gaining prominence. As technological advancements impact various aspects of society, from privacy concerns in surveillance technologies to the ethical implications of AI in decision-making processes, a renewed focus on ethical frameworks and guidelines is essential. The integration of ethical considerations ensures that technological innovations align with societal values, respect individual rights, and mitigate potential harms. Ethical considerations become an integral part of the design, development, and deployment processes, guiding technology towards responsible and sustainable outcomes.

In conclusion, the integration of human-centric approaches in technological advancements marks a transformative shift towards technology that is not only powerful but also deeply attuned to human needs, values, and experiences. Whether in design thinking methodologies, accessibility features, ethical considerations in AI, or personalized healthcare solutions, human-centric approaches prioritize the well-being, autonomy, and engagement of individuals. As technology continues to advance, the success of innovations increasingly depends on their ability to enhance the human experience, foster inclusivity, and align with the values of the diverse individuals they aim to serve.

www.ingramcontent.com/pod-product-compliance
Lightning Source LLC
LaVergne TN
LVHW051429050326
832903LV00030BD/2991